Italy, the Embracing Circle: Il Circolo

Dear Barb —
I hope
you enjoy
my book.
Welcome
to il circalo

Con affetto
Donna Marie

Italy, the Embracing Circle: Il Circolo

My Past, My Future

Donna Marie Ferro

To order additional copies of this book, contact:
Xlibris LLC
1-888-795-4274
www.Xlibris.com
Orders@Xlibris.com
616515

Contents

To my family who brought me into *il circolo*.

To Alyssa Rose and Valentino, my

grandchildren, welcome to the circle.

Ti amo sempre.

Acknowledgments

When I was a little girl, my nonna Maria shared this story. One evening while she was helping her mother peel potatoes to make a soup, she turned to her mother and asked, "Who do you love the most of all your children?" Her mother extended her hands and put them up close to my nonna's face with the fingers spread and asked, "Which fingers should I chop off?" My nonna exclaimed, "None. You need all of them!" Her mother smiled and in a gentle voice, looking deeply into her daughter's eyes, responded, "You have answered your own question."

Each person I have acknowledged has been significant in making my book a reality.

John Ferro, my brother, with your beautiful mind, I phoned you day and night; and you were always able to answer my questions. You are amazing.

Deborah Edginton, you are my Rogers to my Hammerstein, the pianist to my lyrics. May all that you desire come true.

Anita Ferro Paullus, my cousin, where will we go next? My dear Conquistadora, please don't listen to me. Bring the carry-on.

Rose Rusca Belotti, I'm so lucky to share your DNA as cousins. I am your mosquito who pesters you day and night on the history of our family and the dialect. Be prepared. Your cousin La Zanzara will be flying to your villa.

Donatella Betinelli, my dear Italian teacher, you make every moment in class a living experience. You are my *lucciola* of the *bel paese*.

John Masala, thank you, my friend, for your encouragement in keeping my voice authentic and my artistry true to myself.

Mark Greenside, you have shared with me the "Holy Grail." Your wisdom and guidance has been a beacon of light for me as a new author. Maybe in our next life we can collaborate on a book of Brittany and Liguria.

Susan Cecconi–Jacoli, all of our lives we have shared the same circle that our precious parents introduced to us. We are sisters, *credo bèn*.

Milena Cipresso, in Stella San Giovanni, Italy, in spite of twenty-four-hour texting from me, you somehow found a way to respond instantly every time with the answers.

Linda Berry, "Sissipoo," a.k.a. the queen of grammar/editing, your laser skill of turning an incomplete phrase into a literary dream is beyond magic.

Mary Copeland, you have transformed the sea of red-ink edits into the last major revision of this book.

Joe Camara, who came to my rescue and found the manuscript that I thought I had lost on the computer.

Pat Duncan, my first reader, you provided feedback with honesty and clarity.

Terèsa (Bella), my daughter, and Michael Calegari, who likes to remain behind the scenes, your support and encouragement and patience are boundless in the face of my obsession with and incessant jabber about this book. I promise my silence to both of you.

My mother, Rosa, I kept my promise to you and wrote this book. I can hear my father say to me, "Really, you did it, really." Yes, I did.

Last but not least, Yoda, my dog, and Bruno, Boom-Boom Ferro, my cat, who waited in the den while I wrote long through the night and into the morning. Lights out! Let's go to bed. *Buona notte.*

Prologue

"Rose, don't unpack. We're not staying here. This is not the place for us." In the dark of midnight with no moon, the door opened. I could see a room with what looked like a dirt floor and a single lightbulb swinging from the ceiling. It was *miseria*, misery. It was the birthplace of my father's mother, the brave immigrant. No wonder she left.

It was 1971 and my first time in Italy. I was in complete culture shock. I had little concept of the language, the culture, or the people. I was American. I loved the American way of life, loved TV, loved the music, loved shopping, and loved football. I thought this was the only way to live. Don't get me wrong. I appreciated how much my grandparents had sacrificed in order to come to their new homeland, but I thought the American way of life was divine. If I never ate ravioli, never tasted another piece of tiramisu, never listened to opera again or heard the Ligurian dialect, I would have been fine. I was proud of my heritage but prouder to be in the United States of America. I was a Golden Bear, a UC Berkeley graduate. I drove a brand new Ferrari red Volkswagen Bug. Our house was in a good neighborhood. It had a flushing toilet, a refrigerator, and no red-eyed visitors late at night scurrying across my bed. The coast of Italy could be duplicated just by driving down California's Highway 1. I was a happy little American and was positively convinced that I was never going back to Italy. I was just fine here, but my parents wanted me to experience Italy. And so *il circolo*, the circle, begins.

Chapter 1

Never Again! 1971

The first trip to Italy with my parents was more than forty years ago in 1971. I was young, a recent graduate of UC Berkeley, an anglophile, with long straight blonde hair brushing my shoulders. I wore hip-hugger stovepipe pants, a tight ribbed sweater, and granny glasses. We boarded the plane and sat trapped in that metal box for what seemed like days. I had lost count after the first ten hours. It was like a can of sardines with wings. I felt like I had entered the twilight zone and would never arrive. I was afraid to go to the bathroom on the plane because I thought I might get sucked out of the plane through the toilet. So I held it. When I got off the plane, I actually kissed the ground in Rome and ran to the nearest bathroom. I was immediately confused. Should I push a button, pull a chain, or stomp on something? It was a survival test, and I was already flunking a basic skill—how to flush a toilet.

We flew on John Daly World Airways, a charter airline out of Oakland, California, directly to Rome. I was stinky and sticky and felt like I had moss growing on my teeth. In those days, passengers could smoke on the airplane. You cannot imagine what the air quality was like after hours and hours with all those smokers. We all smelled like the inside of an ashtray. We were exhausted, our clothes were rumpled, and we walked like zombies. It was about nine in the evening when we arrived and perhaps ninety degrees or more on a hot and sultry July night. It felt like we were stepping into a steam bath when we walked down the stairs from the plane. At this time, the Red Brigade, an Italian terrorist group, was dominating the headlines; and the airport was filled with armed soldiers patrolling with their sentinel German shepherds. Their presence was intimidating, and I was scared. This was a very terrifying time in Italy, with many kidnappings and terrorist acts. The government was unstable and very weak, with the political parties fighting among each other in an environment of catastrophic unemployment. We were anxious to get out of the airport as swiftly as possible. We gathered our bags, moved like the Roman god Mercury through customs, and took a taxi to the train station.

The exhausting train ride to Genova seemed to take endless hours, even though we arrived at eleven at night. We had studied our cousin Giorgio's photographs on the train. As we entered the lobby of the station, I pointed out a man holding a photograph. He had a medium build, curly dark hair, pearly white teeth, and was waving at us as he called, "Ciao! Ciao! Mi chiamo, Giorgio." He was the nephew of my paternal grandmother Antonietta. We strapped our luggage to the roof of his tiny Fiat and raced up the coast. As we bolted on to the autostrada, Giorgio floored it, and the car leaped forward like we were going to be airborne. I thought we were going to die. My mother had a fear of three things: birds, cats, and speed. She was thrown backward into her seat. Screaming, she grabbed for the dashboard and wet her pants. Of course, my mother wet her pants even on the Dumbo ride at Disneyland. Remember, there were no seat belts in those days. I'm convinced the reason we have seat belts in our cars now is because the vehicle safety board members must have had a ride with Giorgio. My father and I were trapped in the backseat. All my father could say was, "I can't stretch out my legs. It's been twenty-four hours since I've been able to stretch out my legs, and I'm getting cramps." My father thought he had the legs of a Las Vegas showgirl. After a couple of drinks, he would roll up his pant legs and announce that he had the legs of a dancer, better than my mother, who, he claimed, had thick ankles. "Look at my ankles, Rose," he would say. "They're like a racehorse, built for speed. And look at this calf, the calf of a dancer." His knees were up to his chin, and my father was not a tall man.

We couldn't see anything ahead of us. "Donna, don't look. We don't want to know what's going on up there," my father said. Then he leaned over and using one of his favorite expressions said, "Godamita, Rose. He better not lose our luggage." My father used to create words when he was upset but didn't want to swear. My mother glanced back. "I don't care about the luggage. I just want to live." Giorgio seemed possessed, the demon driver from hell, and we thought we were on our way there.

With no warning, certainly no signal, Giorgio careened off the autostrada and headed for the town of Varazze. We continued along the coast for a short time and then headed for the hills. He whipped around the hills on the narrow dirt roads. We never knew which way the car would lean, and we were thrown from side to side, with my mother screaming each time the car shifted. It was now midnight, and I was convinced that I was going to die without ever seeing Italy. And here we were, traveling in complete darkness to the birthplace of my nonna Antonietta, Stella San Bernardo.

As I stared in wonderment at Giorgio, the crazy Italian driver, my stomach was growling so loud I thought even Giorgio could hear it over the racing engine of the little Fiat. A box of See's chocolates had sustained me on the flight; but now as the two-hour drive wore on, I was really counting on the huge table of real Italian food to celebrate the arrival of the American relatives. I couldn't wait to get there. I imagined all the relatives waiting to welcome us, the table laden with rich Italian food, music playing, smiling faces all staring down the road, waiting for the first visit of their American relatives, the son and daughter of the immigrants. Then suddenly, the car slid to an abrupt halt. I looked out the car window and saw the reflection of my own face. We couldn't see anything. There were no lights.

We arrived in the forested darkness some time after midnight, with no moon. My father asked Giorgio where we were. He replied exuberantly, "We're here!" Giorgio jumped out of the car and called out into the darkness, "Gli cugini Americani sono qui." The American cousins are here. Clutching my macramé purse, I stumbled over the rough rocky ground in my platform sandals toward a door in one of the most primitive houses I had ever seen. The Berkeleyite had come to the rural hills of Italy.

They opened the door, and there we were, and there they were. "We are so happy to see you, our cousins from America!" they exclaimed in the Genovese dialect. My four years of Spanish were immediately relegated to useless. I heard my father say in English, "Rose, don't unpack. We're not staying here."

My eyes widened in disbelief. I was staring at people out of the American Wild West from over a hundred years ago. Standing there was an emaciated couple from a bad Western movie. They were my great-aunt Teresa and her husband, Uncle Giorgio. She wore a full-length black dress and was seriously skinny, so skinny that she looked wafer thin to my "fat" size 3. He had on some kind of baggy suit made of a wool fabric that hardly kept his bones from peeking through. When we turned around, Cousin Giorgio had vanished. He had gone back home. We had no rental car. We were trapped. I was exhausted and hungry, and I was to remain hungry the whole visit. They literally had no food.

When I was a child, Nonna Antonietta explained that the village of Stella San Bernardo is one of the five stelle, "stars," that comprise the crown of Mary. Stella San Bernardo supposedly was the top of the pecking order, and yet I wondered, *What happened?* My parents' families came from a region in Northern Italy on the Mediterranean near the French-Italian border called Liguria. Liguria is about the size of the state of Delaware and has a population similar to that of Idaho. It is a small thinly sliced arc of land that the Italians call *mezzaluna* or "half moon," facing the Ligurian Sea. The road leading to its most famous city, Genova, curves along the rugged coast made up of craggy hills and lots of *gallerie. Gallerie* are tunnels cut through the Italian hills.

Oh, Nonna! Where was that villa you used to tell me about? Was this the upper crust of the stelle, stars in the corona of Liguria, that Nonna Antonietta's stories had promised? Was this one of *the* stelle with its "royal Italians"? It appeared that the stelle stories from Nonna's childhood memories had been romanticized with the passage of time.

My grandmother, or as we say *nonna*, Antonietta Rusca came to America to escape being murdered. Born in 1893, she was the eldest daughter of eight children and perhaps the most beautiful. She worked as a maid for a wealthy family in Savona. There in Savona, a handsome young Sicilian man with red hair and blue eyes fell in love with her. The relationship had blossomed to the point where he had met Antonietta's parents. He was a serious suitor. In those days, if a daughter brought a young man home to her village to meet her parents, it meant that there were marriage intentions. At that time in Italy, young men of a certain age were drafted to be trained for the army. One afternoon, she joined the other women who went down to the train station to wish good luck to her childhood friends from Stella San Bernardo who were being conscripted for the army. As she turned and leaned in to give a hug to one of her friends, a shot rang out, and a bullet grazed her ear. Her suitor had followed her to the train station and, in a fit of jealous rage, tried to murder her. At the trial, he admitted that he had been stalking her and indeed intended to kill her. Since it was a crime of passion, the judges acquitted him. While they were in the courtroom, he vowed that he would find her, no matter where she went, and hunt her down and kill her.

Antonietta was now afraid for her life. She knew she had to leave, but where could she go? How to be safe? She had relatives in France but thought that France was too close and that her stalker could easily find her. Antonietta decided to flee to the ends of the earth—California. She made her way to Oakland and first worked as a maid and then later in a cannery. She was the first in her family to emigrate from Italy to the United States. She was running for her life. What an irony! She was forced to leave what she thought was her safe haven, her beautiful villa, to come to a foreign land, which became a land of riches for her.

I looked in disbelief at the light coming from the one bulb swinging from the middle of the ceiling and illuminating the dirty stone floor. The refrigerator was two wooden crates filled with vegetables stored in the bathroom next to the toilet because that was the coolest place in the house during the summer. The bathroom toilet had just been installed because our American Rusca family had sent the money. My bedroom was upstairs, and you could get to it only by going through the bedroom of Giorgio's parents, my seventy-year-old great-aunt and uncle, Teresa Rusca and Giorgio Manico.

That night, as I slipped through their bedroom to get to mine, I noticed that Giorgio's father wore a nightcap and a nightgown as he cuddled with Teresa. I could hear them giggling and making noises with the steel springs of the bed going *cha-ching, cha-ching, cha-ching.* The headboard banging against the wall every night was only one of the things that kept me awake. As I huddled under the covers waiting for dawn, adding to the romantic ambiance of the place, there were scrawny rats glancing at me with their big red eyes as they scurried across my bed. Even if I had been able to sleep, the bells from the church that tolled *bong, bong, bong* every fifteen minutes all night would have kept me awake. I felt as if I were trapped in a bizarre film like *Clockwork Orange* and could not escape—little red-eyed monsters with claws going *scritch-scratch, scritch-scratch, scritch-scratch*; the lovers going *cha-ching, cha-ching, cha-ching* with the headboard banging; and finally God signaling *bong, bong, bong* every fifteen minutes. Somehow I don't think my art history teacher visited this part of Italy.

Adding to my misery each day was the need to scurry like my red-eyed night visitors to find food. I thanked God it was summer, and there were fruit trees in the backyard. I never realized how thin the Italian people would be next to me, and I was always hungry. One day as I was searching for some ripe apricots on the trees, I looked up into the hills and saw a fire coming down the hill at a rapid pace through the brush. I thought, *We must evacuate—NOW.* I was in shock. How? We had no car. I ran to my dad and, with wide-eyed terror, reported, "There's a fire in the hills. It's coming down toward the house and the village. We'd better call the fire department." What a joke! My father calmly replied, "We have no phones here, and there is no fire department." My father turned to Uncle Giorgio and asked, "What shall we do about the fire?" Uncle Giorgio calmly responded, "We let it burn." Eventually, the fire sputtered out but not before it got to the edge of the backyard, a close call; but we were safe. That really confirmed it for me. I needed to get out of there.

While watching the fire getting closer and closer, my mother threw a curve into the mix. "Before we leave," she said, "we have to see my cousin in Stella San Giovanni and see my aunts in Pero." We didn't leave Italy but did leave the burning hills. In Genovese dialect, the word aunt is *lalla*, and in the mother tongue, it is *zia*. Nonna Antonietta, who had arrived earlier and remembered the arduous hikes to the nearest neighbor, announced to my mother that it was too far to walk to Stella San Giovanni or Pero. Cousin Giorgio, the speed demon, graciously volunteered to drive us in the now infamous race car to meet the aunts in Pero: Lalla Albina, Lalla Giuseppina, twin sisters, and the youngest of the family, Lalla Nita. We had no choice. We had to rely on Cousin Giorgio's tiny Fiat and daredevil driving. Giorgio told my mother that she would have to figure out a different way to see her cousin in Stella San Giovanni because he was working.

Although it was just a day trip, I was elated to leave Stella San Bernardo. I thought that it had to be better on my mother's side of the family. This place had to be an aberration, an exception, as it certainly didn't look like the pictures in the tour brochures for Italy. It could not be this bad everywhere, could it? Off we went to Pero, arriving about noon in the heat of a sizzling summer day. It must have been well over a hundred degrees. We were sweltering. Lalla Nita's home and the twin sisters' home were located on the same dirt road a stone's throw apart.

We trudged up a dirt road and saw a house in the distance. It was the Vallerga family home where my nonna Maria had been born. The home was a rustic, crumbling grayish stone house neglected over time by poverty. Here lived my mother's aged twin aunts, spinsters Lalla Albina and Lalla Giuseppina. I stood under the grape arbor and watched as my mother, fleet of foot like Victoria, the Roman god, ran into the arms of her aunts. As soon as my mother reached them, they hugged and hugged as if they would never let go. They were all crying with joy. While we watched them, my father and I had tears of joy for them. It was the first time in my mother's life she actually saw any of her family members beyond her parents and connected with any of her roots. Right then, she promised, over and over, to return; and she did return year after year, with Nonna Maria and my brother John. I should explain to you that my brother, who is four years older than me, was diagnosed with child schizophrenia in the 1950s. My brother spoke both Italian and English by the age of four but ran a high fever because of pneumonia. At the age of five, he regressed to an infantile state and was unable to speak or take care of himself. Eventually, John regained his ability to speak as well as his motor skills, but his social skills would be severely delayed. John would be mainstreamed into a Catholic school and rediagnosed as autistic in the 1990s. My brother lives in our parents' home and has made great strides toward independence. I am happy to report that he was my fact-checker for dates and other pertinent data for this book.

Lalla Giuseppina was a strong, sturdy woman about five and a half feet tall, wearing a flower-printed dress with an apron. Her graying hair was pulled back in a bun. Her face was elegant with fine bone structure and a good nose and pretty gray eyes like Nonna Maria. She had a warm, welcoming smile. She wore sturdy shoes with a Cuban heel. I saw that her legs were heavy and that her ankles were thick, and I noticed that she walked with a slight limp. I found out later that the limp was from shrapnel wounds incurred during World War II while she walked to work as a nurse at the nearby mental hospital. Lalla Albina was much smaller, thinner, and petite, perhaps five foot two. Albina, with a very childlike face, had short graying hair cut in a Dutch-boy style. She had contracted spinal meningitis as a child, which left her mentally challenged. Giuseppina had devoted her life to caring for Albina and the patients in the mental institution. I found out later that the townspeople considered her a saint.

The visit was very emotional for all of us. It was the first time my great-aunts met my mother, their American niece. Until that moment, I had never met any family members from my mother's side. As different as our homes were, our emotions were the same—deep, raw, and real. As we then walked back down the same dirt road, I began to think about my nonna Maria, who had moved into our home when I turned five after her husband, my nonno Edoardo, passed away.

My maternal grandmother, Maria Vallerga, was courageous. She was the only daughter who left the small hill village of Pero, located above the Italian Riviera. She emigrated alone from Italy because she was starving, and she was escaping to a better life. Maria was sponsored to the United States by her brother Tony, who had come earlier but later died tragically in a mining accident.

She traveled in steerage and would go up on deck in the night to get fresh air. While on deck, Maria saw the crew using white sheets to wrap adults and children, who had died during the voyage, for burial at sea. Maria could not help wondering if she was going to survive the trip across the Atlantic. It was a scary and challenging time for her, especially because she could not speak English; however, she was smart, willful, and determined to survive.

As a little girl, I listened many times to Nonna Maria recount her journey to her new home. She would start by saying that she weighed less than one hundred pounds and was really skinny when she came. "I think maybe the ship's captain liked me because one evening while I was on deck, he noticed me. After that, he made sure I was given food. Then when the ship arrived in New York and the immigration service was examining me, they looked at a small cut on one of my fingers. The officials were talking about this and discussing, I think, denying me entry. Suddenly, the captain, who was standing near me, stepped in and persuaded them to allow me entry. They stamped my card, and I was in America!" she would exclaim with a big smile.

One of my favorite stories was the one where Maria took a train across the United States. She would begin by saying, "I rode the train across the Great Plains, thinking how big my new country was, when suddenly I saw creatures on horseback with colorful plumes sprouting from their heads. I thought they were a different kind of species, perhaps birdmen who had feathers growing out of their heads. I didn't know until much later they were Native Americans who had already been here for centuries. When the Indians stopped the train to board it, I was paralyzed with fear. As they walked down the aisle, I sat very still and tried to squeeze into the corner of the seat next to the window to become invisible. I peeked at them out of the corner of my eye and saw that they were emaciated and their eyes were sunken in like mine. I felt fear but also sadness for them and for me. In some strange way, we seemed to connect. Both of us were different. I, because I was a pauper, could not speak the language and did not know the culture. I was looking for a new beginning. They were looking for possessions that could be traded for food. They paused to look at me. We had eye contact. Our eyes communicated fear, despair, and a search for something better. They passed by me and went on to the more well-dressed passengers who seemed to have money." Maria's hope was a still small candle, a fragile dream that could have been extinguished in a moment, but it was not; and she survived again. She had survived the voyage, Ellis Island, and now the train. All she needed to do was to get to her brother Tony in California.

When she arrived in California, Maria was able to obtain a job in the cannery with other Italian women in Oakland and later met Edoardo through common friends. The Ligurian community kept to themselves because they did not speak much English and needed to survive in this new and strange land where Italians and immigrants were so suspect.

My mother always told me, "Your grandparents had a wonderful marriage. They never raised their voices to each other. They were a happy couple and were deeply in love." Edoardo and Maria's first birth was their only child and was a daughter, my mother, Rosa Maddelena Vallerga Bertuccio. She was named after her two grandmothers, an Italian tradition. As I continued to reminisce, I heard my father saying to my mother, "I don't know, Rose. This is *miseria paese*, miserable country."

Walking down the dirt road, in the distance, we saw a small wooden rustic house not far from the Vallerga home. It was nestled into the hillside next to a pig sty and a small vegetable garden. My hopes sank. As we neared the wooden house on stilts, I saw a toothless old man in hip-high boots coming out of a muddy pig pen. He turned out to be my mother's uncle by marriage, Francesco. He was scrawny and skinny; he could have slid through a closed door. He gestured warmly to come inside.

Lalla Nita was standing in the kitchen, cooking. She was in her sixties, the spitting image of my nonna Maria, who was the eldest of the daughters; whereas Lalla Nita was the youngest of the family. Nita's baptismal name was Maddelena. She had the same steel blue-gray eyes as Nonna Maria, a flawless porcelain complexion, the same nose as Maria, with silvery hair pulled into a chignon. In my forty-plus years of knowing her, she never aged, staying mentally sharp and living until she was a hundred. Those Vallerga genes are very strong. Thank you once again for my nice nose which thrilled my mother. They offered us a shot of something that smelled like vermouth and some cookies. I sat there as my mother and Lalla Nita chatted away in the dialect. I was wondering what planet we had landed on. I was glad my mother was able to meet her relatives, but I didn't know what was being said, and I wanted to leave.

As the visit continued, I started to smell something. The stench soon became so unbearable that I became nauseous. Then I heard "the stench" beneath the house bellowing, "Moo. Moo. Moo." There were cows under the house, and that was why the house was on stilts. The cows were their source of heat in the winter, but this was July. It was a hot, stinking nightmare. My visions of "better" evaporated along with the methane gas seeping up through the floorboards. Now I was only thinking about one thing, *How fast could I get out of Italy?* This Italy was nothing like the one in the movies or in the art history classes I had taken in college. I swore that if I could only get out of there, I would never return. My father was repeating and repeating to my mother in English, "Rosa, we've got to go. Rose, we've got to go." I was silently cheering him on. But my mother was determined to meet her family; she dug her high heels into the Italian soil, and we did not leave.

Her nickname could have been the iron lady. She was the iron hand in the velvet glove. She was a force to be reckoned with, exuding self-assurance and confidence. It was a combination of her DNA and a loving family that made her think that she could do anything, and she did.

Rosa was a very loved and protected child. She was a classic Italian princess or *principessa*, as we say. Once when she was three, her parents took her to the circus and denied her a doll that walked and talked that she wanted. She then had what was the only tantrum of her life, stamping her feet and yelling in the dialect that she wanted the doll. She was denied because the "doll" was not a doll but a dwarf, a little person. This was the only time her father talked sternly to her, and her mother gave her a look that stopped her in her tracks. My mother did not speak English until she went to school in Oakland, and the same with my father; but both were glib and could toss out one-liners like Jerry Seinfeld and Whoopi Goldberg.

During the 1970s, my mother was quite a picture. She was glamorous and had a figure that rivaled Hollywood starlets. Her blonde beehive hair was piled high, and she wore the latest fashions. Rosa was, as they say in Italian, *un bel figurino*, "a beautiful fashion plate"; but to the relatives in rural Italy, she looked like a streetwalker. According to her cousin Lorenzo, the word on the village streets was that a high-class prostitute had moved into town. But how did she know the Ligurian dialect? It was a mystery to them. There were no prostitutes in the stelle that they knew. They wondered, "How can she be one of us?" There were no televisions, no telephones, and few radios. She was outside their realm of reality and experience. Nonetheless, my mother was there and was determined to find the rest of her family.

A few days later, while my father and I remained in Stella San Bernardo, Rosa hiked the half mile up the dirt road in her stiletto heels toward the next village. She discovered the bus stop and found out how to get to Stella San Giovanni, where her cousin Maria Ferro Cipresso lived. But that is another story.

The good news is that I escaped. I left for France. *Merci beaucoup!* Ciao, Italy! Hurray! Hot running water! Yum! Real food! I never wanted to experience again a fire coming over the hillside with no fire department to come to our rescue. I never wanted to experience the continuous bell tolling every fifteen minutes throughout the night or rats scurrying over my bed, staring at me with their beady red eyes. I was tired of being hungry and tired of seeing everyone skinny as sticks and dressed in tattered worn-out clothes. It was so depressing, and there was nothing I could do to help. And to top it all off, I could not communicate with them.

I said goodbye to my Italian relatives, and before I left, my father and I made a secret pact never to return to Italy. My father had had his fill of the Stella and was no longer convinced he wanted to see his father's birthplace, Alpicella, which was just up the road.

Thankfully, Cousin Giorgio dropped me safely at the airport, and I flew ecstatically away to Paris. As I soaked in my hot bath in my modern Parisian hotel room, I was determined to never return to Italy. I dressed in my finest clothes and went out to find a delicious dessert and relax. I sat down at a classic Parisian café and breathed a sigh of relief that I was out of the rustic place of my family's roots. I bit into a blissful morsel of Peach Melba and slowly turned to look at the nearby tables. To my astonishment, there was the ever-charming, desirable, enchantingly elegant Maurice Chevalier, the famous French actor from the movie *Gigi*. I smiled at him, and he beckoned to me. I floated over to his table. I lamented, sharing with him my misadventures in Italy, swearing eternal love for Paris and the French. He looked kindly at me and gently said, "But of course." I felt that I was transformed into Gigi and that I was in my rightful place at last. Italy? I just didn't belong. I didn't understand Italy, and Italy didn't understand me. I reaffirmed my promise never to return.

Years later, I gave my father a free pass to return to visit his father's birthplace; of course, my mother had coaxed him into it. He would do anything for his dinky doll. My father visited Alpicella and connected with the Ferro side, but ultimately, he was happy to stay home enjoying his comfortable lifestyle. So my mother, brother, and Nonna Maria would travel to Italy without us. We continually wondered why they wanted to leave paradise for Italy or, as my father would say, "We have football. We have color TV. What more could you want?" It seemed logical to me; we had it all.

While the happy traveling trio was globetrotting, I was working on my master's degree and teaching high school. My father kept busy tending his rose and vegetable gardens and working for the Oakland Scavenger Company. While they were gone, often in the evenings, my father would reminisce and talk to me about growing up on the farm and meeting my mother.

My father, Carlo Ferro, was born in Alameda, California, in an area called Bay Farm Island. From the age of six, he plowed the vegetable fields before and after school, a chore he continued until he married Rosa Maddelena Vallerga Bertuccio and joined her father in the scavenger business.

Carlo was a young man who radiated joy. He had gorgeous curly blond locks, hazel eyes, and a smile that would light up a gloomy day. He was very shy but very handsome. He was intelligent; he skipped two grades in school. He was talented. He could sing with perfect pitch and played several instruments: the accordion (his favorite), harmonica, drums, and piano; but his operatic voice was the most remarkable instrument of all. He was a kind and gentle spirit who deeply loved his mother, father, and brother.

The story of how my parents, Carlo and Rosa, fell in love is special. My father relished telling me about how he met his dinky doll and became her tiger. Because the Italian community was so small, its members attended many social events together. One of the popular pastimes was to gather at someone's home or barn and play cards. One evening when Carlo was seventeen, he went with his family to a party to play cards at my great-uncle Vince and aunt Mary's home. Uncle Vince was a garbage man and Nonna Antonietta's younger brother. My mother, who was then thirteen, came with her parents to play cards as well.

Much to Carlo's surprise, my mother consistently won at cards that night. They fell in love at the dining room table. Carlo sat with his back to the wall where a mirror hung, while Rosa sat across from him and looked into the mirror. It was a very long time before she revealed to him how she was so good at "winning." He was her tiger, and she was his dinky doll. He called himself Tigre. Dinky doll had a full scholarship to Stanford, but the war hit, and she never went. The good news was that she married Tigre, my father. Edoardo, my mother's father, impressed by the young Carlo and his work ethic, sponsored him into the Oakland Scavenger Company. When my parents married, the wedding present from Maria and Edoardo was a new black 1941 Buick. Rosa and Carlo had an elaborate wedding with about eight hundred guests. The vast majority of the Italian community attended. She wore a beautiful lace veil from France that draped a full six steps at St. Elizabeth's Church in Oakland. My parents had a lifelong love affair and an exceptional marriage. It was a true partnership, which I will always admire and treasure.

I loved these special times with my father; while Nonna Maria, my brother John, and my mother returned to the rural hills of Italy. I was happy here, and so was my father. We had no desire to go back to Italy.

Però mi mama è molta furba. But my mama is very cunning.

Chapter 2

The Côte d'Azur Carrot 1989

Fate has a way of turning tables. Almost twenty years had now passed. It was now 1989. My career had taken many wonderful turns, and I was at Butte Community College as director of Disabled Students Programs and Services, near Chico, California. My daughter, Terèsa, whom we call Bella, was about to turn eight years of age. All was right with my world.

My mother had been a widow for five years. After my father's untimely death, she had dropped to ninety pounds and went into therapy but had begun to recover. I had been devastated by my father's death. My light had gone out, so I buried myself in my work. Then one day, my mother phoned and said, "Let's go to Italy." I immediately flashed back to our infamous trip with the aroma of cows, the hillside fire, the bonging of the bells, the rats scurrying, and my incessant hunger. I certainly did not want to expose my young daughter to the same elements that I had experienced. So I made up a story, "Geez, Mom, I am busy because the college staff will be reduced for the summer. It's probably not a good idea for me to go."

She was what we say in Italian *furba* or "cunning." Rose dangled a golden carrot in front of me and used her most persuasive voice, "I was thinking that we would fly into Nice, France. We could get a rental car, stay at the Ritz Carlton in Cannes, and then drive to the relatives in Stella San Giovanni and finally Portofino, staying at the Hotel Splendido." I had never been to either Cannes or Portofino, and they sounded lovely. It was a big fat carrot dangling in front of a very hungry rabbit. My mind started to wander as she continued to hammer at me to go on the trip.

Sigmund Freud would have been proud of her and the Rose Ferro School of Psychology, which she practiced on me all my life. She knew exactly what she was doing, and when she decided to do something, she was usually successful and got her way. I remember each year on my birthday, October 3, she would remind me that God had given her a sign that I would be born that day. The sign was that the roses that usually bloomed in the spring had bloomed again on October 3. That day, when she went to the doctor for a checkup, she told him, "Today my daughter will be born." He asked her how she knew, and she told him it was because "the roses are blooming on the side of the house." The roses signified female and birth that day. Remember, in 1947, there were no sonograms. She went home and ate a big bowl of ravioli to fortify herself. I arrived on cue, at eight o'clock that night. Every year after that, she sent roses to St. Elizabeth's Church in Oakland to grace the statute of St. Thérèse de Lisieux on October 3, her feast day. In fact, in the saint's honor, my middle name is Thérèse.

Suddenly, a staff member came in and said, "Are you off the phone yet?" I could hear my mother on the phone yelling, "Donna Marie, can you hear me? You're not listening to me, are you?" "Uh, yes, Mom, I'm here." My mother continued reassuring me that the living conditions had improved immensely for the relatives. She had made many trips back to Italy, and things had changed for the better. Her cousin, Maria Cipresso, had married very well. Her husband owned a mine and several apartment buildings; and yes, they lived in one of the stelle—Stella San Giovanni. My mother continued with great confidence, "I promise you that the relatives have all the modern conveniences, hot water with a tub and a shower, no rats, refrigerator, marble floors. And below the apartment is a piazza with shops." I cautiously accepted her offer. And with great trepidation and my young daughter in tow, I said, "All right we will go to the French Riviera and Portofino." Somehow I would find a way to deal with the Stella part later.

We flew on Pan Am, where Terèsa, Bella, celebrated her eighth birthday at thirty thousand feet. The copilot came out on his break and, seeing the vacant aisle seat next to me, sat down. He asked if I had ever been to Nice or Cannes. When I said no, he replied, "You will love it." Then he took a little catnap before returning to the cockpit. After we landed and we were beginning to disembark, I heard the copilot announce, "Welcome to Nice, Donna Marie. Have a great vacation." I knew it was the start of a fabulous adventure.

Oh, the airport in Nice on the Côte d' Azur, it is like eye candy. What is there not to love in Nice? You may remember that Italy was not united until about 1861. Liguria and the Côte d' Azur are a mixture of French and Italian. In fact, Menton, nicknamed the "Pearl of France," is the site of the Paleolithic Cro-Magnon Grimaldi Man and many Cro-Magnon and Neanderthal findings. Menton, which is on the French-Italian border, is about an hour and a half from Varazze, the Italian Riviera resort town near my relatives.

Wow. I was in Nice, but I had never driven in Europe. What an adventure for someone who hates to drive. Even after driving lessons, it took me three times to pass the California DMV driver test in Alameda. My French-American driving teacher resigned after he found out that it took me three times to pass the driving test. If only my French driving instructor could see me now as I merged on to the autostrada heading north, hoping to see a sign that said Cannes. I had no directions except my internal Ligurian homing device. I made an instinctive left turn, thinking I was going toward the sea, when suddenly I realized that I was on La Croisette, "small cross," which is the main street in Cannes. I recognized it from the movies and television. It was a miracle as I have absolutely no sense of direction, just ask my family. "Oh, I can't believe it. I'm in Cannes." And, I thought proudly, not a scrape or dent on the car.

The Ritz Carlton is located there as well as the famous Hotel Martinez. The Martinez, where the European stars stay during the Cannes Film Festival, was previously owned by the king of Naples, for decades the social center of Cannes. It is fronted by beautiful beaches, boasting the largest private beach, with gently lapping waves from the turquoise Mediterranean Sea. La Croisette has Salvatore Dali sculptures lining the sidewalks opposite the beach. It is THE place to be seen. Anyone who wants to be seen comes there and promenades, or as we say in Italy, the passeggiata. It is the riviera, where the Cannes Film Festival is held every year in May.

I looked back toward my sleeping mother, "Hey, sleepyheads, wake up." Then voila! There in its opulent splendor was the Ritz Carlton. By this time, I was dripping wet with sweat from nerves and fear from driving. I tossed the keys to the valet and said what was to be my signature arrival statement, "Rose,[1] Bella, we're here. Let's get some champagne." They brought us and our luggage to a very small but beautiful room. I had to crawl across Bella's bed to get to mine. But it was France. I was back in the land of Maurice Chevalier.

I opened the doors to the balcony. The air was soft and fragrant with the scent of blooming flowers, freesia, jasmine, and the salty scent of the sea. The sun warmed my skin, the swaying palm trees lining La Croisette moving in rhythm to the breeze off the sea. I saw little sidewalk cafés and fantasized about sipping an espresso. Who knew who I would meet, perhaps another celebrity?

We went downstairs to stroll on La Croisette and the exquisite beach. Bella went exploring on the beach and discovered topless beach ladies, which she dubbed "Titties on Patrol" (T-O-P). As we walked along, Bella would announce every woman who came along topless with "T-O-P." We began to rate them on a scale of 1 to 10. Once in a while, we would wince. We decided we did not like the Speedos on the men. But hey, we were in France, and they let it all hang out. Every pubescent boy should spend a summer on the Côte d'Azur.

We went shopping on a side street and found a lovely doll for Bella. It was dressed in a pink sailor dress with a small hat that had a front brim turned up. Its cheeks were rosy, and she named it Rose Marie in honor of my mother. And yes, to this day, Rose Marie resides in my home in Bella's old bedroom.

After the beach and shopping, we finally returned to the Ritz. We were wondering how we should dress for the evening when suddenly, there at the top of the grand staircase framed in the double doors of their suite was a couple, the man in a tuxedo with a woman in an elegant but understated cocktail gown. They were walking two standard Italian greyhounds with jeweled collars. I turned to my mother and announced, "The Marines have landed. Get out your green chiffon Carolina Herrera dress. We need to stuff you in it. We're going out on the town."

Upon returning to our room, Bella and I had my mother lie down on the bed with the dress. Then Bella and I pulled and tugged

---

[1] *I began calling my mother Rose when I was quite young. She was so focused on my brother because of his disability that when we went some place and I said Mom, she did not respond. By the time I was in the fifth grade, I had figured out the only way to get her attention was to call her Rose. This annoyed her greatly, but truth be known, it worked.*

and stuffed my mother, who had gained weight, into the dress. After twenty minutes of hard labor and with a few jumps on the part of my mother at the very end to shake things down and in, the dress was on. She looked great with her blonde hair piled up on her head and her perfect makeup, enough to rival the couple and their elegant Italian greyhounds. We were now the Marines, and we were making a beach landing on La Croisette.

Our first "deployment" was to go downstairs to the bar and have a drink. Bella thought the bartender looked like football Hall of Famer Joe Montana and told him so. Each time we returned, she would say, "Hi, Joe." At dinner, the waiters would bring a highchair for Rose Marie, the doll, and the three of us would dine elegantly. That first evening, a waiter accidently touched the doll's cheek with his pen. It was a permanent blue souvenir from the Ritz and the Côte d'Azur, and to this day, it reminds me of the first adventure of three generations of women who would travel many more times together.

We floated in our sweet fantasy bubble of luxury and had a perfectly lovely time in Cannes. We met people from all over the world. Bella would walk around with her doll, Rose Marie; and people would comment on how lovely the two of them were, at which point Bella would bring them over to meet us. Bella and Rose Marie were like goodwill ambassadors, meeting and greeting the visitors of the hotel. One night, my mother decided to "hang one on," and we began our habit of closing the bar at the Ritz. In our fog, we decided that the next day we would go to Grasse to tour the perfume factories. We fell into bed dreaming of the wonderful fragrances we would sniff the next day or actually later that day.

Reality knocked on the door. I dragged myself out of bed and staggered to answer it. In my confusion, I called out, "Who's there? It's late. Why are you knocking on our door?" The voice from the hallway spoke in French. I waited, and then it said in English, "I'm here to make up your room. It is one o'clock in the afternoon." I asked her to come back in an hour. Since we had only three hours until the perfume factories closed, I shouted to my mother and daughter, "Get up. Get dressed. We've got to get out of here. We've only got a couple of hours until the perfume factories close!" As I raced to throw on some clothes, I thought, *Oh no. I don't know how to get there.*

We grabbed a snack for Bella and asked the concierge how to find our way to Grasse. He said in what I have found to be quite the European style, "Just go up the hill." We raced up the hill, and somehow I found Grasse. At one point as we looked for the factories,

Rose screamed at me, "You are going the wrong way on a one-way street. You're going to get us killed. Turn around." We were lucky it was Sunday, and few people were out. It seemed most people were at the beach. We made it to the factory just before closing and left with some delightful perfumes and a working knowledge of how perfume is made. We were impressed with ourselves. We had gone from being comatose to mach speed and reached the factory in less than an hour. The Grand Prix had nothing on us.

I found myself thinking that "Life is good." We were enjoying the best of everything. We were pampered and spoiled by the French as never before. As the sun set, the hour of reckoning was approaching. Tomorrow I would be driving to Italy and had no clue where was Stella San Giovanni. Now it was time to face it. Would there be food for my daughter? Were the rats really gone? Was the Sword of Damocles of the Stella about to fall? Stella San Giovanni was the home of my mother's cousin, Maria, and Zerbio Cipresso; but I had never been there. Would there be hot water, food, a refrigerator, red-eyed friends, or cows under the house with their fragrance du jour? My mother had been there several times, and I thought she would know how to get there. Wrong-o bucko!

As we left Cannes and began heading south, I asked my mother what direction I should drive. She replied, "Just drive opposite of the way you came. I have confidence in you. Wake me up when we arrive." My mother always sat in the backseat and went to sleep, preferring to be awakened upon arrival. It was her ritual all the years we traveled. It worked quite successfully for her. Meanwhile, I was sweating profusely, had a white-knuckled grip on the steering wheel, clenched teeth, and fear in my heart as I tried to keep up with the wild Italian traffic. I raced up and down the winding roads and then on to the autostrada as I sped toward Varazze.

In order to calm myself during my frenzy to keep up with the Italian traffic, I began to recall some research I had done on the people and the region of Liguria prior to the trip. In the beginning, the Ligurians were tribes that dated back to the first millennium BC in the northwestern part of Italy. In addition to being dominated by the Romans, we were also invaded between the fourth and the tenth centuries by the Byzantines, the Lombards, the Franks, the Saracens, the Normans, and finally the Republic of Genoa. The invaders pushed for assimilation but were rejected, and the Ligurians maintained their identity. In fact, the basis of the Ligurian dialect is a Gallo-Romance language that is not only spoken in northern Italy but also in parts of Mediterranean, France, Monaco, and Sardinia. Of the over one and a half million Ligurians that live there today, approximately half a million still speak the original Ligurian-old world dialect dating back to before Christopher Columbus.

Many of my relatives' villages and homes are nestled in the hills above Varazze. The coastal town of Varazze has a population of approximately fifteen thousand, except in the summer, when it can swell to forty-five thousand with tourists. Somehow my relatives were now living in a very posh area and without having to move. The world had come to them.

The first of these little hill towns in which I have a relative is Casanova. My cousin Franca Perata-Damele is the daughter of Lalla Nita. They used to live in the stinky house with the cows underneath. Franca is married to Gianni and has one son, Elviro. No, no one knows where the name Elviro comes from. Maybe Franca had a crush on Elvis as a teenager and Italianized his name. Elviro is a year younger than Bella, my daughter.

From Casanova, the next small town is Pero. This is where Lalla Nita used to live with the cows and the toothless man. As a widow, she now lives about ten minutes up in the hills in a hamlet called Campo Marzio, with her son Lorenzo and his wife, Mariuccia, and their two sons, Maurizio and Damiano. Lalla Nita has moved up in life to a beautiful three-story home with no "moo moos" under it.

Elviro tells the story of Campo Marzio, which he roughly translates as "stinky swamp." Julius Caesar's troops were trained there, marching through the rotten, stinky swamps. Trust me, it does not smell now but has tropical flowers, huge fruit trees, and vegetable gardens. Winding up the road from Campo Marzio is a fork where, if you go left, you will arrive in the stelle; but if you continue to drive straight up, you will go to Alpicella, a burgeoning metropolis of four hundred inhabitants and six hundred *cinghiali* (wild boars). The commune is comprised of the five stelle, with about three thousand three hundred residents, according to my cousin, Milena, who lives in Stella San Giovanni.

Upon arriving in Varazze, we intended to ask directions; but it was siesta time, and stores were closed. There was little to no traffic. Finally, we saw a man in a one-pump gas station and asked directions. He waved his hand vaguely, indicating (you know what) that we should "go up the hill." There were no signs. So we took the road that appeared to climb into the hills.

After a while, we saw a sign saying we were headed to Stella San Giovanni. Then we got to a fork in the road, again with no signs. Once again, my Ligurian GPS instincts had to take over, and I could hear my father's voice in my head saying that the stelle were more toward the left and Alpicella was to the right and straight to the top. Fortunately, I took the left side of the fork, which led to Stella San Giovanni; and yes, the right led to Alpicella. Thanks, Carlo, for being my guiding light.

We had arrived in a small town, so I woke my mother. Groggily, my mother said, "There. There it is. I know those men on the bench in front of the apartment." Across the piazza were a little bakery, a bar, a church, a restaurant, and the apartment building owned by the Cipressos. Men were sitting on the bench in front of the bar, drinking, smoking their cigarettes, and chatting about life. When I tooted the horn, Maria came running out of the building with her daughters, Giovanna and Milena. Maria was calling, "Rosa. Rosa." My mother was calling, "Maria. Maria." Maria told my mother that she was more of a sister to her than her own sisters, and she had eight siblings. This relationship continued throughout their lives, a very special family bond. My mother had found her Italian family at last. She was no longer an only child.

Bella was thrilled to meet her teenage cousins Giovanna and Milena. As we entered the apartment, she made friends with the cat, Romeo. Romeo had the distinct talent of being able to jump three feet off the ground when someone touched the doorjamb. He also had an incredible memory; and for the next seventeen years, each time my daughter came to visit, he ran up to her and immediately rubbed up against her. Because Bella met him when she was eight and bonded with him as she constantly played with him, he always knew her and loved her. He died at the ripe old age of twenty.

The Cipresso family had a beautiful apartment house, marble floors, antiques, modern bathrooms, with a five-thousand-piece jigsaw puzzle of Switzerland that hung over the sofa. It still hangs there today. I could hear a sports' event on their TV; it was July, and the Tour de France was happening. Zerbio was sitting at the kitchen table, cigarette in hand, eyes glued to the screen as if in a hypnotic trance.

I think all Italians are fixated on machines that use wheels and speed: la macchina, the car; la bicicletta, the bicycle; la motocicletta, the motorcycle. In June is the Giro d'Italia and in July the Tour de France, which is on every TV in Italy. If church were the only place that Zerbio or the Italians could see the race, they would all be there. One year during the Tour de France, Zerbio's daughter Giovanna married Gianni in the town of Stella San Giovanni. Maria had to physically drag him away from the TV to make it to the wedding on time, and the church is across the street from their apartment. Zerbio was a wonderful man. He loved his daughters and his wife, and they adored him. I used to kiss the top of Zerbio's bald head just like I did my father. He had such a generous, gentle, kind heart; and Maria would squeeze his arms affectionately after I kissed his head and tease me that he belonged to her. He truly did.

When we stayed with them, they rearranged a huge room, adding three beds for us. One night, as we drifted to sleep, my mother screamed, "He has red eyes. He's on top of my chest." The whole household ran into our bedroom. There was Romeo sitting on my mother's chest, staring at her with his glowing red eyes. My mother hated cats. Romeo was furbo. I think he knew about her disdain for cats, especially ones with eyes that looked demonic at night. Ah, Romeo, tu sei furbo. You are cunning.

Thank heavens Maria loved to drive. We would all pile into her car, and she took us everywhere. She was not a maniac driver like Cousin Giorgio. One day in a weak moment, we decided to return to the infamous Stella San Bernardo, which is five minutes from Stella San Giovanni. It was quite different from Nonna Antonietta's childhood days. When we arrived at the little house, Nonna Antonietta's nieces, Eda and Elena, came out to greet us. They were very jovial and welcoming. Eda's husband, Alberto, was the driver for the sisters. Eda lives with her husband in Muggia, near Trieste, while Elena had an apartment in Genova. In the summer, they converge on the Rusca family house in Stella San Bernardo for vacation and to be cooler.

I wondered if the place still had no refrigerator, one lightbulb, and a dirty stone floor with red-eyed visitors. To my amazement, the home was permeated with the wonderful aromas of Italian cooking. Was this the same house I had visited with my family some twenty years ago? It had real floors, white walls with indirect lighting in the ceiling, a repaired staircase, electricity, and refrigerator; and the rats had left. The place had a living room, a kitchen, nice bedrooms, and real bathrooms on both floors; and it was clean. *Hey*, I thought, *I could hang out here.* The smell of the food was incredible. We were going to eat really delicious homemade Italian food, sitting together at the table in the kitchen. It smelled like my nonna Antonietta had returned and was doing the cooking. Obviously, she must have shared her recipes with her nieces. I was in a state of happy shock and delighted with all the changes.

Later as we walked around the village, we visited the cemetery where my relatives are buried. I recalled walking with my father on that infamous trip down the same dirt road to the cemetery to look for the names of our family. We had been looking for the graves of my father's grandparents, Carlo Antonio Rusca and his wife Maria Zunino. I had learned that Maria Zunino met Carlo Rusca at a *festa* in Stella San Giovanni. He was passionately in love with her, and their passion lasted a lifetime. As I wandered through the cemetery with my father, I looked closely at a tombstone with Maria Zunino Rusca's name. There was a very small picture of her on the tomb. As I stared at her face, our eyes locked, and I jumped back like I had been hit by a bolt of electricity. I turned and fearfully said to my father that his grandmother was a strega, a witch. All my education had disappeared, and I was pulled back into my superstitious Italian roots. My father looked at me and said, with a tinge of sarcasm, "Really, Donna Marie, really?"

Nonna Maria told me scary stories about my great-grandmother (*bisnonna*) Maria Zunino Rusca. One of the stories was how she tried to suffocate a baby by putting a blanket over it, but someone came in the room before she could do it. Another story was that a priest came to do an exorcism on her. Some thought she was mentally ill or suffering from postpartum depression. After all, she did have eight children, one right after the other. True or not, I still get the goose bumps when I think about the time I was in the cemetery and locked eyes with my great-grandmother. Now her tombstone is gone. Her remains are in a small mausoleum, and the photo is gone.

Progress had come to Stella San Bernardo, and it was changing. Many of the homes were being remodeled, and much of the money was coming from Germany for summer homes as well as from rich Italian families of Milan. Yes, things had changed in the stelle; the straw of the stelle had turned to gold. I knew I wanted to come back. I'd had an epiphany. Maybe I was connecting with my Italian roots? My mother's golden Côte d'Azur carrot was beginning to work—furba. It was such fun to be with Eda and Elena in Stella San Bernardo and the relatives in Stella San Giovanni. My pact to never return began to dissolve.

After our wonderful week with the relatives in Stella San Giovanni, we departed for Portofino. My mother had made reservations at a place in Portofino called Splendido. Once again without a map, all

I knew was that I was supposed to drive south toward Rapallo. Who knew where was Rapallo? Not me. It meant that I had to go past Genova and try not to get sucked into the vortex. Genova is a huge city with lots of traffic and lots of signs. The traffic moves fast, and there is not just one sign for Genova but many: East, West, North, South, plus all the signs for the villages and towns that surround her. The last time I was here, it had been midnight, and I was not the driver. I was lucky I did not get sucked into the city center of Genova. She knew she would be my Waterloo many times in the future, and she would wait. Such a vixen!

As we wound down the hills and headed toward the sea, my daughter had been counting the gallerias, *gallerie*, since we had left France. She was up to thirty-seven at this point. My goal was to bypass Genova and keep going until I could see a sign for Rapallo. Rapallo was the key. I took the exit for Rapallo, paid the toll, and very quickly looked for the sign for Santa Margherita. I needed to pass through Santa Margherita to get to Portofino and Hotel Splendido. I could see the Mediterranean as we passed many tiny little villages. Having never been this way before, I kept wondering, *Are we there yet? Are we close to it? Where the #@& is it?*

We knew we were close because we had gone into Portofino, and Hotel Splendido was in the hills above it. We began to look for the Splendido sign. The road was taking me down to the seaport and back up again. I was on a merry-go-round: up and down, up and down. Suddenly, Bella said, "Mom, Mom, look up. There is the sign." The sign, almost completely covered with a lush fuchsia-colored bougainvillea vine, was white with blue lettering and had the Splendido seahorse symbol on it. We took the hairpin turn and headed up the narrow driveway. I tooted the horn constantly as I drove up the hill, and it seemed like it should have been a one-way only. The road bloomed into a park like setting with beautiful landscaping, and there it was, Splendido reigning like an Italian empress in the hills above her subjects in Portofino.

If you can imagine paradise, it would be Splendido. Originally, the hotel was a monastery built in the sixteenth century, but the monks were scared off by the pirates. Then it was abandoned for a while. A doctor from Rome bought it as a summer home, renovated it, and sold it. Eventually, the Orient Express Hotel chain bought it and made the sixty-nine rooms into a hotel during the 1920s. Splendido has its own special fragrance, a mixture of jasmine, roses, freesia, and gardenias. All of it beckons you to stay. The air was soft, caressing me with a sweet gentle scent as though I had entered another realm and was under a spell of some kind. Every time I come, I am transported into a luxurious lull. Time and space are suspended. It is truly paradise for me.

The staff immediately greeted us, took our luggage, and escorted us to suite 108. It was a spacious suite we were to have every time we visited over the years. We walked up marble stairs and down a hallway carpeted with Persian rugs and furnished with beautiful hand-carved chairs, credenzas, tables and lamps, and many old-world treasures. The priceless lamps had been made in Albisola, not far from Varazze. The ambiance was of luxury, comfort, and the best of Italy.

In one direction there was a beautiful bed, an alcove with a desk for writing, a huge balcony with views of the Bay of Portofino and nearby villas in the hills. In the other direction was the living room with Champagne, candy and flowers. As soon as we arrived, my mother and Bella ordered room service, and then we shopped, lounged, dined, and danced. Our every need was met. Splendido reflected its name.

The Hotel Splendido is Ligurian. Ligurian in this sense means simple elegance. For example, if you have a bowl of fruit in your room, it would be an ancient Grecian bowl filled with perfect fruit. So it is not opulent; it is understated pristine elegance. It is feeling the experience: the view, the garden, the food, the sea; everything has its place and is in its place, *tutto a posto*. Ligurians face one another and turn their backs to the sea. I have seen the same Ligurian people for more than twenty years engaged in their everyday work, fishing, selling their handiwork, making focaccia in the bakery, selling their fruit and vegetables, and welcoming us to their small caffès and restaurants. And then I saw these same people, without being asked, stop their work, and come to my mother's aid when she fell during her last trip to Italy. We Ligurians are private and closed, but we will always be there for those we love. We know the sea is fickle, just as the world can be, and so we turn our back to it and embrace our family. We are like grapes, clustered together, hoping the vines will protect us.

I had no idea this trip would be the beginning of my love affair with Italy. It began with meeting my mother's family in Stella San Giovanni, returning to Stella San Bernardo, topped off with the dangling carrot of the Côte d'Azur and Splendido in Portofino. Yes, Mom, you were furba.

Chapter 3

Meeting the Rest of the Family 1992

It had been about three years since my mother had dangled the golden carrot that enticed me to Cannes, my return to the relatives and my first trip to Portofino. She had continued her visits over the years since 1971; and she wanted my daughter, Bella, and me to meet more of our relatives.

The three-generation team of grandmother, mother, and daughter boarded the plane for Milan. It was a different route to Liguria, but I had great expectations for my daughter. She was older then, age eleven; I hoped she would ride shotgun next to me as my navigator, be an extra pair of eyes to look for signs, and keep me awake when I got drowsy. But she was just like her nonna, my mother; she slept until we arrived. As we drove from Milan toward Stella San Giovanni, I felt drawn to some hills toward the east. Suddenly, I began to cry, with tears streaming down my cheeks. I woke up my mother. "What's wrong?" she asked, "Did we have an accident?" I tried to share my feelings. "See over there? That is where my paternal grandfather, Nonno Edoardo, lived as a young boy."

"How do you know that's where my father lived?" she said quizzically. "I know. I don't know how I know. I just know. Trust me." My mother was always skeptical about my premonitions and clairvoyance, but Nonna Maria use to tell me, "Believe in your instincts. They are a gift from God."

When we told Maria Cipresso what had happened on the drive from the airport, she told us that the area I had pointed to was Montessoro, where my nonno Edoardo was born. Montessoro is not to be confused with Monterosso, which is part of the Cinque Terra. Cinque Terra is made up of Monterosso, Vernazza, Corniglia, Manarola, and Riomaggiore. The area that Edoardo came from was inland from Genova, near the Piemonte border; whereas Cinque Terra is on the coast, south of Portofino.

Maria thought my feelings and convictions were worthy of a trip, and she offered to take us there. Montessoro was about an hour and a half away and turned out to be located exactly where I had pointed. It was as though Nonno Edoardo was guiding me and wanted me to find his roots. My relatives opened their doors to us and also opened their hearts. The whole tiny hamlet was filled with Nonno Edoardo's relatives; they were all Bertuccios. No one, except Edoardo, seemed to have left Montessoro.

Montessoro does not have the moderation of the Mediterranean, and so it is boiling hot in the summer and freezing cold in the winter. As I looked up into the hills, I could see the modest white stone houses that were replacing the previous primitive homes. I wandered further up the hill and found the ruins of a castle Nonno Edoardo told me about when I was four years old. He had described the castle to me in detail, and I thought that it was where an Italian princess lived, at least in my childhood dreams.

Nonno Edoardo was a twin. He came from a family of six surviving children. His twin sister's name was Assunta, which means "Assumption"; her nickname was Giulietta. Edoardo made the voyage to his new home because he was starving and as a child had been put out alone as a shepherd boy in the hills in order to earn his keep and get something to eat.

He left Montessoro with just the clothes on his back and sailed to the San Francisco Bay Area, like so many other Ligurians who immigrated around 1910. He was the only member of his family to escape the rugged, brutal terrain of Montessoro. He first found farming work via word of mouth on Bay Farm Island, where a substantial community of Ligurians from Alpicella lived. However, Edoardo had his eyes set upon a different occupation, not farming. He was brilliant but had absolutely no formal education. He taught himself to read and write by using an English dictionary and was determined to be a United States citizen, which he proudly accomplished in the 1930s.

Breaking away from working on the farms, he saw, as a handful of other Ligurians had, the need for garbage pickup. He saved enough money to buy a horse and cart; and he established in Oakland, California, a small entrepreneurial garbage business. During this time, many of the garbage men were scrambling to establish their turf and neighborhood routes. Conflicts and arguments abounded, until Edoardo and a handful of others realized they had greater leverage in uniting rather than remaining independent contractors, and so they created a coop of scavengers about 1915 or 1916. Edoardo was instrumental with the other garbage men in establishing, in 1920, the Oakland Scavenger Company. What an achievement for an illiterate shepherd boy with no formal education, who started his new life with only the clothes on his back.

As the scavenger business boomed, Edoardo felt more secure and ready to provide for a wife and family. Within the closely knit Ligurian community, he met a beautiful young woman with steel blue-gray eyes, porcelain skin, and the most exquisite, as they called it, Gloria Swanson nose. He fell in love with this new immigrant from Liguria, Maria Vallerga; and she became his bride.

As the Oakland Scavenger Company continued to grow, Edoardo and Maria purchased a beautiful home in a good section of Oakland, California, on Prentiss Street. Shortly after they moved in, some of the neighbors placed a large cross on their front lawn and set it on fire. The neighbors felt threatened by these foreigners and thought the Italians would bring down the value of their property. Edoardo responded by sharing his homemade wine and the olive oil he had won by answering opera questions on a Sunday afternoon radio program. He had responded with kindness and made friends. Soon every Sunday afternoon, the neighbors gathered in Edoardo's basement to sip wine and root for him to win more olive oil, and he did.

Edoardo was the soul of kindness. One day, as he was driving his scavenger truck, he heard people screaming for help and saw a young boy trapped under a car. The onlookers seemed paralyzed by the situation; but Edoardo leaped from the truck and, using his shoulder, heaved the car off the young boy, saving his life. Only a little over five feet tall, he was left with a lifelong back-and-shoulder injury. His most precious physical resources were his back and the shoulder he used to heft the heavy metal cans of garbage. He had come very close to sacrificing his livelihood for the trapped young boy. Edoardo was also known for taking young Italian boys off the streets and employing them in the company, rescuing them from a life of poverty and giving them hope. Twenty-five years later, the young boy Edoardo saved that day attended his funeral with close to a thousand others. Edoardo was a pillar in the community.

The harshness of Montessoro made Eduardo strong, resilient, and adept at surviving. His homeland is arid, less lush, and green than the western side of Liguria. It is craggy and desolate, a total contrast to where my other relatives lived. Very simply put, it is hard, and the other part of Liguria is soft. I tried to imagine Edoardo as a boy in this difficult environment, and I could see how he would want to come and build a new life in the new world. Even in the 1990s, Montessoro was rustic and austere. They live the simple life as they eke their living from the reluctant countryside. In contrast, their open arms and generosity reflected who my nonno Edoardo was, and the older relatives still remembered him for his kindness and gentle spirit.

Upon returning from our trip to Montessoro, we stayed in Campo Marzio. As a surprise, Cousin Lorenzo, Lalla Nita's son, contacted Piero Ferro, my father's first cousin, from Alpicella. One afternoon while visiting Lalla Nita's family, Piero arrived. I was shocked to see he looked identical to Nonno Antonio. It was the first time I had seen a relative of my paternal grandfather, Nonno Antonio's family. Piero's grandfather, Pietro Ferro, and my nonno Antonio were brothers. Piero had big blue eyes, a bald head, wiry build, and was soft-spoken, just like my nonno. At that moment, I knew, I must go to Alpicella and meet the rest of my father's side of the family. It was as if my relatives were reaching out to me, and I was reaching out to them.

That same evening, Lorenzo announced that we were to go to a party in Casanova. So I put on my dancing shoes, and the whole family came, including Lalla Nita. We wound down the hill from Campo Marzio; and in fifteen minutes, we were in Casanova, near the seaside town of Varazze. After parking in a large field, we hiked over a small hill. We could hear the faint sound of music. The dance floor was outside, strung with lights hanging from grape arbors and edged with chairs and very small tables. It had a large wooden floor filled with elegant dancers twirling and dipping to the music.

I thought the music would be the Top Ten hits from the United States, and the dancers would "shake their booties." Instead it was like everyone had stepped out of a Ginger Rogers and Fred Astaire movie.

They danced ballroom style. The dancers were fluid and glided around the floor in total synchronicity. They had been dancing the waltz, rumba, mambo, cha-cha, swing, tango, and the polka all their lives. Everyone knew everyone. We were the only foreigners there, but they embraced us because we were family, the Italian family who lived in America. It was like a scene from the television show, *Dancing with the Stars.*

Cousin Giuseppe, young and extremely good-looking, had been a champion ballroom dancer. He took Bella by the hand and began teaching her how to waltz. It was amazing to watch her gain confidence as he spoke gently to her in Italian and guided her through every step. She was only eleven at the time, but she remembers to this day learning to dance with her cousin Giuseppe. Afterward, Giuseppe danced with me under the stars. I thought I was with Fred Astaire, only Giuseppe was definitely more handsome.

My cousins often wondered why I was single and always traveling with my mother and daughter. Why wasn't I married? They had not read *Smart Women Dumb Choices*, my mantra. Lorenzo decided to be a matchmaker at the dance. So he asked me what kind of man I wanted. I always joked, "Io ho bisogno d'un uomo ricco, vecchio e vicino alla morte." I want a man who is old, rich, and ready to die. Even if this is not correct Italian, this is always what I would say, and they would repeat it back to me. And then we would laugh. So every time they saw me and I was still single, they would say, "Ricco, vecchio e vicino alla morte." And we would all laugh again.

At the festa that evening, Lorenzo introduced me to an older man. Lorenzo said that since I had always told him I needed a man who was old, wealthy, and ready to die, he had found me one. According to Lorenzo, he was a widower and owned vast olive orchards, the best in the region. I danced and twirled and whirled nonstop like the Energizer bunny for over an hour and a half with the man. Finally, I had to sit down. My cousin Lorenzo had purposely set me up with this gentleman because he wanted some of that olive oil, but I sat down too soon. Would you believe that the olive oil man died of a heart attack several days later? Just my luck!

Lorenzo teased me incessantly about the gentleman's death and keeping him from getting any of that precious olive oil. Lorenzo would say, "I found you the perfect man, and then you killed him because you stopped dancing with him. You broke his heart." He would add, "You killed off my chance to get free olive oil for the rest of my life." How would I ever live this down? It was the talk of the town in Casanova. This was not the last time this would happen, but that is another story in another chapter.

Before we left the fateful dance, Franca, Lorenzo's sister, invited us to come to her home in Casanova the next evening for dinner. The drive to Casanova is on an extremely narrow road with tight turns. It is steep with a sheer drop-off. One slip and you're airborne. Francesca's home is perched on the hillside with a deck overlooking terraced orchards of olive trees. There was a group of men sitting on the terrace enjoying sangria and singing songs in Ligurian. Of course, I joined them, and we sang and sang. I never figured out what it was we were singing, but it was fun. The lazy summer days in small Italian villages are filled with music, joy, and laughter. These days filled my heart.

The dinner at Franca's home was absolutely delicious. We had pasta with pesto, cantaloupe with prosciutto, green salad with fresh vegetables from their garden, and lots of sangria. There was much laughing and conversation, and then the heavens opened up. The night was filled with thunder and lightning on a major scale. Thank goodness Lorenzo was there to drive us through torrential rain punctuated with exclamations of thunder and lightning. Later, at Campo Marzio, I was reveling in the rumbling sounds of the storm and went to find my mother and daughter to share the excitement of it.

My mother had taken Bella and hid under the bedcovers. When I found them shaking in bed, I could not resist getting mischievous. I opened up the shutters and stood in the window, enjoying the lightning show. The claps of thunder shook the house. The chickens were squawking, and the dogs were barking. It was exhilarating. I was in awe of Mother Nature. There were "le lucciole," fireflies, flitting near the windows. They cast a twinkling, sparkling spell, mesmerizing me. It was magical. The contrast between the lightning strikes and the flickering fireflies was dramatic. There were no streetlights, nothing man-made to mar nature's electrifying light show. The deafening thunder reminded me of how powerful nature is, and the fireflies reminded me of how miniscule our lives are, gone in the blink of a light.

And seemingly in a blink, my vacation was coming to an end. Each time about noon on the day before we would leave, the relatives would begin to arrive to say their farewells. A pall would hang over the house. It was like a wake. Everyone was sad. We felt like our Italian roots were being ripped up again as our part of the family traveled back to America. It was especially hard for Lorenzo and my mother, who cared so much for each other. Some years before, my mother had noticed that Lorenzo, who was a mason, did not have the usual leather belt for his tools. When she returned home, she sent one to him. He used it for the rest of his career and carries the remnant of it in his trunk even today.

As the pall of sadness loomed over us, Piero came down the hill from Alpicella to say his goodbyes and said to me, "Please come and stay with me and Angela." My mother did not have much interest in visiting Alpicella. She was quite content to be with her family. After many trips with my mother to visit her side of the family, I had a growing desire to explore my father's side. For the next dozen years, based upon my work schedule, I would go to Italy with my mother and daughter. Each trip deepened my understanding of the beautiful region, Liguria. It motivated me to want to learn the language, be more involved in the culture, and to gain a greater knowledge of my heritage. The bond grew stronger with my family as I flew across the "pond" with each trip. I learned that I am truly Ligurian and that my immigrant grandparents had planted the seed of this region in me, and my parents had nurtured it by maintaining the traditions that were passed down to them. For example, at Christmas, it was not the tree that was symbolic but the "Presepe," the Nativity. We also had an additional celebration on January 6. Nonna Maria taught me about La Befana, the old woman who gives little presents such as tangerines or sweets to good children and coal to those who misbehave. Apparently, I must have been a good girl as I always received tangerines. Boy, did I fool them!

My DNA kicked in; the ravioli became a staple in my kitchen again. I started to listen to opera again, and I flew the Italian flag proudly. Eventually, I would take my first trip without my daughter, who had her own busy life or my mother, whose schedule rivaled the pope's. On the last trip with them, in 2003, I had asked Piero Ferro of Alpicella if I could come to visit in a couple of years with our cousin Anita Ferro Paullus. His crystal-blue eyes sparkled; and with a big smile, he said, "You are a Ferro. Come home." And I did.

Chapter 4

My First Trip with Anita 2005

Our lives as first cousins had gone in different directions. Anita had stayed in the San Francisco Bay Area; while I had taken jobs in Paradise and Quincy, California, which are nestled in the Sierra Nevada Mountains. It was at the funeral of one of our beloved cousins when I saw Anita for the first time in many years. While we were catching up, I told her about my trips to Italy and said to her, "If you ever want to go to Italy, just let me know." Anita has two different Latin bloodstreams: Spanish, from her mother, and Italian, from her father. Anita has a great smile and beautiful brown eyes that have the twinkle of the mischievous Ferro clan. She has a quick dry wit and is always ready for an adventure.

One day on impulse, I called Piero to confirm whether or not his invitation to come to Alpicella to visit was still good. It was. I immediately called Anita and asked what she was doing and if she wanted to come to Italy with me the next year. She laughed and replied, "Yes, I'll come. All I'm doing is babysitting my daughter's dog."

The flight was fabulous. We met a woman by the name of Madeline, who was our reservation assistant. Anita and I were so excited about our first trip together; she upgraded us to business class. Being bumped to business class was like a dream come true.

It was extreme elegance for us and plush. We had so much leg room we could have been basketball players. The lovely luxury was sipping champagne in the Red Carpet Lounge prior to our departure. Our excitement was so contagious that the other passengers gave us their drink tickets. We were having such a great time we almost missed our flight. Joyously, we rolled as fast as two little hedgehogs to our boarding gate. Upon boarding, we made friends with everyone in business and first class whether they wanted to meet us or not. It was like an extended all-night party, and we were having so much fun that before we knew it, our jet was descending. We were stunned when we heard the announcement that the plane was landing in Frankfurt. It's amazing when you are having fun, time really does fly. We connected to Milan, and our real adventure began.

It started when we went to pick up our rental car. They had given our automatic-shift car to someone else. Eventually, they found us a very small Ford Fiesta. The worst part was that I did not know how to start the European ignition. Luckily, we met a man who showed us how to turn it on. We looked with dismay at the automatic stick shift. I then sighed and turned to Anita and said, "Well, I did drive a VW Bug. Let's roll." There we were, exhausted from no sleep, the wrong car, and the autostrada circus was about to begin. Once again, I was the one and only driver, and off we went heading toward Alpicella, anxiously searching for a sign for Savona. Savona was the key that would tell me we were going in the right direction.

I was feeling so woozy; and now my copilot, Anita, whose job it was to keep me awake, was getting drowsy, so I turned the air-conditioner on full blast to wake us up. Clutching the steering wheel with great fear, I attempted to keep up with the flow of traffic on the autostrada. Driving in Italy is like racing in the Le Mans. First, you run to your car, jump in, and then head to the autostrada, where you join the other racecar drivers all going at breakneck speed. I could hear the Ferraris and Lamborghinis zooming by us, their engine sounds so distinctive as they shifted gears, accelerating up to autostrada speed. It's like no other sound. Vroom! Vroom! Vroom! Then there was our Ford Fiesta: putt-putt, putt-putt, putt-putt. I had the gas pedal jammed all the way to the floor, as we putted along: putt-putt, putt-putt, putt-putt. There are no Sunday drivers in Italy. Even the senior citizens are like adolescent drivers. Italian drivers are eternally eighteen years young.

We left the autostrada and started winding through the hillside towns. It was summer and peak season. Depending on the traffic, we knew it could take anywhere from twenty to forty minutes. I kept telling my copilot to look for a sign for Savona or Varazze. We crossed over toward the Mediterranean Sea and found the picturesque seaside town of Varazze. Varazze was my signal that it was time to start climbing back up into the hills, past the small villages of Casanova, Pero, and Campo Marzio. Eventually, after many tight turns and tooting my horn so we didn't end up in a collision, we arrived safely in Alpicella. We made it, thank God. No dents.

As I gazed at the little hamlet of Alpicella, I could almost see my nonno Antonio Pelegrino Ferro standing there in the piazza. His nickname, Mazzetta, meant "little sledge hammer." He was a small wiry man, only five feet tall but incredibly strong. He had the bluest of eyes, high cheekbones, with a brush mustache and perfectly white teeth. He spoke softly with kindness, and he loved music and dancing. Antonio was born at Christmas time in 1883 and was the first child baptized in the new church, San Antonio Abate, in his village of Alpicella.

Roughly translated, Alpicella means "Little Alps of Heaven." Alpicella is located in a lush forest area near the very top of the hills at the end of some narrow, winding roads. Today the village has about four hundred people who live there year round, many of whom are related to me. It has a tiny piazza with a small church; a bar that, in Italy, is like a very small caffè with benches out front for sitting in the sun; a hunter's lodge that hosts a wild boar-hunting club; Gianni Battista's restaurant, Baccere Baciccia; a bakery shop where they make focaccia; a small alimentari or grocery store, called Ferro Alimentari; and a post office that is open only a couple days a week.

Nonno Antonio emigrated from Alpicella sometime after the turn of the century, around 1917. He made his way to Bay Farm Island in Alameda, California, or as my dad would call, it "BFI." Antonio did the work he had grown up doing in Alpicella: he was a vegetable farmer. It was here on Bay Farm Island that he met Antonietta Rusca, my paternal grandmother, who had emigrated from Stella San Bernardo, a place not far from Alpicella.

According to my grandmothers, a hundred and fifty years ago, Alpicella was a rough and tumble village inhabited by a group of wild mountain peasants who lived off the land. Today, it would take perhaps ten minutes to drive from Alpicella to Stella San Bernardo; but in those days, it would take days by foot or by horse and cart, since there were no roads, just paths through the forest over the rocky ground. If Antonio and Antonietta had stayed in Italy, they probably would have never met and married.

Furthermore, it was unheard of for someone from the corona, the five stelle, to marry anyone from the Alpicella. It was not part of the crown, and the people were considered outsiders and were thought of as wild mountain people. However, fate had its own mind; and so Antonio and Antonietta met on Bay Farm Island, married, and eventually had two sons, Thomas and Carlo Ferro. Thomas was about three years older than my father, Carlo.

The Italians called Bay Farm Island, *l'isola*, or the island. The Ferro home was a small wooden house on a dirt road. Across from them was a road edged with swampy marshlike land where the houses of other Italian farmers were built on stilts. On the other side were farms with rows and rows of vegetables. My grandparents' home was nestled among the vegetables. Near the house was a barn where they kept the horse and later a tractor. In the beginning, though, Antonio plowed the crops of beets, carrots, celery, lettuce, mustard greens, parsley, radishes, spinach, Swiss chard, and turnips with a horse, using a harness wrapped around his shoulders. When I used to follow my nonno in the fields, he would stop and tell me how much he loved to dance. As a young man after working all day, he would stay up all night dancing. I think I inherited my love of dancing from my nonno. He also told me how much he loved music. Once when he played the bugle horn in the Italian Army, he heard another rendition of reveille. He thought it sounded so much better than the one he had to play that the next morning he played the other company's song to wake up the troops. No one woke up. An officer demoted him and put him in jail for a couple of days, but he always thought it was a better song.

One of the saddest memories I recall was the Saturday before Thanksgiving 1959, when I was twelve. It was evening, and the telephone rang. My mother immediately handed the phone to my father, and as I watched his face, I could see something was horribly wrong. After hanging up, he told us that his father had not come home for dinner, and his mother was beside herself. My father said he was going to Bay Farm Island to search for his father. It was a cold, pitch-black November night; and there were no streetlights. All he had was his flashlight to search the fields of the farm for his beloved father. We waited and waited. Finally, he walked through the door crying, devastated beyond words. I can remember repeatedly my father describing how he had found his father felled by a heart attack, lying among the crops with dirt still in his mouth; he loved tilling the soil. Carlo cradled his father in his arms like a child and took him home for the last time to his wife, Antonietta.

Eventually, the farms on Bay Farm Island were bought up by the Utah Construction Company. When the roads were paved and the homes were built, the streets were named for the Italian and Portuguese families who had farmed the land. Who knew that my nonno, who left Italy with only his dreams for a better life, would come to America and ultimately have a street named for him? Currently, I live walking distance from that street, Ferro Court.

There we were, first cousins, and we were entering the birthplace of our grandfather. I drove into the piazza and made a right turn, looking for the monument from World War I. It was the marker that told me I should go straight on to a road that would lead to Piero's home. I began looking for his place, a small compound of three little houses nestled in the beautiful green hills, with arbors of grapes and orchards of fruit trees. I tooted the horn to announce our arrival.

I parked our car under the tin-roofed carport. There waiting for us was Angela and Piero, with his twinkling blue eyes. Angela, his companion for many years, had on her beautiful hand-embroidered apron and was standing beside Piero, who was in his daily summer uniform of red shorts, near Leo, the famous cat of Alpicella, a striped tabby who loved to sashay between our legs. As we entered the house, we could smell the wonderful aroma of the meal being prepared for us. Angela had set the dinner on the terrace, with its view of the beautiful valley below with villas nestled in its lush green forest. That evening, we ate and drank and laughed until the wee hours of the morning. We said buona notte, good night, with many kisses and hugs and went to sleep, actually happily passing out from complete and utter exhaustion.

We woke up midmorning and walked out on to the terrace. There was our "little man," as Anita called Piero, in his red shorts, working on his vegetables and fruit trees. He picked everything fresh daily. Piero made his own honey as well and baked his own bread. I must warn you, though, about his homemade organic wine. Everyone in the village knew not to drink it. Why? It tasted like mouthwash.

After a light breakfast of coffee and homemade bread with honey, we decided to spend time visiting the local cemetery, since there is so much rich history chronicling the lives of our paternal family. These Alpicellians were remote mountain people, and a century ago, it would have been difficult for them to meet people from other villages.

It was the custom that the people from the corona (remember the stelle) never married those from the hills. Consequently, if you visit the cemetery in Alpicella, you will see the last names of my relatives who intermarried, because that is who lived there. The cemetery is extremely well kept, with flowers everywhere. No one in Alpicella ever forgets who is in the cemetery because there is an iron link between those who have passed and those who are living. After wandering the cemetery for a while, we did what everyone in Alpicella does: we went to the local bar. A bar in Italy is not like the average bar in America. It is actually a small caffè, a place to hang out and to visit.

The bar in Alpicella is called Baccere Baciccia Ristorante, a name that does not translate. It is owned by Giovanni "Gianni" Battista Ferro. Giovanni is a handsome man, standing over six feet, with white wavy hair and big Tiffany-blue eyes. He usually wears a blue plaid shirt to complement his eyes. Giovanni's daily ritual is to move from one bench to another. He begins on one bench in front of Baccere Baciccia and moves across the piazza to another bench in front of a little caffè with a green awning, and finally, he moves to a third bench in the late afternoon after his siesta. I am sure that ritual is why he is so happy. This ritual has been going on for an eternity. He does not work in the restaurant; he owns it. You might ask, if he owns it, how can he sit on the bench? His son manages the bar while his ex-wife oversees all the chefs and waiters; that is why he can sit on the bench. He has nothing to do. So he sits with the other men, and they talk about their glory days. Their moves are like clockwork; you can set your watch by them.

Alpicella stories are not the only ones shared. There is much folklore in Italy. I recall that when I was a little girl, Nonna Maria told me a story about a real Casanova who lived near the village of Casanova in the hills. Supposedly, there was a man named Fra Giacomo—Fra means priest—who fathered many, many children and used the names of flowers and trees for their first names. Their last name would be that of the village. Then there was the story Piero told about another priest named Fra Ratte. This priest allegedly bilked the poor people of Alpicella by loaning them money, and when they could not repay him, he took their land. He ended up owning a great deal of the land in Alpicella and had an estate called Castello di Alpicella. This is why many people in the villages are not overly religious. The stories were always the same, even when recounted thousands of miles apart from the men on the Alpicellian bench or from my nonnas (in Italian, *nonne*) in the evening before bedtime, tradition.

A few days after we were in Alpicella, it seemed like we had met nearly everyone in the village. Then, just like Gianni Battista Ferro, we developed our own ritual. Each evening, we would walk from Piero's home down the street to the bar/caffè. We became known, affectionately, as those women who walked to the bar every night, the street walkers. Alpicella was like "Cheers," where everyone knows your name and where everyone is somehow related to you.

It did not take much time in Alpicella before I could look at someone's face, note their features, and accurately guess their last name. For example, the Rattos have bright blue eyes; the Delfinos are thin and wiry in their build; the Dameles have round full faces. I don't know what is in the Peratas' genes, but they all seem to be good-looking. The Ferro side is small in stature, sturdily built, and has mischievous eyes. As one of the relatives said, "We're all related in Alpicella." My genetic pool was expanded by the Vallergas and the Bertuccios. Thanks for the nice nose and my small *culo*, Nonna Maria.

One of the games I developed among the three Ferros (Piero, Anita, and I) was a discovery game called "It takes three Ferros to equal one Angela." Let me give you an example of how this game works and how Angela ended up being the champion. Anita and I drove down to Varazze. We were looking for that difficult summer beach parking spot. We finally found one, and we were elated because they are so rare. It was midday and lucky for us; many people were taking a siesta. We had to figure out how to use the meter. I would put a coin in the parking meter and pull out a ticket. I did it five times and purchased two and half hours of parking time. Now picture the five parking coupons lined up like tiny soldiers on the dashboard protecting the car from the evil meter maid. We felt proud we had worked the machine, and we would keep the evil parking citations from our car.

It was time to buy the limoncello for Piero, Santa Margherita Pinot Grigio for us; and giving in to our sweet tooth, we also purchased several torte, multilayered cakes, from a wonderful pastry shop. Then, lo and behold, no citation for the car! I took a picture to document our brilliance. Apparently, all you had to do was line up a bunch of coupons in your car window, and you would be fine. The grand finale included our departure ritual. I would say, "Anita, go out into the street and act like you are in charge of traffic." Anita would stand in the middle of the street like a traffic cop, putting her life in peril with the Italian drivers and stopping traffic so I could back out of the parking spot safely. As soon as I had backed out into the lane, she would swiftly hop into the car, and we would be on our way home. Good job, Poliziotta Anita.

As we carried our packages into Piero's home, we could smell the aroma of freshly cooked beans, gnocchi with pesto, fresh baked-bread, and yummy prosciutto. We entered the kitchen and, turning to Piero and Angela, triumphantly made our big announcement. We declared that we were the queens of how to park in Italy. Anita explained, "All you have to do is just get those coupons and line them up on the dashboard. Perfetto." Piero was so proud of us he applauded. Angela rolled her eyes and laughed.

As she looked at Piero with amusement, she told us, "You just put in all the coins that you are supposed to, hit the button once, and get one ticket." That's when the game of three Ferro's against Angela began, but at the end of our trip, Angela was the undisputed champion. We decided to keep score on each trip, and the score sheets reside in Piero's home even to this day. Angela continues to win each time we return to Italy and is undefeated. Long may Angela reign.

Angela holds another title within our family. I have anointed her as *La Regina della Cucina di Alpicella anche del Mondo.* She is the queen of the kitchen in Alpicella and also the world. Angela can take anything from the garden, and you will think that a chef from the Cordon Bleu Culinary School has created it. Angela's pesto sauce uses fresh basil from the garden, a little bit of olive oil, a lot of Parmigiano-Reggiano cheese, a touch of salt, with garlic to taste and a few pine nuts. According to Chef Angela, "You must not bruise the basil, even though you are going to smash it when you use the pestle on it." I have never figured out how to do this. Literally, her pesto is to die for. I would lather my body with it if I knew it would get rid of wrinkles, warts, and varicose veins. Maybe I should sell it on one of those TV shopping channels?

The Ferros have a special fondness for the cinghiali or wild boars. We identify with these wild beasts. Why? Piero had been told many times by Angela that he was a cinghiale. She said he was a *testa dura,* "hard head." Cinghiali manage to go through anything, fences notwithstanding, to get to food. Therefore, by genetic default and being a direct relative to a limited gene pool, my cousin, Anita, and I are cinghiali.

We became passionate in protecting these wild creatures from the huntsmen. We decided that we would never eat cinghiale on the menu or attend a cinghiale festa. More important, to honor our new cinghiali family, we would purchase a cinghiale statue for display in our homes. Mine is on my dresser at home. They are held in high esteem by Piero, Anita, and me. We are the cinghiali. We think they should be our family crest rather than the Griffin, the Ferro Cinghiali.

Another example of how we are related to cinghiali is illustrated by Piero's adventurous mountain climbing. When he described his romp in the Dolomites, I asked him, "Who was with you?" He said, "No one." He had forgotten Angela. You see, cinghiali are so focused on what they do that sometimes they forget what is going on around them. Angela brought out a photo showing Piero and Angela in the Dolomites. She affectionately hit him on the head with her hand, exclaiming, "Testa dura!" Then she pointed at him and said, "Cinghiale." Angela and Piero had initially met when they joined the same mountain-climbing club more than twenty-five years ago. It is hard to resist a cinghiale.

The day finally came when the cinghiali had to do laundry. Angela, a nurse, was at work. Piero, a retired engineering instructor turned gentleman farmer, was at home. We asked Piero how to use the combination washer/dryer in the bathroom. He turned to us and looked at us with his innocent blue eyes and said softly, "I don't know." He then proceeded to tell us that Angela did the laundry, cooking, driving of the car, took care of him if he didn't feel well, and he took care of the outdoors. After he prunes, weeds, tills, and picks the produce, still wearing his red shorts, his daily summer ritual is to hose himself down outside near the garden. And that is his day. In contrast, Angela has to drive down the hill from Alpicella and take a train to work, which takes an hour and a half one way. Angela gets up at four in the morning, returns from work about six in the evening, creates an incredible dinner for us, and then stays up to talk with us until at least midnight. I gave her another title: St. Angela di Cinghiali. She holds three prestigious titles: the greatest cook, champion at the game, and a saint to put up with my beloved cousin and us.

Are you wondering if we ever got our laundry done? We did, but the process took as long as flying from Oakland, California, to Anaheim, California, including security checks, or about three hours. First, Piero had to call Angela to find out how to turn on the washing machine step by step and then how to change it to dry mode, since the washing and drying were done by the same machine. Our thorough engineer, Piero, wrote all of this in great detail, as if he were launching a rocket to the moon.

It took three Ferros in place of one Angela to try and figure out how to do laundry. We gave up on drying and just washed the clothes. It was midafternoon by the time we finished the process. We were all so proud of ourselves; the cinghiali danced merrily on the terrace. Happily applauding with our hooves, we opened the washer and found out that the clothes were still dirty. We had not done it correctly and had to wash the clothes again.

After successfully washing the clothes by late afternoon, our underwear was strewn in the grape arbor for all of Alpicella to see. It was dramatic, as some of it billowed like sails. The folks of Alpicella always knew when we had arrived because they could see the underwear hanging in the trees, blowing and flapping in the breeze. It was our cinghiali greeting to the Alpicellians.

We know there are always people of local color in any village. Once, late in the day, as Anita and I were walking to the local bar, we saw a strange man hacking the weeds down at the end of Piero's driveway. We thought, *What a "good Samaritan."* He had the bluest eyes I had ever seen. I tried to speak the Genovese dialect to him. He introduced himself as Lorenzo (Luenzin) Vallerga. I told him that my nonna Maria's maiden name was Vallerga. He told me that we must be related and that he was seventy-eight years of age and lived with his daughter. He chatted away nonstop, like he had not talked to anyone in years. I nodded profusely and interjected "Sì," "Sì," "Sì" every so often. (The dialect pronounces "Sì" as "She".) Anita asked, "Do you understand what he says? He is speaking with such staccato speed, and he sounds so French." I admitted, "No, I just nodded my head." It turned out that he lived way up in the hills beyond Alpicella. Maybe we were his first encounter with the outside world?

Little did I know that for the next six years, out of nowhere, he would appear in front of me without warning, just like magic. One time he appeared at the top of a tortuously steep hill. There is a famous monument of the Madonna above Alpicella, several miles up a steep dirt path laced with scorpions, spiders, and ticks. The name of the monument is the Rock of St. Anna. In the early 1900s, Nonno Mazzetta, with six other young men, used carts and hand-carried the marble for the chapel to the top of the hill. The white marble was carved by local craftsman to create a chapel that contained a statute of the Madonna. My grandfather's name is inscribed in the chapel on the list of the handful of those who built it. The marble is so white you can see it glowing brilliantly in the sun, beaming its blessings down on Alpicella.

In the old days, men and women made pilgrimages to pray, bringing candles and flowers to ask the Madonna to intervene. More recently, you still see the flowers, but now there are battery-operated candles. The Madonna faces Alpicella and protects the Alpicellians as she gazes down upon them. When you reach the top and you look out from the right-hand side of the chapel, you see Alpicella and all of the stelle. On the left you see Campo Marzio, Casanova, and Pero; and directly below is Varazze and the sea.

Late one afternoon, Piero got the notion that we should hike up to the Rock of St. Anna. The hike takes over an hour and is difficult. I only had huarache sandals with cardboard inserts to wear. So I improvised by wrapping my feet and sandals with bubble wrap. Of course, I got blisters, and before we even reached the top, my feet were bleeding. Without Anita's encouragement, I never would have made it. As I was climbing, I could not help but think about Nonno Mazzetta and the herculean effort made by the men of Alpicella in dragging, carrying, lifting, and pushing the huge stones of marble up this steep trail to create the chapel and its Madonna. Surely I could get myself up the hill, and I did.

When we arrived at the Rock of St. Anna, who was there placing battery-operated candles and flowers for the Madonna? Mr. Blue Eyes, Luenzin. He sputtered out a tsunami wave of words so fast that even Piero did not understand him at times. He was a little over five and a half feet tall, very thin, with a full head of white hair. He had the Vallerga nose. Intelligence sparkled in his eyes. He spoke the ancient dialect and probably could have conversed understandably with Christopher Columbus.

As we left the Rock of St. Anna, my bubble wrap was popping rapidly, and my feet were directly on the rocks with little snakes and scorpions wiggling. I wondered if my popping sounds were some kind of mating call for the wild beasts in the hills. By the time I got down the hill, my feet were bloody and throbbing with pain. I felt I had been on a death march. But I didn't give up on the walk because I was a cinghiale, and more important, there was Luenzin. It was kismet. I spent the evening enjoying the beautiful view from the terrace, soaking my feet and medicating myself with wine. Anita was nursing a terrible spider bite, and Angela had to surgically remove a tick from

Piero's calf. Still, it was a great day, spiders, ticks, and bloody feet notwithstanding. We are cinghiali.

Another time, Luenzin showed up unexpectedly, just before we left on a trip to Tuscany. I had gone to my cousin's store for groceries, and who appeared out of nowhere to help carry the groceries but Mr. Blue Eyes. So the legend grew that when I came to town, Mr. Blue Eyes always showed up. My relatives told me that they had not seen him all year; but as soon as I showed up, he was here, there, and everywhere. The cosmic ritual seemed to be that if I was there, so was he.

Fortunately, he never showed up when we tried to take a bath. Bathing at Piero's house is a unique experience. We had not bathed in a couple of days because we didn't want to use Piero's precious fresh water. We turned on the bath water, thinking, *This will be lovely.* I got in, screamed, and jumped out. I yelled to Piero, "There is no hot water." Piero yelled back, "You are right." I explained to him we needed hot water because we wanted to bathe. I asked him, "What's that big tank near the orchard?" He told me it was for hot water. Then he turned on the tank to heat the water but said it would take at least a full day for it to heat up. Brrr, brrr. Now I knew why Piero was taking his showers via the garden hose at the end of the day with lots of Italian sunshine to warm him up.

There is a footnote to this story. In the winter months, Piero, Angela, and Leo, the cat, go down the hill to Varazze, where Piero has a penthouse suite in an extremely posh area. We discovered this because one day we were with Piero in Varazze when he said that he had an apartment right next to the church. Below his apartment are elegant boutiques, fabulous caffès, and bars. The apartment rivals any penthouse in San Francisco. When he showed it to us, I tested the faucet in the bathroom, and hot steamy water came out instantly. I told Anita, "We've got to get down there where the action is and the hot water." So far, I have never used the apartment for a hot bath, and yes, I have continued taking cold baths in Alpicella.

There's never a dull moment with Cousin Piero. Remember the wild ride with Mr. Toad at Disneyland? Take it from me, if my cousin Piero is driving, you're on a wild ride. Late one afternoon, Piero was to drive us to pick up Angela and go to a town named Loano on the Italian Riviera, close to the border of France. This is where Angela's sister, Margherita, lives with her husband Lorenzo and their son Giacomo. We left about three thirty on a sunny afternoon.

We were to pick up Angela about four thirty from work, but our tour guide Piero decided to show us all of the stelle: Gamergna, San

Giovanni, San Bernardo, Santa Giustina, and San Martino. Along the way, we went to visit a friend of his and to pick up a branch of a genealogical tree of our family, the Delfinos. Then he decided to stop and pick up the "Bee" man, Gian Piero. It was now about four thirty, as the conversation ran on and on about honeybees and the production of honey. At that point, I told Piero, "You'd better call St. Angela so she will know we are running a little late." It would now be at least another thirty minutes to Savona, where she worked. After the phone call, Piero decided to take us on a leisurely ride along the riviera. He ended up driving the wrong way on a one-way street with the traffic police at the intersections waving wildly with their hands. It was Angela who usually did the driving, not Piero.

When we arrived to pick up Angela at work, she looked at Piero and said to him in Italian, "Ferro, why are you an hour late?" He tried explaining how he had to meet with the Bee man and introduce him to us, that he wanted to show us the stelle and then to show us the long scenic route of Italian Riviera. He described going down a one-way street the wrong way with the police waving their hands frantically to get him to stop. It was then that St. Angela demoted her Ferro to the passenger seat as she took charge of the car, and we breathed a sigh of relief. The driving talent must run in the family.

I laughed quietly as I remembered the infamous stories about Nonno Antonio's driving history. After saving enough money to get his first truck to drive vegetables to market in Oakland, Antonio decided that he should be the one to drive the truck. Early one morning, he took the truck to market, but he hit the accelerator instead of the brake pedal. In grand confusion, Nonno careened through the produce market at breakneck speed, with the Italian vendors throwing vegetables at him, yelling at him to stop. He was screaming at the truck, "Whoa, Horsey! Whoa, Horsey!" It was quite some time after that fiasco before he was allowed to drive again. Nonna Antonietta usually did all the driving whenever they went out. As you can see, the DNA of driving does have its challenges for the Ferros, and that includes me; but that's another chapter. Whoa, Horsey! Whoa, Horsey!

When I was four years old, my grandparents took me on a week-long vacation to Calistoga. Nonna Antonietta had driven all the way to Calistoga, and on the return trip after crossing the Bay Farm Island bridge, Nonno said he wanted to drive. He held the reins of the wheel as if the machine were a horse and drove us all the way to the brink of the water's edge. He slowly stopped the car just as the water lapped up on the wheels, saying softly in Italian, "Whoa, Horsey. Whoa, Horsey." My nonna affectionately patted him on the shoulder and gently told him to get into the passenger seat. She took over the driving for the last five minutes to the farmhouse. My sweet nonno Antonio, the machines of this new world were not meant for him or for Piero or me.

Our adventure continued with Angela driving us to Loano and Piero sitting in the passenger seat. Loano is quite close to the French border and is part of the Italian Riviera. It is full of graffiti-covered high-rise apartments everywhere you look. To me, the outskirts lacked the charm and vitality that I had seen in other Italian places. It seemed a place to sleep or perhaps to just live. Upon entering the apartment of Angela's sister's family, we felt as if we were in a little tiny carton or box, no room to grow. How impossibly expensive it must be to live in Loano as it is on the Italian Riviera.

We left for the restaurant and proceeded to walk endless miles. At least it seemed that way. We walked and walked and still no restaurant. By the time we finally got there, it was nearly ten o'clock. The restaurant was outdoors, and the people were very friendly. However, we were tired and knew that we had to get up early the next morning to go to Tuscany. After dinner, Anita and I were ready to go home, but Angela's relatives decided to show us the historic center of town. It was so kind of them, but we were exhausted.

There we were at nearly midnight, being shown every window of every shop; and surprisingly, everything was still open. Then we marched back to the apartment, where they decided at one o'clock in the morning to show slide pictures of their trip to Sardinia. We saw every fish and rock and grain of sand in Sardinia until our eyes began to involuntarily close. Americans are not the only people who have lots of vacation slides to show visiting relatives in the middle of the night. We finally arrived home in Alpicella at three o'clock Saturday morning, the same day we were leaving for Tuscany.

Later that morning while we had our coffee, Piero washed our car so it would be presentable for the trip. We said our goodbyes and told them that we would return the following Saturday for the big festa. We left for Tuscany with visions of hot water and siestas in our future. Oh boy.

Chapter 5

"Toodling" in Tuscany 2005

When we planned this trip, Anita and I had been dreaming of a villa in Tuscany, but we were not quite sure how to find the perfect place to stay. Then a friend told me about a website based in New York, called ParkerVillas.com that listed Tuscan villas for rent. We scoped out various places and rented one that looked perfect on the computer screen. Tempus fugit came with velocity speed, and it was time to actually experience and to savor the Tuscan lifestyle.

We waved a temporary goodbye to Piero and Angela and wound down the hills from Alpicella, looking for the autostrada. I could see the coastline, so I knew we were near the entry of the autostrada, which curved to the left and had the sign saying, "Autostrada Entrance." Soon we would be toodling in Tuscany. To my amazement, we did not get lost until the very end of our journey. I took the wrong fork in the road, ending up in front of an eighteenth-century villa. The gracious owner told us that everyone gets confused and ends up in front of her place. She gave us directions to the villa on the hill. We twisted and looped up and up until our eyes could not believe what we saw.

The spired cypress trees lined the road, with a huge villa at the end, surrounded by smaller villas; it was an estate that included a small chapel. We felt so triumphant. We didn't get lost, we didn't dent the car, and we had no causalities. We were so proud of ourselves. Standing in the doorway of the big villa was Marisa, the owner. Marisa was an earthy woman in her late fifties, a little over five and a half feet tall, with brassy blonde hair. Her daily housecoats and the constant cigarette that hung from her red, red lips provided a misperception about her that we slowly became aware of as we noticed the difference between her real self and the portraits showing her posed with movie stars and Italian politicians of the first rank. In these photographs were the images of a fabulously beautiful woman whose looks had gently faded with age. We realized she must have been quite a stunning beauty, not all of which had fled from her. This fact became obvious when we saw the life-sized portraits of her in the foyer and in her office.

She told me she was grateful that I spoke some Italian. What a compliment she had given me. She was tired of having to speak English so much, and while I was there, she had me speak to the visitors in English while she spoke to me in Italian. It was a win/win for both Marisa and me. I cannot tell you why, but she took a liking to us. She decided that we should stay in the villa called *Il Cacciatore*, The Hunter. She handed us the huge skeleton key with several other keys to open our villa. I unlocked two heavy wooden doors, and we entered a beautiful tiled foyer, with a huge bedroom and bath to the right while to the left was a small kitchen. Down a step from the kitchen was a large living room with a portrait on the wall of Il Cacciatore. He was a hunter dressed in country gentleman's clothing from the early 1800s. He looked completely refined. Il Cacciatore had reddish-blond hair and wore a tartan cloth jacket. It was his eyes that caught my attention and captivated me. They seemed to follow me everywhere I went. I am sure you have seen paintings where you feel you are being tracked, and that was the feeling I had with Il Cacciatore.

The stairway across the living room led up to another bedroom with another bath. I opened the bedroom shutters and looked across the breathtaking Tuscan valley. The undulating hills baked in the afternoon sun, roads lined with cypress trees winding between fields and fields of vines heavy with the royal purple of Italian grape clusters. The countryside was dotted with the burnt sienna roofs of villas lounging in a siesta "pomeridiana," late afternoon. On the terraced landscape below us were the swimming pool and the estate's chapel.

We decided to have a picnic outside, as it was about five in the afternoon, and we had not eaten all day. We sat in the warm afternoon sun drinking our Pinot Grigio and eating the fresh fruits and vegetables from Gian Piero's local grocery store in Alpicella. New travelers arrived at the villa. We toasted them, welcoming these new American tourists to their Italian adventures. Then it was eight o'clock, and we had dinner reservations at nine at the Borgo Antico Ristorante, in the old hamlet of Civitella, about fifteen minutes away.

Civitella is a hamlet dating back to feudal days. Upon arriving in this walled village, I found parking in the town square. It was a place where everyone knew everyone else. The town was spotlessly clean; you could have eaten off the cobblestones. We had no idea where to find the Borgo Antico. I saw a young woman wearing a white blouse and black skirt who I thought might be a waitress. Using my best Italian, I asked, "Dov'è il ristorante Borgo Antico?" She told us to go straight up the stairs, "Va dritto, scala, scala, scala." The stairs were steeper than any we had ever climbed. I lost count of the steps, but I figured it was a good cardio workout before dinner.

We walked into the restaurant, and in the center of the dining room's cavelike darkness, there was a huge antique millstone for grinding. We felt the warm and welcoming ambiance immediately, and there was a charming table reserved for us. The other customers were locals; we were the only foreigners. We both ordered steak Florentine, which came on Thanksgiving-size platters, huge. When they arrived, each looked like a whole side of beef. We had enough for the next two or three days. As we enjoyed the scrumptious meal, we planned the strategy for our trip to Florence the next day. Since neither one of us could read a map, it was going to be an interesting day exploring the countryside as we meandered toward Florence. When we returned to our car, we heard thunder and saw bolts of lightning, but this could not dampen our spirits. After all, we were in Tuscany.

The next morning, I opened the shutters as though I were Sophia Loren and was confronted with a dark foreboding sky. How could this be? I phoned Angela to get the weather report. Angela said they were having a hail storm. I asked, "How is Piero?" Angela laughed and then replied, "Ferro è un disastro." This was Angela's standard comment about Piero. He was an accident waiting to happen. It simply meant he was the same. God loves Angela. She is like a shepherd with a lost lamb, her Piero. I think every Ferro needs an angel like Angela; her name suits her perfetto.

In spite of the ominous weather report, it was time to get on the road. Mustering as much courage as we could, Anita and I drove down and around toward the autostrada entrance when all of a sudden the hail storm hit. Across the autostrada entrance was an abandoned gas station with a tin roof protecting the gas pumps. I turned to Anita, "What do you think? Shall we go for the tin carport over there?" She agreed, "Go for it." We took shelter from the golf ball-sized hail pelting the car and listened to the rat-a-tat-tat, rat-a-tat-tat of hail on the tin roof. Then before we knew it, we were not alone. Five other cars had squeezed into the old garage to join us. As fast as the storm came in, it left, and the skies turned blue.

In Florence, I found a parking space near an English-style manicured park. Anita was worried about getting towed. "Do you think we can park here?" I tossed back, "Look at all the other cars. We'll all get towed. There should be safety in numbers." Having absolutely no idea of where we were in the city and relying upon my Ligurian GPS, we began walking toward the center of Florence. After many blocks, we finally reached Via Romana, which turned into the Ponte Vecchio, which ran along the Arno River and was the main thoroughfare in Florence. Anita said, "Michelangelo's David has not changed in centuries. Let's go jewelry shopping." I whispered to myself, "Blasphemy. He has haunted me all these years for not visiting him."

As fate would have it, we brought the thunder and lightning with us; and it forced us to make mad dashes, giggling and laughing, between Florentine stores filled with 18-karat gold and glitz. By the end of the day, we not only had lots of glitz but also a new Florentine umbrella, a true tourist souvenir with Michelangelo's David printed all over it. On our way back to the car, we bought more wine and food, so that if we could not find a restaurant, we would have a great meal at our villa. As we drove away, I was thinking that the David had expected me. I had stood him up for jewelry. Silently, I promised to come back.

As we made our way putt, putt-putting on to the autostrada, I made the sign of the cross, grabbed the steering wheel with Ligurian determination and began our drive back to the villa. To our good fortune, the gods of wine, food, and glitz were with us and protected us as we wound all the way back up the hills to our villa in the darkness of the Tuscan night. We settled into the villa; jumped into our PJs; sat down to a Tuscan feast of good wine, rich Florentine food, and leftover steaks; and admired our glitz.

Anita was sleeping downstairs, and I had the bedroom upstairs. Something felt eerie. Each night I would stare at the picture of Il Cacciatore and watch his eyes follow me as if I were his prey. Even Anita commented that his eyes followed me, and that was before our evening glasses of wine. I kept saying that I felt I knew him, that we had been together but that we had been separated against our wills. Someone had pulled us apart. When I looked at the picture, it was like an awakening. Somehow I thought I have been here before. The next day, I asked Marisa, who the hunter in the painting was. She said, "It was my very wealthy great-great-uncle. You know, the villa you are staying in was his favorite." She further said that on occasion, he appeared on the grounds and sometimes in our villa.

I asked her, "Is it possible there might be some strange connection between Il Cacciatore and, me?" She replied, "But of course, that is why you are staying in his villa. You look like his beloved wife, who died very young."

Every night, I could feel the intensity of his eyes. Perhaps in another life or another matrix, I knew him and had lost him or he lost me. My nonna Maria once told me that she thought there had been a sign when I was born or something had been placed on me when I was a little girl that I would have difficulties in relationships with men. She felt that I was too innocent and would not be able see through them. She said it came from a long bloodline and from some other place in Italy. The more I visited Italy, the more I felt I had a link with Florence or Tuscany. Had I been taken from here against my will? What was this magnetic feeling pulling me toward him that I felt? Maybe it was Il Cacciatore? Could he be part of the sign that had been put on me decades before? Was he trying to tell me something by reaching across the dimension of time?

I awoke from dreaming of Il Cacciatore and opened the shutters to a beautiful sunny day. I went downstairs to make the coffee. How long could it take for two university graduates to make a simple pot of Italian coffee? If you answered two hours, you are correct. Much of our mornings were gobbled up trying to make coffee without burning our fingers or singeing our hair, eyebrows, or any other hair in range. Our other issue was our hygiene. The shower and bath were cold water again. The only warm water was in the bidet. We had both learned to use the bidet for other purposes such as washing our feet, clothes, or shaving our legs. My cousin loves the original purpose of the bidet, whereas I prefer to soak my feet.

We were planning to visit the city of Arezzo, about thirty minutes away if we didn't get lost. The Patron Saint of Arezzo is St. Donatus. Loosely translated, he could be my patron saint. Arezzo is famous for manufacturing jewelry. How amazing, it all fits: Donna, Donatus, Arezzo, jewelry; yes. This is why I love jewelry so much. Well, Rosie, maybe you and the priest were right after all. Now I can hear my father saying, "Really, Donna, really."

My real name should have been taken in the Italian tradition from the first two names of my grandmothers. Originally, my name would have been Maria Antonietta; but when my mother realized the historical consequences of the tragic queen, Marie Antoinette, having a severed head, she went to the local priest for help. With less than two weeks before my birth, the priest and my mother came up with the name Donna Marie. My mother told me that Donata meant gift. I think my mother took some creative license, as my name stirred controversy with my nonna Antonietta. In fact, Nonna refused to call me by my baptismal name until I was in high school; she called me Maria Teresa. When my father passed away in 1984, I decided to honor my mother's wishes and began using my real legal first name, Donna Marie.

We arrived safely in Arezzo. My copilot Anita was able to find us a parking spot so we wouldn't get towed or get a ticket. We walked about eight blocks into the old historic center of town, where we found the piazza was being decorated for a grand festa. Medieval flags from all the Italian regions were flying everywhere. It was a sunny Tuscan day, not sweltering, with a breeze, perfect to wander through the shops that lined the perimeter of the piazza. After shopping awhile for gifts and souvenirs, I found a glitzy pillbox of pink and black crystals for my mother and Italian perfume for my daughter. Then in one of the jewelry shops, I found an antique gold bracelet I couldn't resist. It has alternating gold and semiprecious stones with carvings of the heads of Roman soldiers. Then we needed a break, so we went to the local bar.

I had to go to the bathroom and got a big surprise. The bathroom had a large hole in the floor for the toilet. Be careful when you squat. You'll need good leg muscles in Italy. It had an automatic flush and an automatic dryer for my hands. Technology is sometimes quite innovative in Italy. As you travel through Italy, you will find all toilets are not the same; they are an adventure all unto themselves. Some toilets are like ours in the United States, and some have only a shallow ceramic trough that you squat over. Some are pristinely clean, and some were last cleaned in the days of Caesar. Be careful also with the doors. I was locked in more times than I care to remember. The doorknobs on the insides were so old that many times they did not work. That's when I thought the Italian bathrooms wanted to capture me and make me the "Queen of Italian Latrines." I would tell Anita, if I'm not back out in ten minutes, you need to go on a search-and-rescue mission for me. Call in the Navy Seals and good-looking Italian scuba divers. I think someone should write a guidebook on how to use all the different toilets in Italy. It might be quite useful. Maybe that will be my next book.

After Arezzo, we stopped in Città Civatella on the way back to the villa. We had eaten there the first evening, but it was so dark we couldn't see anything except the restaurant. In Civatella, we found a small museum and discovered the very emotional story of this village. On June 29, 1944, during World War II, 176 townsmen, including the local priest, were taken in groups of five into the town square and shot in the head execution-style by the Nazis. There are statues symbolizing peace throughout the village and a statute dedicated to the one man who survived. He hid—they lost count of the executions—and he fled; and so the story survived. The tiny museum has the bloodied clothes, the pictures of the men and their families with the complete history of that terrible day. It is one of the stories of the war that did not make the history books but remains in the hearts and souls of these people who endured and will always remember the ravages of that tragic day.

Arriving back at the villa, we began planning our next day's trip to Siena. We knew we would have to get up early because of how long it took to make coffee. Our goal was to be out the door by noon. Amazingly, we left on time. As we drove down the hillside, we were immediately blessed with a sign for Siena near huge fields of sunflowers. They were a kaleidoscope exploding with a sea of flowers, and so I stopped to take pictures and then continued our search for more signs to Siena. We arrived midafternoon in the historic center, and it is absolutely magnificent. One literally sighs when one says, "Ah, Si-e-na."

We stood in the piazza, feeling that we needed to stay there at least a week and knowing we had not brought any clothes to stay overnight. The scents, the light and shadows, and the sights of Siena took our breath away. The piazza of Siena is built like a conch shell, curved up and out from the center so that when you walk from the center of the piazza, you are walking up a gentle slope toward the perimeter. In some sections, it is like walking into an Italian deli; first, you smell the prosciutto, and then you look over; and through the windows and the inviting open door, you see cheeses, olives, cotta, stacks of wine bottles, and all manner of food. They are known for their *sugo di cinghiale*, wild boar sauce. The aroma of the freshly baked bread and the plump, vibrantly red tomatoes draw you in to buy the makings of a sumptuous summer picnic; and you do.

Siena is like a magnet drawing to it a collection of rich, diverse abundance. Dotted along the perimeter of the Piazza del Campo is an array of stores: jewelry; leather goods; clothing; antiques; ceramics; shoes; beautiful trays and fixtures for a home; and, of course, souvenir shops. Radiating outward are dozens of vicetti, small alleyways with even more shops. Housing the shops are the antique structures, many of which have been there for centuries upon centuries. The sun hits the buildings in a way that creates soft shadows and glowing spaces of light different than any other *città* in the world. We walked and walked. Then before we knew it, the sun was setting, and we needed to go. We had only scratched the surface of this formidable city, which rivaled Florence. We promised Siena and ourselves that we would return next year; and we did, but that's another story.

I have come to the conclusion that my driving DNA comes directly from Piero. I'm definitely a cinghiale. There I was with my prescription sunglasses, trying to get on the autostrada, looking at a sign that says "closed" in Italian, *chiuso,* with the sun setting rapidly. I had no idea where was another entrance to the autostrada and desperately needed to find a point of entry. I asked Anita to look through my purse and the car for my regular glasses but had no luck. I had left my glasses back at the villa. So there we were in the dark, with me trying to drive using my sunglasses. I had to turn on my high beams to see anything. And to top it all off, the oncoming cars were flashing their high beams to signal me to turn mine off.

Eventually, I found a bar and was able to ask where the autostrada was located. Before this trip, I had practiced a critical Italian phrase with Angela, "Scusi mi, sono persa dov'è l'autostrada?" (Excuse me, I am lost, where is the autostrada?) The waiter came outside and pointed in the direction we had come, saying, "Go back." I finally found the autostrada; and wearing my prescription sunglasses, looking so chic but truthfully blind, I clicked the high beams.

The autostrada was frightening. There were no overhead lights and no center divide. The Italian drivers behind me were practically in my trunk because they thought I was driving too slowly. I couldn't find an exit sign for Città Civitella, so I decided to get off the autostrada at the next exit. I was hoping to find a town where I could ask directions. I wound up into the hills and came upon a small village where the street was filled with children. I stopped for directions, using my Italian to get information from the children. One little girl said that her brother spoke English but was shy because he felt it was not good enough. At that point, I was exhausted, exasperated and frustrated. Finally, a woman came out. I asked her how to get to Città Civitella. She kept saying "diritto," waving her hands straight down the road. Five minutes later, we saw the sign for Città Civitella. Part of the sign pointed left, and the other part pointed straight ahead. I could hear the voice of the lady saying "diritto," and so I went straight. She was correct. We got back around midnight. Il Cacciatore stared at me as we relived the day. He seemed so amused, as if wondering to himself, "What will she do next?"

The next day, we were looking forward to exploring Deruta and Perugia. After making coffee—you know the coffee drill—we laid out a map to strategize our trip and realized we could not read it. We wanted to avoid the midnight driving on strange roads if possible. So we each packed a small emergency brown paper lunch bag with underwear, cosmetics, and a toothbrush. We lifted our heads, sniffed the air with our cinghiali snouts, and pointed our noses toward Deruta. We had no problem finding Deruta, how fortunate. *Che bella fortuna.*

Deruta, famous for a certain style of ceramics, has two hundred ceramic workshops. The design of the ceramics is stylized and has been more or less the same since the Medieval Ages. It begins with a cream background that has flowers ringing a stylized dragon. Typically, the color palette is blue, gold, green, and brown, surrounded with a myriad of black scrolls painted with such fine lines that they appear as if they were drawn with a pen. In one shop, we met the artist, Gian Paolo, the owner, and his wife. On the wall, he had diplomas reflecting the training he had and licensing him to paint in the Deruta style. I bought a blue ceramic holy water holder to hang near my entrance at home and a small ceramic bowl and pitcher. On the bottom of each authentic piece, you will see the last name of the artist followed by their initials and the words "dipinto a mano," which means painted by hand and the name of the città of origin, which in this case would be the city of Deruta, and signed by the artist, Mangaritelli, G. P.

Signore Mangaritelli also gave us instructions on how to get to Perugia. He said to head toward Montebella; and so once again, we wound up into the hills, reaching an area filled with jazz music. There were banners flying that said, "Welcome to the Umbria World Jazz Festival in Perugia." We could hear music everywhere and wondered what was going on as we saw the bright banners and crowds of people. We had somehow found our way to the historical center of Perugia.

We parked the car next to a beautiful hotel named the Brufani Palace. From the hotel, you could look down into Perugia. Originally, the hotel was the resident palace of the Brufani Family. Anita said, "What are you going to do?" I said that I was going to get us a room. She replied, "But this is the Umbria World Jazz Festival. There won't be any rooms. It's got to be a sell out." Anita stayed in the car, while I went in to see what magic I could concoct.

There was a young gentleman named Josh near the revolving entry doors. Josh was a lean Brad Pitt, almost six feet tall, who originally came from New Zealand. He thought I had a reservation. I said nothing. I strode across the black-and-white checkered marble floors to the reservation desk, thinking, *I bet they have hot water here.* There, in his coattails, was an elegant man standing behind the reservation desk. Leaning in closely, I asked softly, "Do you know the village of Alpicella?" He said, "No." I continued, "We've been with the relatives and traveling for almost two weeks with no hot water." Leaning in closer and batting my big brown eyes at him, I pleaded for mercy and a room. He swiftly called Josh over and said, "Take her to her suite."

We not only got a room, but we also got a suite with hot water. Josh came outside with me to get the car keys. Anita looked at me in shock, "Did you get a room?" "No," I purred. "I got us a suite." Josh asked, "Where is your luggage?" I tossed out my answer with aplomb, "We travel light." I handed him the paper lunch sack with my bra, panties, cosmetics, and toothbrush. When he walked into the foyer, the staff just looked at him, but not a peep did we hear. Written across their faces was, "Where's their luggage?"

Josh took us up to our corner suite. As we came to the door, I turned around to see the top of the head of a man walking down the stairs. I exclaimed, "Oh! My gosh! Tony Bennett? Mr. Bennett, I know you're not going to believe this, but I truly am your biggest fan."

He smiled. "What's your name, sweetie, and where are you from?"

I radiated. "My name is Donna Marie Ferro, and I'm from San Fran-cis-co." I asked him if I could take a picture of him. He graciously said, "Yes." My hands were shaking so much I could hardly take the picture.

He then said, "Excuse me, honey. I have to run because I have to make a sound check for tonight's performance." I thanked him profusely and went running into the suite. Josh and Anita were there. I exclaimed, "I just met Tony Bennett!"

Anita was stroking the silk wallpaper, exclaiming over and over, "We have hot water!" Tony Bennett was my hot water. I've had the original 1962 score of "I Left My Heart in San Francisco" with a photo of Tony Bennett. It's been sitting on my piano since I was in high school. I wanted to show them the picture I took of him. But when I tried to show the picture, there was none. My hands had shaken so much I had hit the wrong button. Anita looked at me, and as she saw my tears, she said, "Uh-oh. We've got trouble here. Hey, let's go out into the streets, listen to the music, and buy something to wear tonight." Wallowing in my disappointment, I found Anita's prescription for shopping helpful. I found a dress in a very light and airy fabric in shades of brown with flowers. It was very sexy with its V-shaped neckline and incredibly reasonable because July is the big sale month in Italy. Normally, I would have put it on and floated back to the hotel, but I was devastated. A new dress can't fix everything.

The heart of Perugia was filled with music. It was everywhere, including in the shops that were playing Tony Bennett. It embraced, enveloped, and washed over us as if we became part of the cadence of the music. If you love music, go to Perugia when the jazz festival is there. I promise you will not be disappointed. As I listened to the music, tears rolled down my cheeks. I was heartbroken. I couldn't believe what had happened. How could I have hit the wrong button on my camera? We wandered through the people-filled streets, surrounded by jazz; and after a while, we returned to the hotel. When we entered, Josh looked at my face, and then he said, "What's wrong?" I woefully replied, "My picture of Tony Bennett didn't turn out, and I'll never have another chance to take a picture of him." He looked into my pitiful eyes and said gently, "Stay here in the foyer." I wondered why we had to stay in the foyer, but we waited. When Josh returned, he was accompanied by the one and only Tony Bennett.

"Mr. Bennett!" I exclaimed. "My picture didn't turn out. May I take another picture of you?"

"No," he responded. "I want you in the picture with me." He then handed my camera to one of his entourage. Afterward, I gave him a big hug and kiss. Tony Bennett walked away, up the same stairs by our suite. I had my picture, and all was right with the world again. The gods of music had smiled on me.

That evening, I would bump into Tony Bennett five more times. For me, it was paradise. Ever since I was a child, I have always loved Tony Bennett. Anita said, "I hope Tony does not think you are stalking him." The last time was at one thirty in the morning. He had just returned from performing and was going out to dinner. He had worn an impeccable dark navy suit with a pinstriped tie and crisp white shirt for the performance but had changed into a beautiful white shirt and slacks for dinner. Every time I saw him that evening, he had great decorum and was perfectly groomed. You, Mr. Bennett, are the consummate gentleman.

After Tony left, I decided to powder my nose and see what else there was to do. As I came out of the lobby bathroom, I tripped; and a tall, dark, and handsome man caught me. He followed Anita and me to the sofa to sit and chat for a while. He had eyes like black slate and an olive complexion. He was very handsome, muscular, well over six feet, and was dressed in a silk suit with a Hermes tie. He wore an 18-karat gold Rolex. He looked like he might have been in his midforties. He spoke English in a formal and highly educated manner. We found out he had come from Dubai with an entourage of real estate developers.

I asked him, "Why are there so many life-sized cardboard cutouts of jockeys and horses in the hotel?" He explained, "Dubai and Italy are having horse races throughout the countryside of Perugia." He also took out maps to show us the development plans for homes in Dubai. The map of land was shaped like a palm tree. Then the jockeys came into the foyer and started talking to him. He introduced us to the jockeys. He looked at me and asked, "Would the two of you like to go to Dubai?" I said, "We are teachers and cannot afford it." He said, "Money is no object." But I had read things and said we could not go. He clapped his hands, and a man appeared. He gave orders in another language, and the man left and reappeared later with gifts. He gave both of us a leather case with dates inside and some magazines on the various horse races between Dubai and Italy. Then he gave me the pin off his lapel and finally his personal card. It was about three thirty in the morning, but no one seemed to be going to sleep. Perugia was in its own magical time zone. Off we went with gifts in hand. Who would have thought we would meet an exotic man from Dubai and Mr. Tony Bennett, all in the same day. Only in Italy!

We woke up the next morning in the lap of luxury and gazed fondly at our bathtub filled with hot sudsy water. Before leaving Perugia, we went to the Jean Louis David Hair Salon, and there we met the famous hair stylist, Luigi. He was the owner of the salon, and he spent hours doing our hair. Thank goodness he didn't charge by the hour. He strutted all over the salon, giving advice, checking on clients with their stylists. This was his stage, his symphony, and his show. He was shaping my hair, and he claimed he could tell if a woman was an American by the cut of her hair; it was too masculine. He said that the American woman's haircuts look like they have been done by a barber. Our conversation also included a suggestion that Anita might like to enjoy the company of his police officer friend and that we could all have lunch or dinner together. Lunch in Italy is much later than in the United States, even as late as four in the afternoon because dinner is usually nine, ten, or later at night. We gracefully declined his invitation because we already had plans to shop the sales, have lunch, and listen to the jazz. We had soaked in the bath and had our hair done by Luigi, and it was time to return to Il Cacciatore and the Tuscan villa.

Miracles never cease. We found our way back to the villa and to Il Cacciatore without event. On our way back home, we took a detour to Cortona, the village where *Under the Tuscan Sun* was filmed. Cortona is a beautiful medieval township high in the Tuscan hills. After exploring the little hill town of Cortona, we toodled home to Il Cacciatore. We arrived happily home and relished every moment in this beautiful region. Tuscany has soft rolling hills like the mounds of a woman's breasts, soft, succulent, and nurturing, the bountiful fields filled with vineyards and olive orchards. The landscape bursts with a sea of bright-yellow sunflowers interspersed with golden rolls of hay. Crowning the tops of the hills were medieval little hamlets with the spires of their cathedrals stretching toward the heavens as their bells toll the hours. These small villages are the treasures of Tuscany.

That evening, we were invited along with the other guests for dinner in the main villa with the owners, Marisa and Franco. The beauty of Italy is that it is so relaxed. We were never late for dinner because Italians move on their own time for certain things, like dinner. Before dinner, we sat out on the terrace, while Marisa made martinis. As she handed me my martini, she remarked with a glimmer in her eye, "I've even made these for Brad Pitt." I whispered to Anita, "Do you think she is telling the truth?" She and her husband, Franco, were so welcoming; we all felt like we were sharing our experiences with our family at a Sunday evening dinner. Marisa's perfectly groomed and charming husband was a consummate conversationalist who was fluent in English. He told fascinating stories and was an expert at eliciting travel adventures from the villa guests around the table. I turned to Marisa and asked her how she and her husband had met. With a twinkle in her eye, she said, "No, ask Franco. I want to hear him tell you the story about our love and how he and I met and married."

Franco began by saying he was a poor medical student, and she was at the university and came from a wealthy family with a prominent lineage. The villa and all of its grounds had been in her family since medieval times. Her family was against the marriage, so they dated in secret, but the stress of a clandestine relationship pressured them to break up. Years later, there was a charity benefit, and they both attended. She had grown even more beautiful than she was as a student. Neither of them had found another partner to replace their youthful romance. By this time, he had become a prominent cosmetic surgeon, with a chain of clinics throughout Italy, and knew the crème de la crème in Italy. She was a socialite and knew many of the people he knew. This time when their eyes met, they knew it would be for life. She arranged a meeting with her father and simply announced that he was the man she would marry. Franco was well off but still not in her class. The family finally gave in and blessed them on the condition that he would help with his resources to keep the estate in the family so that Marisa would have the life she had grown accustomed to. He kept his promise, and they had been married for nearly thirty years.

The table was set for twelve with an Italian country theme. The big comfortable leather dining chairs were embossed on the back with Marisa's coat of arms. We met their son, Piero, who was trying out for the Olympics in the equestrian category. He was a tall, lean, blue-eyed young blond in his early twenties. I told him about my daughter, and he seemed quite intrigued by her and the photo I shared. Unfortunately, she had just arrived at the relatives with my mother in Liguria; he was in Tuscany, and they would never meet. We enjoyed every course of the meal, which was superb including a beef dish, and fried zucchini flowers, which are a Tuscan delicacy. But more important was the exuberant company, the conversation, and wine until late into the evening that was so delightful.

It was another special night in Tuscany; however, tomorrow we were returning to Alpicella. As I began to walk up the staircase to my bedroom, I glanced back at the Il Cacciatore painting; and then turning to him, I said, "Ce vedremo un' altra volta. I will see you another time." When I returned to the United States, I would find the original antique skeleton key to his villa in my suitcase.

Chapter 6

Il Papa and Il Cardinale 2005

Surprisingly, after a week of toodling in Tuscany, we had the perfect Saturday trip back to Alpicella. We didn't get lost or have any driving dramas. While winding through the hills, I noticed two men on bicycles who resembled my cousins. Could they be Damiano and his elder brother Maurizio? It was as if they were searching for someone. I found out later it was me. When I walked through the door at Piero's, I could sense something was very wrong. In a somber tone, Piero told me that my mother had been phoning continuously to see where I was and wanted to know why I had not gone to Lalla Nita's house to greet her and my daughter, Bella, upon their arrival.

I told Piero that when I was at the villa in Tuscany, I had talked long distance to my mother in Alameda, California, on Thursday by phone. My mother had said that she and Bella, who was now twenty-four years old, were going to fly into Italy on Friday. I told him that she and I had discussed my Saturday return from Marisa's villa to Piero's house. She had explicitly said to me, "No, no, no, don't worry about us. We'll be adjusting to the time change, and you know how we like to sleep when we first arrive, so we'll see you on Sunday at the big festa in Alpicella. Just drive home safely." Piero responded to my explanation as if my nonno Mazzetta was there, in that soft gentle but firm tone, "You must go and see your daughter now."

Anita then interjected, "Donna Marie is telling you the truth. I heard her telephone conversation with her mother." It made no difference to him. This was serious. I drove down the hill to Campo Marzio with Anita along for moral support. When I entered the house, I felt like a dead woman walking. The atmosphere in the house was frigid. Everyone had their eyes downcast. No one looked at me. I turned to my mother and asked, "What is going on?" She said, "Your daughter has been crying for two days. I even gave her a tranquilizer on the airplane." I looked at my daughter and asked what was happening. Bella told me that she had gotten exhausted and had a crying jag. She went on to say, "Nonnie had given me a tranquilizer." Then she said, "I can't understand a word they are saying, and when you are here, you translate for me. You are a buffer for me. So I kept crying for you."

As I listened to my daughter, I looked around the room and saw the piercing steel-gray eyes of Lalla Nita staring through me. I realized then that I was in deep trouble. There was now an iceberg, Lalla Nita, in the room; and I was the *Titanic*. My mother's furba had set me up. She had not known how to handle Bella and was putting it all on me. In the years that I had been visiting the relatives, my mother had never translated for me. I was thrown into the lake of the *bella lingua* without knowing how to swim. Usually by the third day, I had retreated into the bathroom, locked the door, and was crying my eyes out because my brain was on overload as I tried to understand the language. When I was there with Bella, I always translated for her and led her into the language gently. Now she'd had two days with my mother's Language Immersion Program and had crashed royally. But nothing could be done. I just had to "suck it up" and take whatever was decided to be handed out. My mother's furba had won out once again. I was cinghiale, and I would be strong.

Realizing that Lalla Nita had misinterpreted what had truly happened, I knew that she was going to call me out of the room and chastise me. Within minutes, she had called me into the hallway, saying in Italian, "When your family arrived in Italy, I expected you to be here for them." I knew to keep my mouth shut, say nothing, and to say in Italian with downcast eyes, "I am sorry. Mi dispiace"; even though I was not at fault. Then I raised my head and looked into her eyes, saying, "Lei è ancora Il mio Papa?" You are still my pope?

When I was a young woman, I had nicknamed her "the pope." She was the head of the family, and she had given me the title, "Il Cardinale." She gestured to me to come closer, "Vieni da me per un abbraccio." Come to me for a hug. Lalla Nita encircled me with her arms and looked into my eyes, "Tu sei il mio Cardinale." You are my cardinal.

I was relieved and happy. With our arms around each other, we went back into the warm sunlit kitchen where everyone was laughing and talking. There was wine and food; all was forgiven. While we were chatting away, Lorenzo, our cousin and truly like a brother to my mother, disappeared. He is a quiet, elegant, and handsome man who seems formal when you first meet him. He has a full head of glistening hair, a perfect Vallerga nose, big hazel eyes, slender in build, about five feet seven, with a great sense of humor once you get to know him. He was gone for about fifteen minutes. Where was he? Nobody knew.

He reentered the room with great style in one of my mother's elegant flower-print bathrobes, wearing bright red lipstick, a mole on his cheek like my mother and Marilyn Monroe; and to top off his look, he wore one of my mother's blonde wigs. He introduced himself with a high-pitched voice, saying, "Mi chiamo Margheitin." (My name is Margaret.) He went into a complete imitation of my mother. We were rolling on the floor with laughter. He informed us that "Margheitin" knew my mother when she first came to Italy and that when he (Lorenzo) first saw her thirty-four years ago, he thought, like the villagers, that she was a street walker. That evening was absolutely grand; both sides of the family went to a restaurant in Alpicella. The story at the dinner table centered on the visit by "Margheitin." I passed my digital camera around so that the more than thirty members of the family could see "Margheitin," the femme fatale of Campo Marzio.

You might be wondering how the sound "ING" becomes part of an Italian name. No one seems to know other than it is unique to our little part of Italy. As an example, if your name is Giuseppe, your nickname in Italian might be Peppe. But in Liguria, it would be Peppin. Another example would be Caterina; in our region, it is Catainin. Antonio becomes Tognin, with the emphasis on the second syllable. Almost everyone in Alpicella has a nickname with the sound of "ing" at the end of it. That is how Margherita became "Margheitin." I have a theory. When my daughter Terèsa was in first grade, she learned about the "ing" in reading. It comes from a land called "ing" and has a king, the king of "ing." I think that Lorenzo is the true king of "ing," and that "ing" is actually Liguria.

If you don't have an "ing" in your name, oftentimes your nickname would have to do with your work or a tool or something about you. As an example, my nonno Antonio was called "Mazzetta," which comes from the Italian word, mazza, which means sledgehammer. So "Mazzetta" roughly translated means "little sledgehammer." The reason my nonno was called Mazzetta was that while he was small, he was very strong. He would take a sledgehammer and break the marble that was used to make the chapel for the Rock St. Anna.

After enduring the two-day Rose Ferro School of Language Immersion, my daughter decided that she wanted to stay with Angela and Piero. Angela could put an extra bed in with us, and we knew it would work. I also knew that Piero would be happy; now there would be four women instead of one. After we returned home about two o'clock in the morning, Angela said she had a surprise. We had fallen in love with her cheese grater, and she had purchased the same cheese grater for both of us. We were so excited; we loved it. It was always the little things that mattered. As we drifted off to slumber, all was right with the world, once more. "Tutto a posto." Everything was in its place.

When we woke up the next morning, we could hear the church bells of St. Anthony, the patron saint of Alpicella. For more than a hundred years, the third weekend in July has been dedicated to Madonna Del Carmine. All the hamlets that surround Alpicella celebrate saints' feast days in July and August. My nonno told me that as a young man, he and his friends carried twelve-foot-high gold crosses, parading them up and down the dirt roads. The crosses are in leather holders, strapped to the young men who have their hands behind their backs during the whole procession. They are not allowed to touch the crosses. Surrounding the cross are more men to keep it safe from falling. If the cross begins to sway or has to be passed to another man because of the weight, then the other men rescue it. As they file through the streets, six additional men carry a platform covered with a bevy of flowers, usually roses and lilies, which has a statue of a Madonna holding the child Jesus. After they parade up and down all the roads, they enter St. Anthony's for mass, and then the fun begins.

Since my nonno's time, the festa has changed. Now on Saturday night, there is a huge dinner and dance in the piazza, starting at seven in the evening, ending around two in the morning. Lots and lots of young people dance in the street to music, old and new. Sunday, the ritual remains the same as in the days of my nonno, with the parade of crosses. After mass, there is another huge dinner and dance until the wee hours of the morning. Monday evening, a small gathering of people read poems and perform gymnastics. Italy loves a party, and so do the cinghiali Ferro Family.

After we had attended many *feste* (festivals) in the surrounding towns, we planned a day at the beach in Varazze to recuperate from all the dancing. However, when I opened the shutters, it was a gloomy, gloomy day; so I suggested a change of plans. "Let's go to Monte Carlo." I phoned my mother and told her our plans and said to be sure to pack an overnight bag. We packed our bags, more than our brown paper "Perugian" bags, and swung by Lalla Nita's house to pick her up. The drive was about an hour and twenty minutes. It was rain and fog all the way. I had my own radar channeling Grace Kelly. We took the hairpin turns, winding down and down until suddenly we arrived in Monaco. No fog. No rain. Just beautiful sunshine!

We found our way to the historic Hotel de Paris built in 1864 in the Monte Carlo district of Monaco. My mother asked, "How in the world are you going to get us into this hotel?" It was high season. Anita replied, "Watch her." Our Ford Fiesta was parked between a Lamborghini and a Ferrari. I was dressed to the nines and looked as if I owned the place. I strutted through the doors and was greeted as if I were a queen. Alongside me were two American tourists: he in Bermuda shorts and she in a tight T-shirt with Levi's, taking pictures of the foyer. Security came over and asked them what they were doing. They said that they were just taking pictures. They were told, "Our guests do not appreciate it. You are disrupting the privacy of our clientele." And they were escorted out. Mr. Security turned to me and said, "I apologize for this disturbance, Madame." I nodded.

I glided up to the reservation desk. Once more, I batted my big brown eyes and said I wanted two adjoining suites. The man asked if I had reservations, and I said no. I asked him, "Do I remind you a little bit of your late Princess Grace?" He agreed, and yes, we got the suites. I returned to the car, tossed the key to the valet, and told my mother we had adjoining suites. She said, "I don't believe it." Anita looked at her, thinking of the Brufani, and said, "Believe it." Our suites had a panoramic view of the famous Monte Carlo yacht harbor, and on top of the hill was the palace of the Grimaldi Family. Our room was filled with flowers; elegant pastries; bottles of champagne; and most important, hot water in the tub.

As I gazed at Bella, from the balcony suite, I realized she had transformed into a beautiful young adult woman. I was amazed at how sophisticated she looked in her twenties. Terèsa (Bella) is part Sicilian and has gorgeous catlike eyes a là Sophia Loren. She is tall, about five feet, seven inches, and has high cheekbones and thick, lush dark brown hair. Usually when we are in Italy, the Italians automatically speak to her in Italian, thinking she is one of them. And when they look at my mother and me, we are viewed as foreigners. Some years earlier, as we exited the hotel in Rome, we had been stopped when she was twelve by a movie director who wanted to test her for the cinema. They had wanted Bella to play a young Sophia Loren in the movie. My mother, who is ferociously protective of her family, had gotten upset and chased him away. She did not want her granddaughter in motion pictures.

Just like any tourist, we went to the Café de Paris right across the street from the hotel, which is next door to the legendary Place du Casino, yes, the famous Monte Carlo casino. We tried to count the Lamborghinis and Ferraris on the way, too many to count. That evening, we went to an elegant restaurant; and later on, we decided to go to the landmark Monte Carlo casino. Anita and I were looking at the Salvador Dali exhibition in the casino foyer; my mother was wandering and people-watching.

My daughter decided to play roulette. Within a few minutes, Bella returned. We thought she had lost. It was now about two thirty in the morning, and we were feeling comfortable sipping our wine. And then my daughter said softly, "I won." She had no idea how much; she had played one number, her dog's birthday. She came back from the cashier white as a ghost. She had won more than €1,800. Later at our hotel, she bought champagne for us. The rest of her winnings were spent in Portofino on designer clothes. Lucky girl! And Lucky Nonnie! Bella bought her a pair of Ferragamo kitten-heel sandals made with sateen fabric printed with exotic flowers on a pale cream background.

The next day, we had lunch in Monte Carlo and then started the scenic journey back to Campo Marzio and Alpicella. The most difficult part was not the driving because we had sunshine and clear skies. It was that we had to say goodbye to our families and then go to Portofino the next day.

When Anita, Bella and I arrived back in Alpicella, we began packing. Bella said, "I can see you two are really cousins." I asked her, "Why?" She said, "You two literally go in circles around the room before you begin putting anything in the suitcase." Anita and I do perform an unusual ritual as we begin packing. We begin circling around the room as if we didn't know what we were doing. Meanwhile, Bella is calmly and serenely packing and is finished while we are still circling one another looking for our clothes. Anita would say," I can't find my shoe. I can't find my shoe." She lost one point in our game because I was the one who found the shoe. Anita and I believe that this is a cinghiali ritual. I didn't know that cinghiali even had suitcases.

As a parting gift, we gave Angela and Piero a large modern coffee pot that Anita had purchased in Florence. We thought it might cut down on our two-hour coffee marathons. We told them to save it for our return. I knew that they would take good care of it, as they still had the slippers my mother and daughter had worn here on a trip from six years ago. As we sat on the terrace that warm summer evening, all the Ferro relatives came to bid us goodbye. I looked around at each one. It was as if one heart was beating among all of us. I reflected that even though these families were separated by miles, age, and cultural differences, nothing could break our bonds. We are all truly one and the same family. I thought no one can explain the thread that binds us, our voices, our gestures, and our emotions: it seems as if we are all one and the same person. I was going to miss them terribly. Then reality set in: tomorrow I would have to drive. It was time to go to bed.

In Italy, we seem to dream more vividly. One night, very late, Anita's cell phone rang, a cousin from the States wanted to talk with her. The ring woke Bella, and she told us that she had dreamed she was talking with Paul Newman. I, on the other hand, was dreaming of hot, sudsy bubble baths.

Before we knew it, the sunshine was streaming in the windows, and it was morning. It was time to get up, check, and tally our points of who won the Il Punto game. It is based upon accuracy of knowledge; for example, how to use a combination washer-dryer. Two points for Leo the cat just because he is the coolest cat in Alpicella; 4.5 *punti* for Anita, 5.5 for me, 12.5 for Piero, and the champion Angela, 21 punti. None of us had ever beaten her. Piero gave us jars of his award-winning honey, and I was trying to think of who I could give the honey to because it was too heavy to pack and take on the plane. Since the four of us and our luggage would not fit into the compact car I had rented, my mother had hired a driver to bring her to Portofino. Bella came with us to Santa Margherita and then took a taxi to Portofino, joining my mother who would already be there.

While Piero was washing off our car, we were marking our territory throughout the house. I took a pair of my slippers from Monte Carlo and left them under the bed and left a sweater in the closet. Bella left a little souvenir from Monte Carlo on the dresser. I hope Anita didn't leave one of her shoes. All of this was to let them know we would return. So we gave our hugs and goodbyes and started down the winding road. And who, you may ask, was coming toward us in his car? Cousin Giacomo!

He was tooting his horn, calling, "Ciao! Ciao!" We blew kisses to him, and then I went back to the reality of driving. We wound down the hillside until we were flagged down by the carabinieri at a security checkpoint. The police randomly select tourists based on the rental car, which is typically silver, to check that the driver has the appropriate documents: international driver's license, passport, and rental agreement. Officer Stefano was quite handsome, while the other was not friendly and wanted all my documents. The grumpy carabiniere was taking his sweet time to check everything out. Then Stefano asked, "Where are you coming from?" I replied, "Alpicella." He said, "Don't tell me. You're a Ferro." He had overheard Mr. Grumpy say my name into the dispatcher. I told him he was so cute that I would put him in my suitcase and take him with us. He replied, "I wish I could, but I have to stay." Then he gestured toward Mr. Grumpy.

We were down to our last week in Italy, and it was to be in paradise at the Hotel Splendido in Portofino. It was a wonderful way to finish our trip, and I was looking forward to the fresh linen beds and hot sudsy baths. But first, we had to run the Genovese gauntlet to get there.

Chapter 7

Il Bacio e Il Colombo—
The Kiss and the Dove 2005

Have you ever been sucked into a vortex? Mine happens to be the city of Genova, and I am not sure why, but she has a love/hate relationship with me. Since I was a young woman driving through Italy, anytime the sign for Genova appeared, I would take a wrong turn and end up in some part of the city. Thank heavens for my cinghiale nose. Relying only on instinct, I was able to pull away from the vortex and took the correct road to Santa Margherita. After a few more twists and turns, we arrived at our Hotel Miramare. We wanted to explore Santa Margherita for a couple of days and then make our entrance at the Hotel Splendido. Prior to our arrival at Splendido, the order of the day was to take warm sudsy baths and get our hair done. We had a lot of dirt to get off our hooves. Our room, at the Hotel Miramare, had a substantial balcony overlooking the bay; and yes, hurrah, we had hot water.

Santa Margherita is a seaside port that has been invaded by everyone from the French to the Romans. With lots of shops edging the harbor, it is one of the more beautiful resorts on the Italian Riviera. It was late in the day, and we hadn't had lunch. We found a little spot for an al fresco snack, since dinner would be in the hotel. While we were eating lunch, a lady who had been pacing back and forth nearby suddenly turned, came up to us, and, leaning in with intense eyes, said, "Do you know I got pregnant by Michael Jackson?" Anita and I looked at each other, and Anita exclaimed, "Really?" After the lady left, I turned to Anita, "What's up with that?" Anita just laughed. "Crazy," she said.

That night, the warm water of the bath was glorious and relaxing. But later in the evening when we went to sleep, I was suddenly awakened by loud bursts of sound. Boom! Boom! Boom! I opened the shutters to see fantastic fireworks over the bay. It was the festa of Santa Margherita, but I fantasized that the fireworks were to welcome us, the Ferro cinghiali.

The next day, we did our favorite thing: window shopping and exploring the glistening jewel of Santa Margherita. Sometimes shopping is misunderstood as an activity. It is actually a good form of exercise and a great way to explore a new area. Some don't understand that when we go shopping, we don't always go for a specific item but simply to look; and maybe, just maybe, we'll find something and maybe not. While most tourists seemed to be lying on the beach or taking a siesta, we walked our hooves off until we finally stopped in a little park overlooking the bay ensconced with a life-sized statue of Christopher Columbus. The statue looked out over the water with one hand extended, as if he were saying, "Benvenuti nella bella Italia." Welcome to beautiful Italy. I was taking photos in front of the statue when Anita warned, "Watch out. A pigeon might drop a present on your head." I laughed. "With my luck, it will."

As we sat under a tree on the park bench, Anita's forecast came true; a Ligurian bomber with feathers dropped a present smack-dab on my head. I think it was a dove, which in Italian is *colombo*. While I tried to figure out what to do about my hair, I noticed a woman having a conversation with no one nearby and without a cell phone. I realized that this was the same woman I had seen the day before who had claimed she had become pregnant by Michael Jackson. She was crazier than a loon. But this was only the beginning.

Anita turned to me and asked, "What are you going to do about your hair?" I announced, "Nobody is in the park. Everyone is at the beach or taking a siesta. I am going to climb into the fountain and wash my hair and pretend I am Anita Ekberg in the movie *La Dolce Vita*." After I had thoroughly rinsed out my hair and was peering through the sopping strands, I noticed a small caffè across the street with a sign Colombo Ristorante. I told Anita that the word *colombo* in Italian meant "dove." I felt it was an omen, a sign of something to come in the near future. "Let's go to the restaurant and have a late lunch in the sunshine so my hair can dry."

We met a lovely maître d' named Camillo. He was a strong muscular man between sixty and seventy, with a welcoming smile and hazel eyes. He reminded me of my father Carlo. He seemed like such a gentle, jovial soul. He brought us minestrone soup just like what the Nonne Antonietta and Maria had made for us as children. He loved talking to us in Italian; even Anita could understand a little of what he said. When I asked him where he lived, he replied, "I live alone in Rapallo in an apartment with my cat." He asked if we planned to come back that evening. We thought, why not, the soup was delicious and he was so warm and friendly; and so we said, "Yes." He brought us some complimentary cookies and said he was looking forward to our return and would reserve the best table for us.

Around nine that evening, we made our way back to the restaurant. He seemed to light up like the fireworks at a summer festa when he saw us. He had reserved a beautiful outside table and greeted us with a big kiss on each cheek. Right next to our table was a young lady sitting alone. Anita engaged her in conversation, and it turned out that she was an architect from Australia. The young lady was sad and told us that she and her fiancé had recently broken up. She was in Italy to salve her wounds. As the night went on, we talked with other people at the intimately arranged dining tables in the restaurant. Nearby was a table with a group of Norwegian tourists. I brought up the name Hans, a Norwegian officer I had met on a cruise. They reacted as if I had met one of the "ten most wanted" criminals. They told us he was infamous in all of Norway and had been on the news many times.

Here is what happened. I seemed to fall into situations. I was on a Caribbean cruise with my mother and daughter, who was four. My mother and daughter would go to bed around eleven or so, while I and my cruise-ship buddies would go off to have a drink at the bar and dance. One evening, as I was coming out of the ladies room, I was trying to step over the abnormally high doorjamb, which was required on ships at that time. I tripped, went airborne, and landed in the arms of an officer. For the next six nights, we would dance and talk into the wee hours of the evening. He had piercing eyes, blue as the Arctic Ocean. No warmth. Some years later, he was wanted in Norway for pilfering funds from wealthy women on cruise ships.

Ironically, he never asked me for a dime. Maybe it's because I had mentioned I was a schoolteacher. No big money here.

My mother, who met him on the cruise, saw a television show that featured a story about him. He supposedly jumped ship in the Caribbean just before the authorities boarded to arrest him. He was never found. The six Norwegians at dinner at Il Colombo knew all about him. It made for great dinner conversation, interspersed with Camillo's wonderful attentiveness to all of us. The Norwegians said good night; and since it was so late, Anita suggested that we walk the Australian architect to her hotel, the Hotel Suisse.

The route back to her hotel included some small dark side streets. I had only one concern. I felt we were safer on the main-street sidewalks rather than taking vicetti or small alleyways. They were not well lit and were quite deserted at this late hour. It might be longer my way but would be safer. We said our goodbyes to Camillo and exchanged hugs and kisses, promising we would return some day and thanking him for such a wonderful evening.

We went down the dimly lit side streets, block after block, until we arrived at the Suisse Hotel and waited for her safe entry. Continuing on to our hotel, all of a sudden, I heard someone whistle from on top of the hill to catch our attention. There he was, Camillo, standing with bravado, looking like Superman with his hands on his hips. He came running down the hill to us. I was thinking, *This man is out of breath.* He was wheezing like my father did shortly before his heart attack. In any case, wasn't it nice he had come to walk us to our hotel? We each took an arm and proceeded down the street. But the sidewalk was too narrow, so I broke off and walked ahead of them. We were at least six blocks from our hotel. I kept walking at a quick pace because I thought maybe, even at one in the morning, there might be music at our hotel. I walked ahead until I heard a bloodcurdling scream behind me.

"Donna, Donna." I ran back to see Camillo face down on the pavement. I looked at Anita and shockingly screamed out, "Oh my god! You have been injured!" Apparently, when Camillo fell, he had knocked her down, hitting Anita's head on the curb and causing a black eye. Camillo was not moving. There was no sign of life. What to do? Anita said, "I will go for help back at the hotel." Meanwhile, I wasn't sure he was breathing. Because he was a heavy man, I kept trying to roll him over. Over and over and over again, I tried. Finally with every bit of energy in me, I was able to get him face up. He looked peaceful, but he was not breathing. I then started doing everything I could think of to revive him, but he was completely still, not a twitch or the faintest of breath. While I was trying to roll him over and finally started CPR, I straddled him with my legs on each side of him. People were passing by and looking down the dark alley in disgust, thinking we were engaging in sex. It seemed that it took forever before help came, but it finally did. Sirens blaring from fire trucks and ambulances and the police.

All this time, I was screaming for help, "Aiutami, aiutami!" Help me, help me! "Lui è morto." He is dead. Finally, a young man on a Vespa heard me and used his cell phone to call for the police. My words flashed back to haunt me. "Lo bisogno un' uomo ricco, vecchio e vicino alla morte." I need a man who is rich, old, and ready to die. I could hear Lorenzo's voice in my head, "Donna Marie, remember you live your words." I vowed never to use those words again, not even in jest. I would not tempt fate again. Or maybe, after all, I am cinghiale.

When the two police vans and two ambulances showed up, they swung into action. Anita had gotten help at the hotel, and the young man's call had resulted in help as well. The paddles were used over and over and over again on Camillo to jolt him back to life. A crime-scene investigator, a woman dressed in white looking like an angel to me, tried to divert my attention from Camillo and get my story. Before they put him in the body bag, the female investigator said, "We're escorting you back to your hotel."

I thought, *Mother Teresa would never have abandoned someone who had just died.* I felt sorry for poor Camillo and for the poor cat sitting alone in Rapallo waiting for Camillo, who would never show up again to feed him. At the insistence of the police woman, I returned to my hotel. There I saw Anita with the biggest shiner and a huge ice pack on it. Poor Anita!

We returned to our room but could not sleep. So Anita told me the rest of the story. She said that as they were walking together, Camillo began to give her little kisses on the lips and had become quite amorous. With a fatal last kiss, he dropped dead. I kiddingly asked Anita, "Are you the black widow of kisses?" We finally fell asleep, wondering and worrying about Camillo's cat.

The next morning, we awoke to the phone ringing; it was my mother saying, "Well, you've made all the newspapers. Did you kill somebody?" Bella had gone down to the lobby in her bathrobe to have her usual early morning coffee with Ermes, the hotel manager. Since she had grown up at Splendido over the years, she thought of it as her home. Ermes showed her the morning newspaper with

Camillo's death on the front page. She took a copy of the paper up to my mother who immediately got on the phone.

I snapped back, "No, I didn't. Anita did." I told her the whole story and asked how she found out. She said that Ermes had told her that Camillo was beloved and had apparently been with a blonde; and he thought it was you. Ermes remembered that I used to joke and say I wanted a man who was rich, old, and ready to die. This was always a joke with me and never really serious. I simply wanted a man who loved me deeply. Was this the curse that Nonna Maria used to talk to me about when I was a little girl?

Ermes didn't know it was Anita's fatal kiss, not mine. He told my mother it was in all the local papers because Camillo was famous in Liguria in the hotel and restaurant business. The irony was that Camillo had been the maître d' at our Hotel Miramare for ten years where we had stayed. So even if we had not had the chance meeting because of the dove's gift on my head, it seemed that Camillo's path and our paths were meant to cross, no matter what. His destiny was by appointment.

Reeling from the traumatic drama that had unfolded the night before, we sat by the pool in the afternoon. Anita iced her bruised and swollen eye, while my thighs and knees were bruised from trying to give CPR. We were like two washcloths wrung-out, flapping in the Ligurian breeze. My mother came over with Bella from Portofino, and we recounted the story once more. We were still worried about the cat. Toward the early part of the evening, to heal our wounds and repair ourselves, we went to get our hair done in Santa Margherita. Fortunately, the shop was not by the vicetti where he fell. Everyone in the shop seemed distraught and was talking about Camillo's demise. They were saying in the dialect that they had heard there were supposed to be some strange or foreign women with him when he died. I announced in my best Italian, "Eravamo io e mia cugina." It was me and my cousin. The shop fell dead silent. Even the blow dryers shut off.

I quickly added that he had been escorting us back to our hotel for safety and that he was such a gentle and wonderful man. It was my cousin who called for help, while I was giving him CPR. We were now heroines in their eyes. But we were still worried about the cat. I asked about it, and they told us they didn't know anything about a cat. They said he had been married for more than forty-five years and had three children, two girls and a boy in their thirties or forties.

I said nothing, and later outside the shop, I told Anita everything:
There was no cat.

All of this was reconfirmed the next day in Portofino when Ermes
greeted us with the newspaper article, including Camillo's photo and
the fact that his wife had waited up for him. The article also stated
that he had had bypass heart surgery six years before and then a
pacemaker, which explained the wheezing. He had been wheezing
so much that I had thought he was a walking time bomb, ready to go
off at any moment.

Sitting on the balcony at Splendido that evening, I thought about
how we cannot control our outcomes in life. Some people call it
destiny, and others may call it the luck of the draw, but at the end of
the day, we must savor and value every moment we live. Even sorrow
and pain have their positions in the universe. The last evening with
Camillo was definitely out of our control, like Camillo. The universe
put pain in our hearts for him. I believe that in his last moments, he
was a virile and vibrant young man again, full of passion and life.
Long may he live in our hearts and memories.

In contrast to our tumultuous evening with the late Camillo,
there is nothing more serenely beautiful to my eyes than to be in
Portofino overlooking the bay. I love watching the sailboats gliding
by as I am sipping a glass of wine and listening to Vladimir play the
piano in the background, knowing that we are soon to get ready for
another sumptuous Italian dinner and evening.

I have known the cast of characters, the staff at Splendido,
for more than sixteen years. The irresistibly handsome Ermes has
moved up the ranks to be manager of the hotel. Antonio has been
in charge of bar services and seems to never age. The title of this
book was inspired by the assistant bar manager, who I call Signor
Rossi. Then there is handsome Carlo, who is my daughter's age, who
blossomed from being a water boy to being the manager of both
hotel restaurants, Splendido and Splendido Mare, which is near the
port. Then there is Vladimir, who is Italian and whose mother loved
a Russian composer and bestowed his name on her son. He dressed
like Liberace and has been the pianist at Splendido for all the years
I came with my mother and daughter. We met when I was forty years
old; and each evening after dinner, Vladimir would play my song, "I
Left My Heart in San Francisco." Since I sing off-key, he would wait
until late and the patrons were in a very happy state of mind. Then
he would invite me up to the piano, and I would do my thing. Dad,

with your perfect pitch, I can see you putting your fingers in your ears and saying, "Do you know the song, Far, Far Away?"

The most colorful and flamboyant person at Splendido was Marisa. Petite and thin, always tan from her winters in the South Pacific, she wore tons of bangles and would make sweeping gestures in that grand manner everyone expects from Italians. She loved swimming in the nude and posted her topless photos in the dressing room of her very small boutique, which was attached to the hotel. She loved my mother, and they would spend hours chatting in the dialect. They both had adored their husbands but were widowed. Marisa's boutique was my mother's Waterloo. Marisa would fill bags with beautiful irresistible, casual chic clothes for my mother to try on in our hotel room. Yes, of course, my mother always found something to buy. Her suitcase was bulging after her Waterloo encounter with Marisa, but those clothes lasted her for years, and she was complimented all the time.

Splendido is a perfect piece of paradise, where we always felt like we had come home. Splendido restored me, infused me with a glow of wonderment. In the world of Splendido, life is perfect. It is a place where one belongs, where one is always welcomed. It is the home we all wish we could have in our fantasy world. The staff is like the perfect family, always welcoming, always there. It is amazing how Splendido lives its name.

Reality had jolted us. This time, it was different. Ermes handed us the newspaper, saying, "Girls, you need to go down to the church and light a candle for your souls and for Camillo." He had a smile playing on his lips, but we did it anyway. Call it heavenly insurance.

Each day, we would go into the little town of Portofino and see the same ladies making the same handkerchiefs in the same way forever, speaking the dialect with one another and recognizing my mother, daughter, and me. In the old days, there were no vans to take one down the hill into town. One walked. Splendido is part of the Orient Express Hotel chain and is quite secluded. That is why so many famous movie stars have stayed there: Madonna, Ingrid Bergman, Elizabeth Taylor, Rod Stewart, Robert De Niro, and Denzel Washington, to name a few. Whether famous or not, everyone is treated like they are a star by the Splendido staff.

One night, we were sitting at dinner when an entourage entered the terrace restaurant. Terèsa said, "Mom, do you know who that is? That is Anastasia, a very famous singer in Europe. She is American." Before we knew it, two tables became one table, and we were part of the group. She was going to be appearing in Rome the next night.

That night we met everyone, from her business manager, to her secretary, choreographer, even her own sister. We had retired when about one o'clock in the morning, there was a knock on the door. It was Terèsa, asking if we wanted to join a private party downstairs. We partied until a little after three in the morning, and I am happy to report that no one dropped dead that night.

When I think of the Hotel Splendido, I think of the very handsome waiters, one of whom stood out, Francesco. Francesco had chiseled features like a Greek god, with green eyes, curly blond hair and flashing brilliant white teeth. He moved with a certain elegant swagger and charisma that swept away the heart of every woman he passed. All I can say is that every time I hear the song "Come Prima," I know that somewhere hearts are beating faster or melting. That's one of the perks of coming to Splendido; the eye candy is delicious.

My mother and daughter had left the day before, and they were safe and sound back in California. The next day, Anita and I left Portofino for the Lago Maggiore region to visit our cousin's villa. Our cousin Rose is the niece of our nonna Antonietta. She immigrated to the United States as a teenager, graduated from the University of California at Berkeley, and eventually married an economics professor originally from Bergamo, Italy. They live in Los Gatos, California, but like to visit Italy as often as they can, which is why they bought a villa in the Lake District in the village of Lesa across Lago Maggiore.

When we arrived at the villa, we discovered that it had been originally built in 1914 and bought by King Farouk in the early 1950s. The ambiance of the villa is eerie. It resembles a Bavarian Castle. The grounds have a gate and fence with black spires and spikes that soar into the sky and look to be at least twelve feet high. Rose and her husband, Mario, had purchased two apartments of the original villa. The bedrooms and bathrooms for each of the apartments are underground. The living area and kitchen are upstairs. Our cousins were kind enough to give us our own apartment, and we stayed for several days.

Rose and Mario took us on a tour of the estate. We saw cement benches and life-size statues all over the grounds. The benches seemed to be stationed at close intervals. Rose told us that the spacing of the benches was because of the mega-rotund size of King Farouk. Apparently, walking any distance was a challenge for him. As we walked the grounds, we could see Lago Maggiore across the street. As I stared at the lake, I was struck by how calm and still it was, but it was not for me. Except for the movement of the boats and the gentle little lapping waves, it had no movement, no rhythm, and no surprise; it seemed like dead water. I need excitement, I need movement, I need surprise, I need adventure, I need something I cannot tame and which cannot tame me; but I will respect it, and it will respect me and that is the sea. When I was young, my nonna Maria told me that we came from near the sea, which has constant movement, not from the stillness of the lakes. I looked into her steel-gray eyes and asked, "Am I the sea?" She leaned forward then said, "No, ti hai rispetto per il mare" (No, you have respect for the sea).

That evening, we went to dinner at a restaurant on the lake. As we ordered dinner, we were attacked by clouds of mosquitoes. We spent the dinner slapping each other in defense. Soon we were quite bloody, and Anita had sixty-two bites. Rose finally suggested that we move indoors. The only one who didn't get bitten was Mario. Now I know why we like the sea, no mosquitoes.

When I was a little girl, my father would always talk proudly about his uncle, Bernardo, who died during World War I. I never knew the full story though, until Cousin Rose told us about great-uncle Bernardo Rusca, who was the eldest child in the family and a brother of Antonietta. Apparently, Bernardo (or Nadin as he was called at home) was shot in the head during World War I. He survived the wound and was able to return home for two weeks' leave. While he was polishing his boots to return to the front lines, he collapsed and died. We think it might have been an aneurism or a blood clot. He was only twenty years old. Bernardo is listed on the fallen-soldier monument in Stella San Bernardo. Many villages have these monuments in their piazzas. The monument in Alpicella is of a soldier with his hand stretched out, holding an angel of freedom.

Rose went on to tell us that many years ago, there was another Bernardo, who was our great-great-grandfather and who became the mayor, *sindaco*, of all the stelle. He married into great wealth, but he gambled. He didn't realize that some of the other players had signals to reveal all of his cards, and eventually, he lost all of his possessions and died in his early forties.

One of the most heartfelt stories Rose shared with us was when she was a child and the Germans occupied their home during World War II until 1945. Starting in 1941, the Germans would knock on the doors in the hills of Liguria, asking how many people were in the house. They would then tell the Ligurian that they were taking possession of specific rooms, saying, "Remember, you may be our

Allies, but you are not our friends." The Italians lived in fear of the Germans. The Germans lived with Rose's family during the war. They needed to occupy the hilltop homes because they could see the Allied planes coming through, and they would shoot them down. According to our cousin Rose, one Allied plane crashed in Stella San Bernardo, but no one would talk about it.

I can remember Nonna Maria and my mother telling me stories about the impact of World War II on my family in Italy. In fact, one of my mother's cousins, a young boy of twelve, was walking to the grocery store when he was killed by an Allied bomb. During that same time, my maternal great-aunt, Giuseppina, who worked as a nurse in a mental institution, ended up with shrapnel in both of her legs because of another bombing incident. There were more horrific stories. As the adage goes, "War is hell."

The stories went into the night, but we couldn't sleep anyway because of the mosquito bites. Finally, we went to bed, and as we were finally drifting to sleep, Anita had her first nightmare. She was making frightened noises in her sleep, as though something was going to harm her. I was awake, feeling a heavy weight on my chest the size of a small child, pinning me to the bed. I struggled to raise my arms and pushed it off of me, turning to Anita to shake her awake from her nightmare. I said, "There is something haunted about this place that feels . . . not good." Anita felt it, too. What was happening to us?

Sipping coffee the next morning, we were exhausted by the hauntingly strange and disturbing things that had occurred the night before. Rose could sense something was amiss. I began asking questions about the villa. Why was it so different from other Italian villas? What is this strange architecture? She looked at me and calmly said, "You know there are strega (witches) in our family." Was I sensing something about this villa? Did something happen here? Thinking of my experience at the cemetery and my great-grandmother Maria Zunino Rusca in Stella San Bernardo, I replied softly, "I know." Then I asked Rose what happens when someone dies in Italy. Rose became curious about why I was asking so many questions about the burial process. So we shared the story about Camillo, and she said, "You should write a book." I did and I hope you are enjoying reading it.

Rose became our tour guide extraordinaire throughout the Lake District. We toured Isola Bella, which is filled with huge villas nestled in the hills overlooking the lake. The villas are perfectly groomed and are a dramatic contrast to the softness of the Tuscan region. The sheer vertical walls of granite containing the lakes have a strength borrowed from the nearby Swiss Alps. It is a glorious resort area in the summer. I think the lake region is one of those areas not to be overlooked in Italy. We visited the famous gigantic Statue of St. Carlo Borromeo, who is a popular saint in Italy. We went to Lago di Maggiore, Lago di Como, and the "Pearl of the Lake District," Bellagio. Sorry, folks, no George Clooney; but we did see the Palazzo di Rusca. We saw many cathedrals, and I actually found a job I could have done at a cathedral in Como.

A lady stands inside the cathedral doors, and if you want to light a candle, you give her the money. She lights the candle and hands it to you to place on a rack. I was afraid of the hot wax and bought the battery-operated candles. I thought, *Hey. This could be a new career for me.* I could be the lady in charge of the battery-operated candles. I know I wouldn't make much money, but I would have beautiful art work and architecture surrounding me. The whole time we were there, we were scratching like two mad dogs with fleas, and the irony was that we had thrown away the mosquito repellant before arriving at the lake. We thought we would lighten our luggage, and Anita asked, "Do you think we need this mosquito repellent?" I replied, "Well, we haven't used it yet." Within twenty-four hours, we had named the mosquitoes the swine bastards.

Itches and all, it was time to go, and all good things must come to an end. It was time to say goodbye to our perfect hosts and begin our journey back home. We reminisced about how it took two hours to make coffee, Bella winning at the famous casino in Monte Carlo, Angela being the champion of three titles, Cousin Piero's Mr. Toad's wild rides, my near demotion from being Cardinale, and having my photo with my musical icon, Mr. Tony Bennett. We laughed about how we slapped ourselves silly in the onslaught of the night of the swine bastard mosquitoes, our driving escapades, and lastly, we prayed for Camillo's soul.

Chapter 8

Life Is a Collection of Experiences:
Venice and Moe 2006

I found myself planning next year's trip to Italy as soon as the plane touched down in California. By the time September rolled around, I was on the phone to my cousin Anita to confirm the arrangements for our travels. For me, half the fun is planning the trip, and the other half is the anticipation. We called it the walled-cities tour; even though Venice, where we started, is walled in by water.

The year went fast, and suddenly, we found ourselves on a vaporetto with a gorgeous young boatman who gave us a tremendous tour of Venice. Anita and I rode the vaporetto around the islands of Venice. We saw multistory Venetian apartments standing tall, rising out of the water, some of them dilapidated and centuries old, which made me wonder why they hadn't melted into the canals years and years ago. We passed under many bridges, some small like footpaths connecting homes and others larger and longer like arteries connecting to the heart of Venezia. We marveled at the mixture of Gothic, Moorish, Byzantine, and Venetian architecture that frames the living museum that is Venice. We watched as people went about their daily business. We gazed at the many flags hanging on the multitude of windows and buildings, showing the proud Lion symbolizing San Marco, and inhaled the sea smells punctuated by the calls of the hundreds of seagulls. We began to absorb the energy of daily living in this Venetian water world. Venice is like a majestic woman, bejeweled by the sea and crowned by her old-world elegance.

The vaporetto brought us to the Bauer Hotel situated very close to San Marco Square. The hotel is a former Austrian Palace now owned by Francesca, an Italian woman whose family originated in Genova. Her grandfather was a ship builder who found his love in Venice, ultimately married her and bought the Bauer Hotel, which his granddaughter Francesca inherited. She set up a cottage industry for women who are in prison to make organic toiletries, which we sampled in our bathroom and could buy in the hotel boutique.

As we entered the hotel, we were greeted by a young man named Marco. I watched him as he escorted us to our suite. He was over six feet of elegance with porcelain skin, green eyes, and dark curly hair, and glided down the hall like a swan. The mini suite, room 156, became our favorite in the hotel. We were enthralled with our suite. The satin wall coverings, marble floors and baroque fixtures, elegant old-world furniture, and hot water baths pleased us immeasurably. The suite was above a side canal, where the gondoliers were lined up, singing and talking in a musical way found only in Italy.

The hotel's terraced restaurant faces the Grand Canal with a stunning view of Isola Giudecca. There is a gigantic statute about five times life size of an ancient woman holding a torch that is lit in the evening. She reminds me of the goddess Minerva. She is a pillar of power, protecting and guiding the boatmen, welcoming them as they come in for the night from the sea. She is a visible landmark. As we dined, we watched the gondoliers come in to tie up for the night below her welcoming gaze. In perfect harmony, the little splashes of their oars and the lapping of the waves mixed with the music of the hotel softly drifted up to our table as we dined. We merged with Venice, and she transported us to another time and place. Washed away was the stress of the trip and our cares. Whatever they had been, they were gone.

The next day, we walked out on to San Marco Square. As I wandered ahead of Anita, I heard her scream my name. The tone of her voice reminded me of the infamous night of Camillo. I thought, *Oh no.* I raced back to her, calling, "What did you do now?" I frantically looked to see what was wrong. She was standing like a scared little girl pointing down to the ground. There was a bloody pigeon that had been impaled on one of those spikes they use to protect the eaves of the building. Suddenly, it hit me; this was the anniversary of Camillo's death, July 6. Was it an omen? Was something going to happen on this trip?

After exploring the square, we meandered down one of the side streets and discovered a small jewelry boutique. I asked the woman, who looked familiar to me, "Didn't you make masks some years ago?" She said, "Yes, about fifteen years ago." As we chatted, I recalled that I had purchased a harlequin mask from her. It was the very first mask I had ever bought, and I had watched her make it. I realized it must have been on one of the very early trips I had taken with my mother when Bella was very young. The woman warned me the business had changed. She told me not to buy any masks for less than €100 and to buy only from places where you actually see the masks being made on the premises. She told me that many masks are made in other countries but still carry the "Made in Italy" label. Since then, I have heeded her advice, which unfortunately turns out to be true.

We bought a light lunch of mortadella sandwiches cut into small triangle pieces called cichetti. We walked down a vico, a small alleyway, and sat on a bench to people-watch. As we munched on our delicious little sandwiches, Anita remarked, "Look at how elegantly the Venetians dress, and they don't even perspire. They are so regal." I nodded my head. "It's muggy. It's hot, and if you look at all the tourists, they look sweaty, disheveled, and have wrinkled clothes." Then as we looked down the alleyway, to our surprise, a huge dog left a rather large pile nearby to mark his spot. It was a dump and run. I had taken care of Camillo, I took care of the pigeon, but I wasn't going to take care of the Venetian dog dump. Anita again made an observation, "Look, the Venetians, they have poop radar. They never look down, never look at their feet, and never step into the dog's gift." I responded snidely, "That must be your astute cinghiale wisdom coming out." We decided to track who navigated the poop island. We knew when a new herd of tourists were coming because the little wheels of their rolling suitcases made a rum-pum-pum rum-pum-pum sound as they staggered down the street over the cobblestones. Their eyes were glazed, their clothes were rumpled, and they had the zombie walk of the newly arrived. We laughed and laughed as people made it or not: rum-pum-pum, rum-pum-pum.

Then we noticed a handsome Italian man on the third floor of an apartment building across the vico (or alley), watching us, watching the tourists trying to dodge the brown island. He laughed and then took pictures of us laughing. He came down the stairs and took more pictures of us and the tourists trying to dance around the pile. He gave us a big smile, a wink, and then returned to his apartment. He never spoke a word to us, but we knew that we had bonded in some wordless way. As cinghiali of Alpicella, we have found some strange ways to amuse ourselves. It's probably an accumulation of all those centuries when we were so isolated in the hills.

The sun was dropping into the lagoon, and it was time to return to San Marco Square. We found some seats, had our glasses of Pinot Grigio, listened to the music in the piazza, and engaged in watching that great Italian pastime of the passeggiata. As Napoleon said, we were in the "drawing room of Europe." I glanced at my watch. It was one in the morning, and we were in the Venetian flow. Time had no meaning; it had been suspended.

Life is a collection of experiences. Some are painful, others joyful. All are snapshots in the cinema of life. When I left home for Venice, I gave my dog Moe a kiss goodbye. I had found him sixteen years before on the Fourth of July on the French island of Moorea (hence the name Moe). He was in the lagoon, catching fish with his paws and eating them. I had never seen a dog like him in my life. He looked like a medium-sized shepherd/husky mix black and tan. As he came out of the lagoon, he looked at me with his soulful dark brown eyes and knelt at my feet. I knew instantly that he would be my Tahitian four-footed black pearl and that we would never be separate again. It was by appointment.

A young man had been watching the feral dog and how he came up and laid down beside me into the white sand. He asked what I was going to do about the dog. I said that I didn't know, that I didn't speak French, and that I only knew one person in Tahiti. He did speak French and offered to be my translator. I brought the dog to my bungalow, taught him to climb the stairs, tied a red handkerchief around his neck to show that he belonged to someone, and began the process of getting him back to the United States. It took a village of many people to bring Moe home. He arrived one day after I did. He was complete joy, my four-legged best friend.

Then on July 6 in Venice at 3:15 a.m., my daughter phoned me to say Moe had ascended from earth to the stars. She went to check on him, but he had passed away in his doggy bed. I lay there crying with my hand over my eyes, when suddenly there was a dramatic bump to the bed. It was something Moe had done every night. It was Moe. He was bumping my bed one last time as he usually did every night when we retired for the evening. He had come to say a final farewell. My relationship with Moe was forever one of love and, simply put, perfect. The first twenty-four hours after Moe's death was filled with relationships of the human kind, a collection of life experiences.

Some relationships are full of drama, some clandestine, some tedious, and some glorious. Our Venetian vignettes began the next day when we met a woman in charge of the hotel boutique who told us a story about herself. She had been married for twenty-five years in a relationship that was increasingly tediously boring. Her stale relationship had deteriorated to the point that she was going to divorce her husband. She wanted a fresh new relationship and was in a major transition. She was rolling the dice, giving up a safe albeit boring relationship for something that would be exciting and new. Would she get a winning seven or craps? Is safe better? Sometimes you have to roll the dice of life to find out.

That evening at dinner, we witnessed a relationship that seemed just the opposite. At a nearby table sat a couple who were so obviously in love they glowed. You could see it in their eyes, their glances at each other, and their conversation. In the pathway next to the outdoor restaurant was a woman selling watercolor pictures. I purchased one of her spectacular watercolors of the Piazza San Marco, and the couple next to us asked to see the painting, which is how we met.

The woman at the table was Finnish, and the man was German. They had met in Venice. She was a teacher of languages and he, a banker. However, the story took a turn when he excused himself to go to the bathroom. The woman told us that they were not married to each other, that both had two sons, and that both were deeply in love with each other. She couldn't leave her husband because he was dying of cancer. The man's wife had discovered their relationship, and the man had promised to stop seeing her but was unable to give her up. They made meeting in Venice an annual event, just like the movie, *Same Time Next Year.* When he returned to the table, our friendly conversations continued, and they decided to walk us back to our hotel.

When we parted, there was thunder and lightning in the sky, which seemed foreboding about the future of their clandestine relationship, and I wondered what was going to happen to them. I watched them walk away from our hotel into the darkness, into their invisible relationship, which was lit only briefly by the lightning of their passion. The storm seemed to be a metaphor for their relationship. It was better than Italian opera because it was true.

With the thunder and lightning still rolling across the skies, and because we were so wound up by the couple's revelation, we went down to the hotel bar for a nightcap. In the bar, we met a young couple on their honeymoon. They were in Venice for a few days prior to a cruise. Love radiated from them. They were drinking a very expensive bottle of champagne and asked us to share the bubbly with them. They came from Connecticut and had been married for one week.

Sometime later, another couple came into the bar, a man in his late sixties with a beautiful woman, perhaps in her forties. Before we knew it, we were all chatting and laughing together. After a while, the newlywed husband left to smoke, and within minutes, the beautiful woman went outside to smoke as well. After about ten minutes or so, they returned, and then the older man and the beautiful woman finished their drinks and left the bar. As soon as they were gone, the young husband turned to us and said, "You won't believe what just happened. Out on the balcony, that woman just propositioned me."

Ah, relationships. One was new, young, and bright, shining with honesty, loyalty, and faithfulness. The other was new but already old and jaded, teetering at the edge of dishonesty and betrayal. Relationships—complex, hurtful, clandestine, sacred, and then, some are for all of eternity—Moe, I love you.

The next day, we experienced a fine Venetian tradition, high tea at the Caffè Florian. It is an experience reminiscent of the days of the infamous Casanova. The Caffè Florian was established in 1720, named after its owner, Floriano Francesconi. Among those who frequented it were the playwright Carlo Goldoni, Goethe, Lord Byron, Marcel Proust, and Charles Dickens. Another frequent patron was Giacomo Casanova, who was attracted by the fact that it was the only coffee house that allowed women to patronize it at that time and was the place to be seen in the 1700s.

Imagine having high tea with scrumptious scones and clotted cream, fingertip sandwiches of salmon and prosciutto piled high on silver trays. It was the height of elegance. Please note that the cinghiali cousins did not break anything, make any messes, or embarrass ourselves. We were on our best behavior as we listened to the waltzes wafting in from the orchestra in Piazza San Marco. My mother would have been proud I didn't make a scene. Perhaps I would have if Casanova had made an appearance.

The Queen's Venetian serenity was about to be disrupted that evening in a dramatic way. Venice is unique, so mesmerizing, that

somehow I was surprised when it was taken over by the frenzy of the
World Cup Soccer tournament. I had underestimated the Italian
love of il calcio (soccer). Nothing comes close to it except maybe
the Tour de France or that firstborn son. The World Cup Soccer
Championship game was being held in Germany and was the buzz
on everyone's lips all over Europe. It was the only thing talked about
by everyone we encountered. Only the Italians and I expected Italy to
win. Everyone expected either Germany or France to be the champ.
On Sunday, July 9, 2006, in the evening, with the *bandiera* (flag) of
Italy flying high on the gondolas, dipping but never touching the
sea, the championship game was heard around the world. It didn't
matter where you were. The sportscaster's voices floated on the water.
Everyone was wearing green, white, and red. Then life soared to a
new level when Italy beat France. I had been told by someone that
France calls Italy her poor cousin on steroids. We were there to
witness this incredible event, and we shared in Italy's wildly intense
celebration and its universal hangover the next morning. I'll bet the
French had to rethink their comment about the Italians. "Viva La
Forza d'Italia." Long live the Force of Italy.

As we sat on our hotel terrace listening to the victorious
celebration, boats tooting their horns in jubilee, I became a bit
melancholy that I would be saying goodbye to this Adriatic jewel.
Truly there are no words to adequately describe Venice, this "queen
by the sea." Venice is like a burst of beauty after a long drought of
dullness. Venice captures your heart from the moment you see her
from the vaporetto. She glistens, she beckons you, and you succumb
without resistance; you become all hers. Then before you know it, you
become a part of her irresistible charm, and you are on the Venetian
stage. Now you have become one of the actors, one of the many
people who for hundreds of years have lived their lives in Venice. You
hear the same church bells toll, taste the same Venetian foods, smell
the same sea scents, and watch the children feeding the pigeons in
the piazza. You are, for this brief magical moment in time, a Venetian.
In our hearts, my cousin and I know we will return to the majestic
queen as she expects us to.

Chapter 9

The Walled Cities 2006

In the morning, we moved gingerly after all the celebrating. Loud sounds made us cringe, and the light of day made us wince. When we walked into the San Marco Airport, we found that half of the employees were still celebrating and not at work. Our plane was delayed more than two hours; luckily, our flight was to Milan, and we had no connections to make. However, the connecting passengers on our flight were so upset they were yelling and shaking their fists at the flight attendants. We almost had mutiny on Alitalia.

We were to pick up a rental car for the drive to Lucca. Yes, once again, our rental car had been given to someone else; and we were told that all they had left was a stick shift. The gear shift in a European car has always been a mystery to me. Nonetheless, we finally chug-chug-chugged on to the autostrada, albeit with a burning clutch and smoke fumes coming from the transmission; but we were on our way.

As I got into the rhythm of shifting gears, we were merrily speeding down the autostrada whereupon a white van came out of nowhere. If there had not been an open lane next to me, we would have had a horrible collision. It was the fast-fast lane that ironically saved us as it was wide open. And rarely do I ever drive the fast lane. But the angels of tourism protected us, and we made it into the other lane safely. To top it all off, we discovered that the autostrada throughout Italy was under construction. In Italy, there are certain years where the government decides to work on the roads. This year, they decided to work on the north-south autostrada roads from the heel of the boot, stivale, to the cuff at the top. My formula for driving was to prepare for last-minute lane changes plus reckless speed on the part of the other frustrated drivers. So last-minute lane changes and speed were the order of the day.

After hours of agitated and aggressive driving, we made our exit for Lucca. It was now twilight, and no one was at the toll gate to collect the money. Instead, there was a sign in the window that said "*SCIOPERO!* STRIKE!" I thought we had saved €10, but no, I got a bill several months later at home for €50. They took a picture of us going through the toll without paying, even though no one was there to collect the money. I guess Italy has invisible toll booth collectors. Because of construction and the narrow roads, it had taken almost seven hours to arrive in Lucca, where normally it would have taken five hours or, for an Italian, maybe four hours.

As we approached Lucca, we saw a sign for East Lucca and West Lucca. We made an instant decision and went east because we were nearly on "E" for empty. It was now evening, and we were driving through a walled city. People were yelling at us in Italian, but we didn't know what they were saying. It turned out that it was, "Don't drive in the walled city!" We finally found our hotel and, around the corner, a parking space. I was delighted to see there were two other cars parked, so I assumed it was safe (like safety in numbers) and legal to leave the car there.

The Puccini was a modest no-frills hotel. And we were met by a happy young man who helped us with our luggage. I immediately ordered a bottle of wine to destress us from the long journey. Our room was so small we could barely stand up together to get around the bed. After we freshened up, we went to dinner at an outside caffè. It had been an exhausting day, with many driving challenges. And so we went back to our room to change into our pajamas. Suddenly, there was a knock on the door. Who could it be? It was our young man, the desk clerk, with another bottle in hand to wish us "Un bel sogno di Lucca." Beautiful dreams of Lucca.

The walled Lucca is an enchanting medieval city with quaint outdoor caffès. It is the home of Giacomo Puccini, so naturally there is music everywhere. They also have a wonderful jazz festival in July. The locals were still celebrating the soccer win and continued each night. As we meandered around the piazza, I noted that they were setting up for a festa. I asked a woman, "What is happening?" She told me it was a festa in honor of Santa Paolina. I was so excited I could hardly wait, another festa. I had no idea who she was, but if there is a party, we are there. Grazia mille, Santa Paolina.

The smells of the bakeries permeated the air, and peering into the bakery shops was dangerous. Once we glanced into the bakery, it beckoned us; and hypnotically, there we were, munching on freshly-baked rolls. From the mouth to our waistline, we expanded like our suit cases. As we meandered from shop to shop, this was one place you did not wear stiletto heels because the ancient cobblestones were torturous on one's feet. I was on a mission to find a special gift for a dear friend who had cancer. She had asked me to find her an Italian angel. I found one, and her daughter placed it on her bed until she died. My mother was going to host the first gay wedding in Alameda, California. She believed that if people love each other, they should be together and be blessed. I was looking for a dress to wear to the wedding soirée. I found a beige chiffon cocktail dress with the faintest of cream polka dots. It had an empire waist with a loosely woven matching bolero sweater. The mission was accomplished, an angel for my friend and a new dress for the up-and-coming soirée.

While walking around, we were amazed to see everyone on bicycles: grandfathers, grandmothers, fathers, mothers, and children, all on bicycles, no cars or trucks. I kept thinking, they are so environmentally conscious here. But our packages were getting so heavy; I could not wait to get to the car. As I passed our hotel and turned the corner, I said to Anita in complete shock, "Where is the car? There is no car." Had someone moved it? Had our car been stolen? Was this a joke? We went back to the hotel to find out what happened to our trusty steed. There, our sanctimonious manager told us that our car had been towed and with a serious look on her face said, "You cannot drive or park in the walled city." This had to be the omen from the bloody Venetian pigeon. Our mode of transportation was dead and gone, just like the pigeon.

Sylvia, the manager, made calls to locate our car. Finally, at eight thirty that night, with a smirk on her face, she said, "You have to pay a €103 fine for your violation of no driving in our walled city." Now smiling as she happily noticed our growing dismay, she went on and shared with no small amount of smugness, "Your car has been put into a junkyard." I was so upset that I was completely and utterly speechless. Anita, who I had nicknamed La Conquistadora, took over with great calm and clarity and found out what to do and where to go. Then, like an angel, the desk clerk swooped in as if he had some important information. He said with some excitement that he knew where the junkyard was and even knew the owner. I quietly cheered, thinking he would talk to the man at the junkyard and rescue the car and us. That was it. He simply knew the man who owned the junkyard and was unable to help any further. I silently removed his angel wings and noted the growing tarnished area on his halo.

It was getting dark as we began our hike to the police station. We waded upstream through the festa-di-Santa-Paolina crowds. The streets were literally wall to wall with people in medieval costumes, ball gowns, and Robin Hood-type outfits. Everyone was walking in a procession to the cathedral, after which they were to have a big celebration. We were so disappointed to miss the festa. The bands were playing, crowds were jamming the streets, people were laughing, and city torches were lit on every street corner. The cathedral glowed in the medieval flickering light. It was going to be an incredible citywide party, and we were going to miss it. Curses to the Venetian pigeon and its omen!

We put on our Ligurian cinghiali armor, lowered our *teste dure*, hard heads, and with snouts out, proudly pushed through the throngs who were going the opposite way. It took us at least thirty minutes to get to the police station, only to find the door was chained. No lights were on. Obviously, the place was deserted because all the police were out watching the party. In my frustration, I began pounding on the doors like a mad woman. At that point, I didn't even care if I got arrested. I was so angry. Then all of a sudden, a beautiful blonde policewoman came out of a side door and with a snide look said, "You are those American women." I said with a Ligurian accent, "Sì, sì, sì." She was in a hurry to get to the festa, and we were delaying her. We paid our ticket, €103, and she called a cab to take us to the junkyard.

We paid the tow-truck driver and owner of the junkyard €65 but paid only €25 to Antonio, the cab driver. The cab driver was a saint. For this €25, he drove us to the car (thirty minutes), led us back to a legal parking place outside of the walled city (another thirty minutes), and then drove us back into the walled city to our hotel and finally agreed to pick us up in the morning to take us back to our car. We nicknamed him St. Antonio because of all he did during the party time without charging us extra at this late hour of the evening. We were like Blanche Du Bois who relied on the kindness of strangers in *A Streetcar Named Desire.* There were more occasions than this one when we became Blanche Du Bois, but that's another chapter.

By the time we got back to Lucca, it was ten thirty, and we still hadn't eaten dinner. I found a restaurant, only to be told that they were closed. But people were still eating so I asked the waitress, "Who is the manager?" It was her mother, who was the owner, cook, and manager. I asked to speak to her. In my best pleading voice, I asked for mercy. I said that we were starving and had just had quite a stressful experience. I saw a light of recognition go on in her eyes, and she said, "You are the two Americans who drove in Lucca and got towed." When we sheepishly nodded yes, the whole restaurant got silent. After telling us we were the talk of the town at the festa, she took pity on us and fed us. We will be eternally grateful to her. She was our Santa Paolina that night.

Finishing dinner and with complete and utter exhaustion, we slunk back to our room, hoping to take a hot shower and get some rest. We got our hot shower, as opposed to our previous years of cold showers. I stepped into the hideously blue-tiled stall, pulled the chain, and got one minute of boiling hot water, period. I will definitely take the cold baths of Alpicella any day over the scalding hot water at our hotel.

The next morning, St. Antonio picked us up and drove us to our car; and off we headed to Perugia, and the Umbria World Jazz Festival. Having paid our karma-driving debt, we drove directly to Perugia, arriving in record-breaking time without being lost even once. I wound round and round the hills, finally entered the historical Perugia piazza, and arrived at the Brufani Palace Hotel. To my amazement, there were no parking places. Having fresh wounds from the previous parking in Lucca, I was determined to be sure we parked legally. Then, like magic, the doorman appeared. It was Josh, who remembered us immediately from the previous year with Tony Bennett. He told us not to worry about the car; he would take care of us. Once again, we were relying on the kindness of strangers.

Oh yes, I thought as I checked in, a suite with hot and cold water. I loved this place. It was a former palace and a gorgeous hotel with an old-world feel to it. We had a corner suite, like last year, room 237. From our suite, we gaze down upon Perugia and three beautiful churches. We could hear their bells toll, one after the other. They are sending their comforting message of protection and care, creating tranquility for its beloved Umbria people. The caroling of the bells cradles the local citizens blessing them with each toll. And for one magical moment, we are in the right place at the right time, listening to each bell with its hymn tolling into the heavens. We briefly become an Umbrian blessed to hear these bells, and just as quickly as they start, it ends. Like the lucciole, firefly, we light up for a brief moment and then we are gone.

When I think of the province of Umbria, I think of incredible sunsets with blazing reds and oranges, terra cotta-tiled rooftops, straight lines of green cypress trees reaching to the heavens, and caroling church bells morning, noon, and evening. The Umbria Jazz Festival rocked from morning to night; there was music about eighteen hours a day. When we opened the windows of our suite, we could hear it, and the Brufani Palace was the venue for the festival celebrities. The previous year spotlighted Tony Bennett. This year, it was to be Carlos Santana.

We had a ritual every night, sort of like our ritual in Alpicella. Around nine thirty, we had dinner at an outside caffè. We would listen to the jazz, walk around the piazza, and eventually make our way back to the hotel bar, where we became regulars. The doors of the bar were wide open, and you could hear the music into the wee hours of the night while sitting and enjoying a last glass of Pinot Grigio.

One night, what we thought would be our last glass of wine turned out to be quite an interesting event. It was a night that lasted until about three thirty in the morning. It started with the phrase sì-sì-sì pronounced she-she-she in Genovese dialect. There were three French men who sold shoes for babies and children sitting at the bar next to us. We thought they were speaking French; and so Anita started saying sì-sì-sì, and I joined her, sì-sì-sì. One of them turned to us and said, "Are you making fun of us?" I replied, "No, I have relatives who talk like you." One thing led to another as I told them about meeting Maurice Chevalier and how much I loved France, Paris, Nice, and Cannes; and soon we were singing French songs, patriotic and love songs. Of course, I can't speak French, but the dialect sounds like it, so I faked it. Everyone in the bar joined in.

One of the men turned out to be a polygamist with wives in Tunisia and Paris. At one point, he asked if I would join his harem; but I'm not used to playing third fiddle, even though he did live in Paris. One of the men lived in Normandy; another lived in Marseilles and was the spitting image of Peter Lorre, the actor. They invited us to their hotel for a midnight swim, but it was nearly three in the morning, and we declined graciously. We don't swim. We are cinghiali. They planned to be on the road at five that morning. All I can say is Viva la France. Those baby-shoe salesmen sure can party.

During the festival, the caffès named their food after the performers. We ordered the pizza named after Eric Clapton for lunch. We had just missed his performance, and he had left for Lucca. Following our usual routine, we made our hair appointments with Luigi; and then we went to dinner at Caeserino, an outdoor restaurant. Performing nearby were American gospel singers followed by Ray Gelatto and the Giants, who did a tribute to Louie Prima and Stan Buterra and the Witnesses. It was an incredible night of impossibly good food. For example, they served me a sliced potato that had been roasted with olive oil and garlic until the edges were toasty, and Swiss chard sautéed, then drenched with balsamic vinegar and olive oil and sprinkled with garlic and sea salt. These were paired with a steak so perfectly tempered with not too much salt that I could cut it with my fork. Delicious food and great music, Perugia is on our permanent list of places we love.

The next day, we saw the incredible New Orleans Street Parade. They are called the New Wave Brass Band of New Orleans. The funds from this world jazz festival were going to the victims of Hurricane Katrina, 2005. We tried many wonderful restaurants, thanks to Josh, one called Il Sole Ristorante. I don't think there is a bad restaurant in Perugia. Speaking of food, because my Italian is not fluent, there were times we ordered things when I didn't know what they were, like the time we were served egg soup with truffle frittata and the time a steak came that was so rare I thought it would walk away. Even though I did have some linguistic culinary challenges, I could point and say we'll have that. One of my best pointing dinners was a veal steak, Swiss chard, fried potatoes, a crisp salad and, of course, vino.

After midnight, we ambled back to our hotel to find our rightful spot at the bar. We had become friends on a first-name basis with a bartender, a young man named Alessio, who was studying to become a pharmacist, and the head bartender Antonio. Alessio was a very good student but was worried that even though he might graduate with honors, he still might not have a job. In Italy, such professions are traditionally handed down from generation to generation, and his family members were not pharmacists.

When I think of Perugia, I always think of chocolate. The chocolate makers in Perugia do something very special. It is so unusual they have a story about it. There was a young man whose father owned a chocolate shop. The young man fell in love with a young woman, and the only way he could communicate with his love was to put a note in the chocolate. The note I found in my Perugian chocolate was "Anything done for love is beyond good and evil." The chocolates that have the messages are called Baci. Baci means kisses. The other delicious eye candy is in the pastry shops. I saw such incredible art work made of pastry: faces of famous people, animals, flowers, everything you can imagine, almost too perfect to eat; except we did. Our taste buds exploded with heavenly flavors. Don't go there on a diet.

Shocking as it may sound, we did some cultural things beyond shopping, eating, drinking, while listening to jazz. We visited several cathedrals and lit candles for family and friends, the sick, and for those who had passed away, including Camillo. Near our hotel was an escalator that took us to an Etruscan archeological dig. The artifacts are exceptional. The contrast between riding an escalator down to the remains of an ancient civilization that existed before Christ and then returning to a contemporary jazz festival all in the same day was mind-blowing for me.

Our last day in Perugia, we had hair appointments late in the day because the next day we were off to Siena. We went to Luigi, the cat of Perugia—*il gatto di Perugia*. When Luigi was blow-drying my hair, there was a tap on the window by Alessio from the hotel. We knew we would have to report to him that we were safe from the claws of the cat, Luigi. Luigi loved to flirt, strut, and parade himself through the salon with great bravado. It is part of his persona, and it is like watching a performance of Casanova. If the salon staff wore white, he would be in black. If they wore black, he would be in white. He was the center of attention at all times. But he was great with hair, and we looked divine. When we walked into the salon, our hair smelled stinky, was sticky, and looked like something could grow in it. When we walked out of the salon, our hair was shiny, clean, and no one was nesting in it.

Alessio was waiting to hear about our day and whether il gatto Luigi had come on to us. I was trying to speak to Alessio in my Genovese dialect, when a man tapped me on the shoulder and said, "Excuse me. I know you are an American, but you are speaking an old-world dialect." He introduced himself, saying his name was Roberto, and handed me his business card with his cell number. He was CEO of a very large corporation, lived near Genova, and spoke the same dialect. He was a medium-sized man with mischievous eyes, very soft-spoken, quite captivating, and very bright. We talked until four in the morning. Roberto had driven two hours to get to Perugia and still had to drive back that day. He asked if he could take us out to dinner in Siena, our next stop, or perhaps in San Gimignano. We said yes. We thought he was quite an interesting man and that there was more to him than met the eye. It was time for dreamland, and as I was drifting off to sleep, I remembered my mother telling me how my nonno Edoardo would say when I was a baby, "I hope she isn't going to be like some of our relatives with big bones, a big nose, and a big *culo*, a big 'butt.'" He would look at me and hold my face in his hands and say, "Faccia fritta." The literal translation is that you have a fried face, but to my nonno, it was a term of endearment as he thought I had a beautiful face; and with that and a smile on my face, I thought, *Who was that man I met tonight?*

Packing our clothes the next morning, we thought they had mushroomed sort of like our waistlines from all the great food. It took us until one in the afternoon to zip our suitcases. We went to check out and to say goodbye to some of the staff, who seemed like friends. In my daughter's last phone call, she had said, "You haven't met anyone famous this year." Then as I was checking out, I turned around, and there was Carlos Santana. I asked to take a photo; and he graciously agreed in his soft, gentle voice. Remembering Tony Bennett and my near camera fiasco, I handed my camera to Anita, who had steady hands. It became my Christmas card. Oh, the magic of Perugia.

Off we went speeding down A-1, Florence to Rome and then on to Siena, we hoped. Somehow the signs for Florence had disappeared, and we were definitely heading in the wrong direction, toward Rome. As the adage goes, "All roads lead to Rome." After about an hour driving south, we made an executive decision. With our cinghiali noses in the air, we headed toward Orvieto, hoping for the best. One of the small towns we passed was named Bastardo. We laughed hysterically as we wondered how we would tell someone we came from the town of Bastard. Does anyone get married there or is buried there? And how did it get its name? I still need to research these questions on another trip. Once I find out the answers, I will post it on my blog. As we approached Bastardo, there was the customary sign with the town's name; but in Italy, as you leave the town area, there is another sign with a red line through it showing you have left. Darn, I should have taken a photo of it, but I was driving. Next time, I will pose next to the sign for everyone to see. Who knows, maybe I will make it my Christmas card next year. It could read,

"Wishing you a wonderful holiday season, Love, Donna Marie and Bastardo." I'll have to work on it, but you get my drift. After leaving Bastardo, we experienced many hair-raising twists and turns as though we were threading a miniscule eye of a needle. One wrong turn and we would be carted off to the hospital. Thankfully, this is something, so far, we have not experienced. While driving along the countryside, we saw many quaint hilltop medieval towns such as Todi and Orvieto, their medieval stone buildings and churches glimmering in the sundrenched Umbrian summer skies. Contrasting the Umbrian skies are the terra firma burst of colors: rich hues of olive green, sienna brown, sunglow gold, and yellow, yellow, yellow everywhere. Sunflowers, vineyards, olive orchards, and fields dotted with golden rolls of hay. I have often wondered why we don't roll the hay in the United States. I am sure it is for economic purposes, but aesthetically, the rolling of hay is much more picturesque and has a circular elegance to it. Practical, I am not, but beauty is divine. After all, I am Italian.

Somehow the gods of driving kept us on track. We wound through various villages. We arrived safely in Siena. Our hotel was St. Catherine of Siena, outside the walled city center. After our experience in Lucca, we now knew that when you saw the word "Centro," it meant that you should not park your car in the walled center of town unless the signs were very clear. We checked in and cleaned up.

We decided to walk through one of the porticos and have a late lunch in the Piazza del Campo, the main district of Siena. When we entered the Piazza del Campo, we stopped and just stared because it was simply beyond belief. It is shaped like a seashell with the edges curling up like a conch shell. As I stood and looked at the Campo, I wondered if this was the place that rivaled Florence. I raised my cinghiali snout and I wondered how were they rivals when they are so much the same. They are different as foes, but they are equal in their beauty. They have majestic architecture, culture and people, and Italian ghosts from the past that love them. I think they should have the titles La Regina di Siena, the Queen of Siena, and L'imperatrice di Firenze, the Empress of Florence.

After bestowing upon them their titles, we shopped for a few items for dinner and ate in the courtyard of the hotel. The view was spectacular. Looking at the tranquil rolling hills, the spiraling cypress trees and the magnificent villas etched into the hillsides, we sighed with bliss and relaxed completely. As we sipped wine, one of the hoteliers brought us a note from Roberto, the man from

Genova we had met the previous evening in Perugia. He wrote that he would contact us to arrange an evening to take us to dinner. But for now we were happy just absorbing the beauty of Siena and all that surrounded it.

The next morning, as we sat in the courtyard sipping our cappuccinos, we could hear the birds chirping and the dogs barking; the nonna next door was watering her vegetable garden. Everything was in its place, tutto a posto. Before I go on, perhaps I should share a bit of Italian coffee culture. Cappuccino was named after the Capuchin monks because their habits are creamy white and tan, just like a cappuccino. It is only to be drunk in the morning, never in the afternoon or evening. If you ask for caffè lungo, you are asking for a large cup of coffee. If you say caffe Americano, it is coffee with cold milk. Italians drink coffee with hot milk. Why ruin a good cup of coffee with a cold liquid? In the afternoon, you will see the Italians drinking their espresso. It is rare to go to a caffè bar to sit to drink your coffee. Italians stand to drink their libation. If you need to sit, you will pay extra for it.

After our coffee, during one of our repeated searches for the elusive ATM machine, we stumbled upon the Cathedral of St. Catherine of Siena. St. Catherine is considered to be at the top of the pecking order for female saints in Italy. Anita asked me to translate a sign she saw under a relic. I read it as, "The police are around the corner at the right-hand side." Then Anita saw something quite peculiar in the relic case below the sign. It looked like a shriveled-up index finger. She began laughing hysterically and, pointing to the relic, said, "Are you sure that's not a finger?" Well, once again, Anita was right. It was a finger. Please do not ask me how I came to this translation, as I know I am quite imaginative; but this was a first for me and probably my worst Italian translation, at least so far!

You would think that since I was surrounded by Italians, I would be fluent in the dialect and the mother tongue, but I am not. Why? In the early 1950s, the doctors kept telling my parents, "You must not speak Italian. It is confusing your son John." At that time, the doctors really had no clue that John is probably near genius and being bilingual had absolutely nothing to do with his disability. Nevertheless, they followed the doctor's orders and spoke only English in front of both of us, while my nonne Antonietta and Maria spoke to us in the dialect. Today I can truly say that I am highly creative when I am speaking the Genovese dialect mixed in with some of the mother tongue and can certainly get my point across with extremely competent Italian gestures. I think of my Italian language proficiency as if it was like making a minestrone soup, a concoction of many ingredients.

Adding insult to injury following my mistranslation of St. Catherine's relic, there were some men with binoculars peering up at the tabernacle. In my best Italian, I turned to the gentlemen with the binoculars peering in reverence at St. Catherine's head, which was encased in glass at the altar, and asked, "May I borrow your binoculars?" I wanted a closer look at St. Catherine's head, since to my naked eyes it looked like a bejeweled ceramic head. Knowing Anita so well, she was probably thinking, *There she goes again. I hope she doesn't get us thrown out of this cathedral.* Well, I'm happy to report we didn't get into any trouble. The men were truly in awe of this miraculous relic and were whispering prayers to it. I gave the men a big smile and "grazie" for the use of their binoculars.

Anita looked at me, and I knew she was thinking, *She's up to no good again.* I whispered, "I've got something to tell you." Anita frantically ushered me out of the cathedral before I could make a scene. Out on the church steps, with hands on her hips, she turned to me and laughed. "Okay, Sherlock, what did you find out?" "See, I told you so that wasn't a real head. It was a ceramic." I was so proud of my investigation and my super sleuthing. How could I know that St. Catherine was not pleased with me for interfering with her faithful flock? She would have her ways, and she would take revenge.

The cinghiali cousins decided to enroll in a Tuscan cooking class that evening. There were fourteen tourists in the class. The best part was eating a multicourse meal from antipasto to dolce. A big bus picked us up and the other members of the class from their various hotels. When we arrived, I reviewed the menu and decided that I was going to spend as little energy as possible. I spotted the chef and wondered if I should play helpless so he could come to help me or just allow him to do his own job. After noticing his wedding ring, I took mercy and allowed him to roam and just be the chef. Anita and I were assigned to the dolce, dessert, which was whipped cream with strawberries, a mindless task allowing us to drink more vino than the others. We were happy, so very happy.

After the meal was prepared, we went out on the terrace to eat our feast at a long banquet table set with wicker chairs. The sun was setting, the view was fabulous, and the mood was tranquil. Then a breeze came up, and a paper napkin flew into the citronella oil and caught fire. Another tourist threw more paper napkins on it to put it out; but much to his surprise, not to ours, the flames grew. I was immensely entertained. I moved some critical things away from the fire when Anita turned to me and said, "You know what to do." So before the flames could jump to the wicker chairs and create a bonfire, I covered the fire with a large ceramic dinner plate, and it was out. No one was injured. Dinner was saved.

The evening was filled with laughter, joy, and contentment as we new chefs bonded over the delicious dinner. I got to keep my souvenir apron. I kept my apron on as we returned to the hotel and told the manager that I would be the chef the next day and would prepare breakfast around nine thirty or ten in the morning. She laughed and handed me a message from Roberto. The note said he would phone in the morning.

Many of our days in Siena were spent watching people, eating, and drinking our way through the many restaurants. One of the best bottles of wine we discovered was Vernaccia di San Gimignano. It was a lovely crisp white wine from the Chianti Region in Tuscany. Once again as we sat in the courtyard sipping our morning cappuccino, the staff assistant brought me a phone. It was Roberto. I could tell he was driving as he talked. He asked if he could take us out to dinner that night. We said yes. I asked the hotel staff to recommend a restaurant for us, and they made reservations.

Our first priority of the day was to buy more Vernaccia and take a tour of the Chianti Region. Late in the afternoon, with our tour guide, yes another Josh, we joined another group of tourists and rambled through the hills of Tuscany. Anita noticed that Josh had pretty blue eyes; and, like the chef of the previous night, he was quite a hunk. As we walked through the vineyards, the mosquitoes began attacking Anita. She is truly a magnet for mosquitoes. In less than ten minutes, she had thirteen bites. We beat a hasty retreat to the wine cellar for protection until we could return to the hotel. Aren't wine cellars the best?

After the tour, we returned to the hotel and freshened up. Anita went down first to meet Roberto, and then I made my grand entrance. As I glided to my chair, Anita whispered, "I'm glad that you didn't let your heels clack on the stairs, so you appeared graceful." It is hard for cinghiali to be graceful. Each of us took one of Roberto's arms and strolled to the restaurant in the heart of Siena, near the Il Campo. I regret that I didn't make a note of the restaurant's name because the meal was delicious, and the restaurant was in a cavelike setting I thought was a former wine cellar. Love those wine cellars.

Before we knew it, it was two thirty in the morning, and Roberto was giving us lessons on the Ligurian dialect and sharing stories about his work. We told him that Anita had the "kiss" of death and told him the story of Camillo. Roberto said he believed he was still safe with us, at least for the time being. He was highly educated in the classics. In addition to Italian, English, and the Ligurian dialect, he knew Latin, Greek, and French. He was studying Spanish. He had a degree in engineering and was totally charming. He didn't mind our frivolity. As Anita said, "He was a classic, elegant gentleman, the real deal." So we thought.

We made our way back to the hotel; Anita said good night, and the evening deskman acted as our chaperone. It was now early morning, and Roberto had a long two-plus hour drive back to Genova; but he stayed. We sat on the sofa and talked until nearly dawn about the people of Liguria, and I learned so much about my heritage. He said he would contact us, since we were going to Portofino, which was close to where he lived. I was looking forward to seeing the villa he talked so much about and wondered if it might be the same villa I had been coveting for so many years from the balcony suite at Splendido.

The following day, we roamed Siena, listening to the chaotic noise of the delivery trucks and bustling traffic, a counterpoint to the exquisite surroundings. Later that evening, a ragtag band of young kids marched around the Il Campo, wearing the colors of their contrade (the district of their birth) and holding up the *bandiera* (flag) of their soccer team. A boy who led the group had on a T-shirt that said, "Frank Sinatra's All Star Band." The Senesi people are very proud of their heritage; and it is displayed throughout the city, with their *bandiere*, "flags," and statues of their district symbol.

Twice per year, Siena has a Palio, horse race; the first takes place on the Feast of the Virgin Mary July 2. Then the next Palio is on August 15, the Ascension of the Virgin. There are seventeen contrade or neighborhoods in Siena. Each one has a bandiera with an animal or object of some kind emblazoned on it and enters a horse into the race. The horses are taken into the church of its contrada to be blessed before the race. It is considered good luck if the horse leaves a pile in the church. The winning horse determines which contrada's banner or bandiera is displayed throughout the city and which contrada wins the bandiera of the Madonna. The bareback riders race for less than two minutes. If they fall off the horse, the horse can win the race without its jockey. There is much loyalty to one's contrada. You are born there, raised there, married there, and buried there with your contrada banner in your casket.

On one of our late-afternoon food explorations—yes, we were eating again—we met a fascinating American couple. Their names were Bill and Sandy; they had been married for four years and were in their middle sixties. He was a chemistry professor. His area of expertise is arsenic. They were traveling to the island of Elba. He was going to the Island of Elba to explore the possibility of Napoleon being poisoned by arsenic. Later it was found not to be true. While Napoleon had absorbed arsenic throughout his life, it had not poisoned him. Instead, it had promoted cancer of the stomach, which is what killed him. You never know who you will meet when you are traveling.

We discovered two popular folk tales in Siena. The first was told to me by a wine shop owner and was a story about a black rooster in Siena. It goes like this: Siena and Florence were rivals on every level for over four hundred years. The major rivalry centered on which city was more beautiful. So the people agreed that each would take a black rooster and see how long it could be kept awake. The rooster that stayed awake the longest would win. The Florentines were sweet to the rooster, and Sienese were mean to the rooster. The Florentine rooster was so happy with the petting and soothing sounds and the wonderful food that it settled down and went to sleep. The Sienese rooster was taunted and starved and was so unhappy that it stayed awake. Siena won the competition and is considered the most beautiful, at least to the Sienese. Surely the black rooster may have won for Sienna; but Florence had the gentle, loving rooster that one would want to hear when one wakes up because it was well fed. Sienese celebrated by making a new wine: The black rooster wine is a dark, red, robust wine from the Chianti Region. You will know it by the black rooster on the label.

The second story is called Mangiaguadagni. There is a statue in Il Piazza del Campo with no arms, called the Mangiaguadagni. Mangiaguadagni is the nickname of a bell ringer Giovanni di Balduccio, who was slothful. He was given the nickname because he spent all his money on food and ate all the time. The bells were rung to regulate the timing of business transaction payments that took place in the Campo, but he never rang the bells on time, so they couldn't do business on time and be profitable. Consequently, they called him the profit eater because he reduced the business transaction payments that were to take place in the Il Campo, and they made less money. Next to the statue, there is now a restaurant called Mangiaguadagni, and the food is wonderful. We heard this story from a waiter at the Mangiaguadagni Ristorante. We smiled at him and were rewarded with the story. In Italy, it is important to smile. Everyone loves a smiling woman, and the Italians don't care about age. Lucky us!

In sports, it was a good year for my countrymen: Italy won the World Cup in soccer, and the United States won the Tour de France and the British Open. Once again, we had to celebrate, and we did until about two in the morning. Ah, Siena. What a place to celebrate and to revel in our championships. Unfortunately, later, the U.S. team was disqualified because of the doping scandal.

After four wonderful days in Siena, we were about to move on to San Gimignano. St. Catherine had not taken her revenge yet, but it was time. We were packed and ready to go, but the man who was to get the car was not to be found. I told Anita to wait outside by the curb with the luggage, took a deep breath, walked down to the garage, and decided to drive it myself. St. Catherine was starting to smirk.

The car was parked in an open-air garage squeezed in between an ancient stone wall and the neighboring car, so that even I had trouble getting into it, and I am petite. In addition, the garage was at the bottom of a gravel road that in my mind appeared to have the steepness of Nob Hill in San Francisco. At the top of the gravel road was a busy street with heavy traffic, and the rental car was a stick shift. For me, it was the perfect storm.

I was sweating like a cinghiale being hunted. After a full ten minutes, I finally wiggled my way into the driver's seat without damaging the other car. I carefully edged the car out of the parking space. I threw it into first gear, stomped on the accelerator, and raced up the gravel hill, only to have the powerless "slush bucket" whimper and die just before reaching the very tip top. The car fishtailed all the way back down, slamming the passenger side into the wall, ripping off the passenger side mirror, and giving the car a new silvery finish on the right side with all the paint scraped off before coming to rest back into the parking spot.

Now I was mad. St. Catherine was cackling. I was determined to get the #&%# car up on the road. I threw it back into first gear and, with the engine racing, shot straight up the hill like a cannonball and straight into oncoming traffic. St. Catherine had had her fun. As I neared the hotel, I could see Anita standing at the hotel entrance with the luggage. When she saw the car, she looked horrified as she stared with raised eyebrows and wide-open mouth in complete disbelief. I rumbled through clenched teeth, "Don't say a thing, throw the luggage in the back, and get in." She got in silently and held on, and we took off.

We were finally on our way to San Gimignano. And except for one challenging round-a-bout, we had a safe trip out of the clutches of St. Catherine of Siena. The countryside was magnificent, with its undulating hills, rolled hay, and fields of shining sunflowers glinting in the sun. As we approached San Gimignano, I saw a policewoman directing traffic. She told us we could drop off our luggage at the hotel and bring the car to a place outside the city and pointed to where we might park. We made a right-hand turn up the narrow cobblestone road toward the Hotel Antico Pozzo. We drove for a short time when suddenly I saw an ambulance speeding toward us. There was no place to turn around. I had come around a turn, and directly behind me was an outside caffè filled with people sitting in the street. I barely managed to back the car and turn it to the side enough for the ambulance to pass by. I asked Anita to get out of the car and look for the hotel sign because we should have been there by now. She finally found the miniature sign hidden behind the bushes of the topiary trees in front of the hotel. We unloaded the luggage, parked outside the walls, and hiked back to the hotel. Phew. We were in San Gimignano, ready to relax and try not to let our wounded steed ruin our trip.

We were so wrung out that we only had the energy to go to the caffè next door, the one where we almost ran people down trying to get out of the way of the ambulance. After decompressing and getting something to eat along with a couple glasses of wine, we were ready for action. But the action was not what we thought. Cars began to roll by, obviously looking for Antico Pozzo. The first was a big black Mercedes. The driver was a woman, and we felt empathy, so we decided to help. We called out to her, pointed toward the hotel entrance, and yelled like the cinghiali we were, "It's here, Antico Pozzo." She turned her head away from us, put her nose in the air, and drove onward. About ten or twelve minutes later, she came back by; and we repeated our act, pointed, and yelled. She looked away again. The third time, we were well into our wine and again pointed and laughed and yelled. The fourth time, her husband was driving, she was yelling at him, and we called to him, trying to show him the entrance. He got the message, but it had taken them forty-five minutes. The next car got it right away. Such was our entertainment that first evening.

San Gimignano is noted for its towers. Over time, the wealthy residents built towers as symbols of their wealth. By the end of the medieval period, the residents had built about seventy-two of them. Torre Grossa is one of the towers that you may climb to get a panoramic view of the Tuscan countryside. Many were destroyed in World War II. Now San Gimignano is an artist's colony. It is only a day trip from Lucca, Florence, Arezzo, and Siena. The food is delicious; the people are warm and wonderful.

One evening, we had dinner at Il Castello. It was a lovely, leisurely paced delightful dinner. Afterward, we decided to take a stroll and found a place to rest a moment in an alcove. We were sitting in an alcove on the street when two men sat down next to us. One of them turned and said, "Don't be afraid of us." They showed us a Puglia police ID. Anita's cinghiale instincts rose up, and she gave me the eye that it was time to go back to the hotel. Anita and I were in sync and didn't always need words. A look, a subtle gesture, a feeling, and we knew what to do. We set a record. It was the first evening we were not the last to come in for the night, such a novelty for the two of us.

In the morning when it was time to depart, the hotel staff brought us our car, carried down our luggage, packed our car, and gave us perfect directions to Portofino. The Antico Pozzo Hotel is a family-run business. The staff is made up of the parents, their two daughters, and their two sons. San Gimignano is simply a charming place to go. As usual in walled cities, no vehicles are allowed, and walking is the mode of transportation, so we've learned the hard way.

We felt fine, had no worries in the world except when we looked at the side of the car. We wondered how much it was going to cost when we returned the car to the rental agency, but that would come later when we got back to Milan. Now finally it was time to go to Portofino and Splendido.

Chapter 10

Returning to Splendido 2006

I always knew when I was getting closer to Portofino because I began to get glimpses of the wonderful azure sea, to smell the salt air, and to find myself driving through galleria after galleria along the zigzag coast. As I wound up the curves to Splendido, I realized that I had never arrived in a rental car that had so many bumps and bruises. Fortunately, I knew the staff, and they knew me. They had seen my mother grow older and my daughter grow up and knew I was usually a bucket of nerves from driving. There stood Giuseppe, waiting as usual to park the car. He was clearly shocked by the condition of it. When he saw me, he immediately said, "Scignua Ferro, welcome home." Then he hugged and kissed me.

Giuseppe knew me well after one of the adventures with my mother and daughter that had us driving on an illegal spare tire on the autostrada. Some years before, we had come to Portofino from Venice. Our first mistake was to ask a Venetian for directions to Portofino. Venetians do not usually drive cars because they have canals, not roads. We ended up in the vicinity of La Spezia but still an hour away from Portofino. Wham! A tire exploded, and we were stranded. We pulled over and began to attempt changing the tire but with little success. We were wearing shorts, and nearby was a small house with two old men sitting on the porch ogling us.

Since my mother spoke the dialect, she asked them if they could help. They said they would try but had not read anything mechanical since World War II. They could not understand the manual, and so they went back to sitting on the porch, watching the show. My mother remembered Claudette Colbert in *It Happened One Night,* so we struck poses next to the car in our shorts; and sure enough a young Italian man in his forties riding a Vespa stopped to help. He was unable to decipher the manual but did go into the next town for help, and soon a tow truck came to assist us. Now we were desperate to get to the hotel as we had not eaten, we were dripping with perspiration, and we needed a bathroom. When we arrived at Splendido, Giuseppe took care of the car, the tire, and us.

Here I was again with a car ready for the junkyard. Giuseppe looked at me and then the car and asked, "What happened?" I told him I had hit the wall in more ways than one, and then I told him all the gory details. As I told him the story, all I could think of was that he had called me *scignua* and that was extraordinary. In my time at the hotel, I had never heard the staff use it with anyone else. They had only used the title with my mother because she engendered great respect and spoke the dialect.

The word "scignua" goes back to around the thirteenth century. It is a term from the Genovese dialect. It is a special title given to a refined woman of knowledge and elegance. It embodied respect, deference, and great reverence. My mother was the scignua. Now I was being called la scignua for the very first time. I could hardly believe that this cinghiale had arrived, and in a car with scrapes and dents.

As I entered the lobby, Ermes, the general manager, and Luca, the concierge, welcomed me home. Ermes escorted us to our suite, the room I always had with my mother and daughter and now with Anita. The welcome basket had pink and white lilies; the fruit included cherries and strawberries; and, of course, there was champagne. I could recall when Ermes barely spoke English, and now he was perfectly fluent. As he opened up the double doors to the terrace, I looked down on the villa that I had fantasized about for years. Ermes told me it recently sold for €32,000,000. I sighed. On one of our first trips, it had sold for US$8,000,000, such a bargain.

At seven o'clock every night on the terrace below, Vladimir's piano music wafted over the Bay of Portofino. Vladimir would play until close to midnight. Dinner for us was always at eight forty-five at our usual corner table overlooking the bay. It was our ritual. On stormy nights, we moved indoors. We still had not heard from Roberto, who we thought was coming for cocktails with us. But just being in Portofino was perfection.

In the olden days when we shopped, we had to hike up and down the hill from the hotel into town. At sixty-eight, my mother was like a mountain goat and had still been hiking the hill. Now Splendido had a shuttle. I knew many of the shop owners, especially the ladies who sold linen handkerchiefs, baby bibs, tea towels, aprons, and small tablecloths that they had made during the winter. Of course, the fancy high-end stores were there too, but the true people of this region were noted for their embroidery. They still spoke the old-world dialect, and time had stood still. Even the local shoe store owned by the Mingo family, where my mother and I had shopped for many years, was still there. Nothing had changed, and that was fine with me.

There are some things that always remain the same: the food of Liguria, its focaccia, and its pesto. I would put pesto in everything, but that's just me. There is an Italian warning about eating too much pesto. One evening, my mother ate two plates of pasta with pesto, and she had horrific nightmares where her arms were flapping around in her sleep. It was as if she was fighting some beast. The staff had warned her about overeating pesto. The apple from Rosa's tree has not fallen far from it. While I was there, I overindulged with pesto and dreamed about the rental car and George Clooney, who looked like a bloated pig. I am not sure what the symbolism was in that dream. Maybe George was a cinghiale coming to invite me to roam with him at one of his villas? My nightmare went away when I confirmed that I had collision insurance. A fender bender is almost a sure bet in Italy. It is always prudent to have a credit card that has collision insurance when you travel. Sorry, George, I have no idea why I had that dream about you. Blame it on the pesto.

We had lunch in the picturesque town of Portofino. Portofino is a tiny fishing village of about 240 families and is comprised with many al fresco restaurants and handiwork shops as well as designer-label stores. In the winter, it is quiet; but during the resort season, it just literally bulges with tourists. The harbor is so small that the cruise ships must use tenders to bring visitors to shore so they can walk the streets. Originally, it was a simple little village used by the Romans who named it Portus Delphini, or Port of the Dolphins, because of the large number of dolphins there. Then the movie people and celebrities found it in the 1950s; and suddenly, it was discovered. As we sat al fresco and sipped our Bellinis made of Prosecco and peach juice, I wondered, *Where did the Bellini drink originate?* The waiter told me this story. "The drink was concocted by Giuseppe Cipriani, founder of Harry's Bar in Venice. The pink color had reminded him of the color of the toga of a saint in a painting by fifteenth-century Venetian artist Giovanni Bellini, and so Cipriani named the drink the Bellini." After reminiscing at lunch and thinking about Camillo, since it was the anniversary of his death, we went to the church to light our candles before we went off to window-shop for "bling." We assisted a woman and her husband—it was their wedding anniversary—in purchasing a special ring covered with amethysts, rubies, and diamonds in a hunk of elegantly crafted gold setting. The ring looked magnificent on her finger. We gave two thumbs-up, and as an added bonus, we were helping the Italian economy.

Late that afternoon, I took a bath and turned on the Jacuzzi but was unable to turn it off. The bubbles rose all the way to my chin, then my nose, then my eyes, and finally all over the floor. I felt like I was Mickey Mouse in the film *Fantasia*. I was the apprentice who had lost control. I frantically called, "Anita! Anita!" Finally, the sorceress came in to work her magic. She struggled to keep her balance on the slick bubble-covered floor. Then she reached deep into the mounds of bubbles, finally finding the handle and giving it a masterful turn to shut it off. La Conquistadora looked at me with a wicked smile and a glint in her dark, brown eyes, saying, "Well, Ms. Bubbles, were you planning to flood the place?"

Once again, this little cinghiale with her curly pigtail between her legs tiptoed down the hallway in her bubble-covered bathrobe and humbly asked the maid, who had just finished cleaning the room, if she would please come back and mop up the flood. She declined my offer of a tip, saying, "I am happy to help. You are at Splendido." Leaving a trail of suds in the hallway, I squished back down the hall in my sudsy and soaked slippers, and I slunk back into the room, where I noticed a blinking light on the phone.

I had received a message from Roberto, who said that he was attending the birthday party of a child of one of his employees. He said he would be late. Roberto was coming from Rapallo and had been delayed by a car accident as well. He finally arrived at midnight, and we stayed up talking into the wee hours of the morning. He said he would contact us on Sunday to show us his villa, but he had a trip to Milan to fit in beforehand. We wondered if he ever slept. The next day, I was on the phone talking with the insurance company about the car when there was a knock on the door. It was a message from Roberto that he was delayed in Milan and would not be able to return to Portofino. The gods of travel snapped their fingers, and in a couple of days, our trip would end.

The irony was that we would leave Portofino to go to Milan on Monday to connect to our flight home, and Roberto would be going from Milan to Rome on Monday. Like two ships that pass in the night, so close, and yet so far. He came out of nowhere in Perugia and seemed to have disappeared back into the beautiful Ligurian landscape. Who was this man?

A few days later, we said our goodbyes. Ermes gave us beautiful bouquets of flowers from the Splendido gardens. Several of the waiters wished us safe passage home and fond greetings to my mother and to my daughter, whom they had known since she was a little girl. Leaving Portofino and all the wonderful memories was difficult, and that was amplified by its incredibly serene setting. Entering on to the frenetic autostrada and heading back toward the big city catapulted us back into the harsh stark reality of life.

We took our bruised and battered car and left. As we arrived in Milan, I was getting more and more nervous about facing the music at the rental agency regarding the car. As Anita would say, "Reality was about to smack us in the face."

As I faced the car rental agency staff, there was not a snide remark or even a question about the crumbling car. No one was aghast at the sight of the wreckage. It was business as usual for them, another tourist driving in Italy. Welcome to the club. I had joy in my heart. I did the cinghiali tarantella, kicking up my dainty hooves. I had gone in with gloom and come out shining. We happily boarded our plane in a state of euphoria.

There I was at thirty thousand feet again in the miraculous flying bucket of bolts. I thought about all the wonderful people we had met along the way. I could hear the sounds of the gondoliers calling out to one another. I reminisced about purchasing a small headstone for my Moe, the San Marco lion. I could hear the church bells tolling and the music of the fabulous jazz festival in Perugia. I loved the Ferro game of which Angela reigns as champion, the incredible Il Campo of Siena, and Splendido. Thoughts of Italy bring a Perugian chocolate quote to mind: "Un bacio proibito brucia piu del fuoco." "A forbidden kiss burns more than fire." Was this an omen?

Chapter 11

It's All Style and Weight, Baby.

There are some things I have learned about traveling in Italy, especially in the summer. For example, do not wear stiletto heels or a high-wedge sandal when you are getting into a vaporetto to explore Venice. Remember that those of us who were not born in Italy are not meant to wear high heels on Italian cobblestones. We don't have enough practice. I have watched many American women twist and fall in the name of fashion. One time, I was trying to step on to the vaporetto while wearing very high heels, and if not for a game-saving catch by the boat's crewman, I would have ended up in the canal. One last piece of advice: do not wear flip-flops on cobblestone streets. It is an accident waiting to happen. You will sorely damage the arch of your foot. Oh, woman! Thy name is vanity! I have seen many ankles wrapped in bandages, not a good look. So take good care of your feet, be kind to them, and in turn you will not end up tripping or injuring yourself.

To achieve the Italian bella figura, one must master the gentle art of dressing as an adult. One of the worst sights is the American woman tourist wearing jeans two sizes too small with giant tennis shoes meant for the gym and an ill-fitting T-shirt with the American flag emblazoned across her chest. This eyesore is unfortunately usually found in restaurants, churches, and museums. We seem to have forgotten that wise old adage: "When in Rome, do as the Romans do." In the summer, the Italian woman wears flowing dresses and skirts. She is graceful even when riding her Vespa, her hair streaming behind her, her skirt rippling in the wind, taking her basket of fresh vegetables and fruits home. Note also that adult Italian men do not wear shorts in public but stay with long pants earned through the rites of passage into their adulthood. I am dismayed that it seems we adult Americans have forgotten the gentle art of grown-up dressing.

There is another art; it is how to pack for travel to Italy in the summer months. Think in terms of where you are going to be, what sights you plan to visit, and what the climate will be. Will you be in the city or in the countryside? Are you planning to visit churches, museums, the opera, the symphony, or will you be hiking, skiing, engaging in water sports? Plan ahead. Start the month before you leave, checking the weather report at ten-day intervals. The week before you actually leave, I recommend checking the report every day. Use the Internet to inform yourself. After all, you want to look your best, and you never know who you might meet along the way. A friend of mine researched seeing the Pope and asked every Italian American she knew what she should wear on her trip. The outcome, you ask? When women on her tour group asked the tour guide what to wear for a high mass at St. Peter's, he pointed to my friend and told them to dress like the signora.

Remember, Italy is not a third-world country. It is steeped in history and civility and prides itself on the bella figura. Bella figura is an attitude, a way of being. It is the impression given by you to the outside world. It is not based on your figure or how much money you have, but a combination of the elements that create you. It is that intangible quality that emanates from a person who you instantly know is a gentleman or a gentlewoman. It is more than a person's outward appearance. It is how one chooses to present oneself to the rest of the world. Conjure in your mind the elegant Italian woman or man dressed appropriately with everything in its place. Tutto a posto.

Now that we have the Internet, go online to see what the "Romans" wear. Remember places plus temperature equal clothes. Two weeks in advance make a list of what you will pack and what you will carry on. Pick a place in your home where you can start stockpiling clothes, shoes, and sundries that you think you might want to take or could use during the trip. One week before, divide your clothes into daytime wear and evening attire. Bring costume jewelry sparingly; remember, it weighs more than you think. Then divide all your clothes and shoes in half. If you have packed for fourteen days, take for seven days. Finally, beware of shoes. They can make you or break you, weight-wise. Do not take new shoes. Shoes will determine whether or not your feet will have a new close personal relationship with blisters.

Now some critical but mundane things about packing for travel. It is essential to research and buy the lightest most durable suitcase possible when traveling overseas. Because it's all about the weight, baby. Remember to pack light because you may want to bring home some Italian treasures from your journey. I had to learn this the hard way. Many times my daughter had to sit on my suitcase and my mother's suitcase to get them shut, and this was before the airlines became strict on weight.

The essential "beyond the clothes and suitcase" checklist includes passport, local driver's license, contacting your bank and credit card company to tell them you will be using them in another country so the company doesn't block usage. Be sure to make copies of your passport, credit cards, ATM card, and driver's license. Place one copy in your suitcase; carry one copy with you; and leave one copy each with your selected trustworthy at home, friend, or relative, (who is not traveling at the same time you are). If your things are stolen or lost, you will want someone to call to get relevant numbers. Also, keep a hard copy of a telephone number list: credit card companies, bank, insurance travel and car, critical contact persons such as doctors. Leave an itinerary with someone who knows your schedule: when and where you are expected to be.

Take euros, at least enough to get you going until you have a weekday where you can get to a bank. Beware of ATMs that are offbeat, the same as you would here in the United States. Take your medications in your carry-on. Use an airline that has a track record of flying on time. If you want a particular seat, do not wait until the last minute. Good fares and good seats during the peak seasons are hard to come by. Reserve your airfare early. The airlines with the best travel records and with on-time flights are booked early. If you have a particular ritual that you perform before boarding, do it. I knock three times and give two pats on the side of the plane's door before entering. My goal is to make the plane and me one and the same. I am thinking, *Here we go, baby. We're off to Italy. Let's have a good time.*

I've created a "Checklist for Traveling" in this chapter. The list is the result of me trying to pack smarter, not harder. For years when I traveled, I seemed to be putting things together as if it were the first time I had ever traveled. One spring day, I finally decided to bite the bullet. It was time to organize myself. I have a special travel drawer, the bottom drawer in my dresser. I had a habit of throwing all the articles, scraps of papers with notes, booklets, and other pieces of information that I collected over the years into the drawer. Information about hotels, airlines, trains, boats, and lists of what to pack, plus any other tidbits of trivia that I thought that might be useful. I called it my "travel tickler drawer." From this mess, I organized and compiled a list of the essential items that I needed each time I went to Italy. I found that it saved my traveling culo. You don't have to reinvent the wheel because I've included it in this book. I hope it helps you in your planning. Please go ahead and modify it to fit your travel needs. Copy it and share it with family and friends. Buon viaggio!

Checklist for Traveling Overseas

Carry the Following:

- ☐ Passport
- ☐ Local driver's license
- ☐ Information for contacting credit card companies
- ☐ Information for contacting banks
- ☐ Euros

Make Copies of:

- ☐ Passport
- ☐ Credit cards
- ☐ ATM card
- ☐ Driver's license
- ☐ Important telephone numbers
- ☐ Insurance company
- ☐ Doctors
- ☐ Lawyers
- ☐ Contact persons (e.g., family member, close friend, business associate)
- ☐ Bank
- ☐ Itinerary

Location of Copies:

- ☐ Suitcase
- ☐ Carry-on, include copies of important papers (see above), carry-on medicines, cell phone charger and adapter, camera and adapter
- ☐ With another person who is traveling with you
- ☐ Someone at home (not traveling)

Photos of Family and Friends

The marriage of Edoardo Bertuccio and
Maria Vallerga, my mother's parents

Ferro Family Portrait, Antonietta Rusca Ferro and Antonio
Ferro with my father Carlo with big brother Tom standing.

June 21, 1941. My Parents' Wedding, Carlo Ferro
and Rosa Bertuccio with wedding party.

My brother John and adorable baby,
me on Lyon Avenue, Oakland, California

Me and John at Bay Farm Island

Cousin Etero, John, Rosa and my mother

Our First Trip – Three Generations

Lalla Nita and Bella

Bella, her cousins Elviro is next to her,
his father Gianni and Lorenzo

Cousins Franca, Mariuccia and Lalla Nita

Bella learning to dance with cousin Giuseppe

The Dynamic Trio in Capri

Me, Mom and Marisa at
Il Splendido Hotel

Our First Trip, me and cousin Anita

In the kitchen with cousin Piero,
wearing his red shorts with Angela

Piero and his pet chicken Henrietta with me

Bella with cousin Damiano

Bella with cousins: Maurizio, Lorenzo,
Giuseppe, Monica and Damiano

My mother with Mariuccia

The infamous Margheitin, aka, cousin Lorenzo
with mom. Notice the family resemblance!

My beloved Moe with me.

"The Living David", Lucky me!

Bella, all grown up in Monaco – and,
of course, on the phone.

The Alpicella Poster advertising The Madonna,
Del Carmine Festa.

The Procession with music and gold crosses

The Procession of gold crucifixes

The Madonna and Child carried with
a laden of lilies and anthuriums

A banner with The Madonna carried
during the procession

"The Bench" with cousins Lorenzo, Fino,
Gianni Battista and Anita.

Anita on the balcony in Alpicella

Me on the balcony waiting for the festa to begin

Me and Mr. Blue Eyes, Luenzin

Cousins Piero, me and Gian Piero

THE FERRO COUSINS – Taking a break from the festa
with cousins Piero, Anita, Giacomo and Gian Piero

Anita and me cooling off, Roma, Italy

Anita starting the new trend of the "Shower Cap Society".
Note the bangs soften the look.

Cousin Giacomo, hat reversed, ready to speed
down the Ligurian hills

My Julia Child's moment, cooking for the family: Gianni,
Giovanna, Maria, Milena, my mother and Giacomo.

Carlo, "La Scignua" and Ermes at
Il Splendido Hotel, Portofino.

Vladimiro accompanying my mother and me as we sing
"I Left My Heart In San Francisco," Il Splendido

My mother and cousin Maria – truly they were sisters

Chapter 12

Ah! Venezia! 2007

The highlight of our 2007 trip was Venice. We connected through Germany. I have found that the Frankfurt Airport is one of the busiest in Europe. Changing terminals for flights, departures, and arrivals is a constant practice here. One time my cousin and I waited at the boarding gate where the name of our destination city, flight number, and correct departure time were showing, only to be rejected when we presented our tickets. We were told it was another airline, and ours was not only at another boarding gate but in another terminal. We had ten minutes to get there. We were the last ones on the plane. It was a miracle because if there had been anyone waitlisted, they would have given our seats away and closed the doors.

About an hour and a half later, we breathed a sigh of relief as we saw Venice below us in all her serene majesty. I even successfully boarded the vaporetto without falling into the canal or into the arms of the crewman, since I wore sensible but stylish shoes this time.

As we entered the Bauer Hotel, we were greeted by Gian Carlo, who was as gorgeous as ever, rivaling any major movie star. The sparkle of his smile could have been used in a dental commercial. He was superbly elegant, bella figura.

Our usual suite was ready, and our welcome was absolutely ostentatious, including a bouquet of Bianca lilies. Bianca lilies are my favorite, white and long-stemmed and not so good if you have an allergy. At the Bauer, these flowers are usually over two feet high and snowy, snowy white. On the table was a bucket with chilled Prosecco, a box of beautifully wrapped hard candy, and an exquisite box of chocolates. The cinghiali had arrived.

It was late in the afternoon, and even though we had been traveling since the previous day, we joyously felt it was time to go out. Leaving the hotel, Anita asked, "Which way should we go?" I said, "Well, since we're in the Moise District, we are close to the Piazza San Marco, so let's go pay homage."

In the piazza, I bought a pendant of a winged Venetian lion that was carrying an open book. The lion represents St. Mark, patron Saint of Venice, and the open book represents peace. Saint Mark, the winged lion, is protecting the Bible. "Pax Tibi Evangelista Meus." Peace be unto you, Mark, my Evangelist. This is the motto of the city state of Venice. It was the anniversary of my dog Moe's transcending into the heavens, and the pendant represented Moe to me, my protector. Afterward, we selected a restaurant named the Quadri. Steeped in history, it is the first caffè to introduce Turkish coffee to the Venetians in the 1700s. The maître d' led us to a wonderful table with a view of a stage being set up in the piazza. We wondered what performance would be on the stage.

Then, as we sat at the Quadri, trying to recover from our journey, we noticed that the square was filling with scaffolding, perimeter fencing, guards and crews setting up for what looked like a huge concert. Since I always try to speak Italian, Anita suggested that I ask someone to find out what was going on.

I approached the maître d', who was talking with some American men wearing Bermuda shorts and their wives wearing jeans. They could not seem to make up their minds about what to do, to stay or go, to make a reservation or not to make a reservation. I asked the maître d' in Italian what was happening. He told me that it was a huge world event with a concert being held on all seven continents. This venue was Venice; and performing on July 6, 2007, was Peter Gabriel. It was a benefit to raise awareness about global warming. He asked, "Do you want a reservation for this evening?" I immediately exclaimed, "Sì! Sì!" He was delighted with my bella figura and my decisive la scignua presence and allowed me to pick the table. He then reserved it for us for the entire evening. The square was filling with tents bearing huge red crosses, representing the emergency being experienced by the earth and our need to save her. It was amazing, a worldwide festival being held on all seven continents, and we just happened to walk into the event being held in Venice.

The moon came up; and it was full, beaming its blessings down upon us and all of Venezia. The concert's opening act was a wonderful jazz group, and then Peter Gabriel entered upon the stage around nine thirty. Both sides of the stage exploded with huge flares. It was electrifying. The crowd went wild, jumping up and down during the whole concert. He performed for about two and half hours and had at least six or seven encores. He then topped off his performance by speaking flawless Italian with gratitude to the audience. Oh! How I wish I could speak like him.

We couldn't believe that we had the opportunity to select our table, no. 111, within the square before the area was cordoned off; and we managed to have it for the concert. We were able to leave and go back to the hotel to change our clothes. Security was on high alert and the check points required: our table number, restaurant, name of maître d', and our name. It was one of those perfect Venetian evenings that become so addicting, so much so that you don't ever want to leave. The concert ended, and we left with the crowd. Even though we were only five minutes from our hotel, we got swept away by the huge number of people; and before we knew it, we were on the wrong bridge heading toward the wrong district. But the moon gave us enough light to bring us home. What more could you ask, an incredible event, a full moon, Peter Gabriel, and ah, Venezia.

As we fell into our beautiful white linen beds, chatting about the unbelievable first day back in Venice, her highness, La Serenissima lulled us into a blissful restful sleep. What is there more to life than to be happy? Venezia! You make us so happy.

Startled, I awoke to an important-sounding knock on the door. Who could it be at this hour? What time was it? It was dark. I opened the door. It was the maid. I asked her in my best Italian, "Che ora è?" What time is it? It was about eleven thirty in the morning. I apologized and asked her to return at one thirty that afternoon. I opened the shutters and the windows, and the light streamed into our room. I could hear the conversations of the gondoliers. I gave them my customary wave and greeting. "Ciao! Sono Maria Teresa Ferro, Lo Americana." The blonde from America was back. The gondoliers shouted back, "Benvenuta!" Welcome! I thought to myself, Nonna Antonietta must be beaming down from heaven. She would have said to my mother, "I told you, Donna was not a saint's name." I was finally using my rightful name, albeit not the traditional grandmother's names but good enough for Nonna.

Anita and I made our annual bet about whether the waiters would be able to get up the nine narrow and steep steps, spiral staircase, carrying our room-service breakfast, and not drop anything. I think this staircase was made for extremely skinny people from the eighteenth century or earlier. We never won the bet; they always succeeded, and we tipped them heartily. We dressed, had our room-service breakfast, and went out for the day. Gian Carlo had made our evening reservations at Harry's Bar, Ernest Hemingway's old hangout.

Later, while we were exploring Venice, we met a woman named Margherita, who designed and sold purses. While we were in her shop, a young woman came in who spoke absolutely not one word of Italian. Margherita said to this woman, "You have been in Italy for a year and still do not speak the language." Then gesturing to me, she said, "This woman is Americana. She doesn't even live here, but she tries to speak Italian." Another woman came into the shop. She had been attending a language school and had only been there for four weeks and spoke very good Italian. Again, Margherita admonished the other woman to learn Italian. I watched Margherita open up to those who came into her store and tried to speak Italian. For Margherita, someone trying to speak her language was like a gift of understanding and respect. Respect is a cornerstone and an integral part of bella figura.

The Italian word meaning "to try" is *provare*. So if you want to get the best from Italy and Italians, try. Use whatever Italian words you can and make an effort (to) provare. It will make a difference. By the way, Margherita was a beautiful young woman who spoke impeccable English. She walked her talk.

We continued to explore, window-shop, and then we discovered an antique store. I went in and tried to speak some Italian. The woman in the store suggested that I try on an antique diamond necklace and the matching antique bracelet. She kept saying, "Just try it. We are just having fun dressing you up." The necklace and bracelet were priced at about €60,000. Venice was making a queen out of me, if only in pretend because I tried, io ho provato.

The saleswoman in this antique jewelry store had lived all her life in Venice. All the items were one of a kind, and so was she. She was a stately woman with a smile that lit up a room. She had deep, simmering dark brown eyes. Her silver hair was pulled back into a ballerina chignon. Her understated dark green dress with Cuban pump heels complimented the minimal, but real, antique jewelry she wore. What an experience. Oh, how I love Venezia.

We sauntered along, taking in the sights and smells of Venezia, and came upon the Venice Gallery and met a charming woman in her late forties with flaming red hair and freckles scattered across her face. I tried speaking Italian and found out that she was really Irish. She had come to Venice to teach English, had fallen in love with a Venetian, and stayed. I bought a small watercolor from the Scuola S. Zaccaria of the Studio d'Arte, entitled, "Remembering the Venetians." The setting was the Piazza di San Marco. In the foreground was the Harlequin and his love, Colombina, two characters from the romantic tales in the Commedia del Arte during the Italian Renaissance. The story was said to have originated in Turkey four thousand years ago. She invited us to visit her at her villa when we came the next year, and all because I tried to speak Italian.

As we continued to roam around, we discovered a *farmacia* (pharmacy) dating back to the fifteenth century. The place looked like a cathedral. They had shoes! Yes, shoes in a pharmacy. Anita bought a couple of pairs of sandals, which made her cinghiale hooves quite happy. We asked about the fact that they were open twenty-four hours a day, which was highly unusual. They told us it was because they lived upstairs on the premises and that's why they did it; and in the winter, it is cold and rainy, and there are not that many people. We serve the community. If you have an opportunity to visit this farmacia, you must make a special effort to look at the wood carvings on the beautiful counter, which might have been part of the altar of a church. It is to the left as you are leaving the Bauer Hotel, down about five bridges or so.

Across the farmacia, I had found an interesting shop the year before. Through the window, I had seen some very dusty but interesting brass sea horses that appeared to be bookends and might have been smaller replicas of the oarlocks I was seeing on some of the gondolas. Everything had faded price tags as if they had been there since the time Napoleon visited Venice. A man had been standing in the middle of the shop smoking a cigarette and reading a newspaper lying on a small table. Unfortunately, I'd had an appointment and was unable to stop in and shop. Afterward, when I returned, it was closed. Now a year later, it was open again, and the man was standing in the middle of the shop smoking a cigarette and reading a newspaper from a table top. Was I a time traveler? I felt a little intimidated, and yet the shop was open, and there were the dusty old sea horses I had seen the year before. It was déjà vu.

The man turned out to be the owner. When I asked to look at the sea horses, he got them out and stood there polishing them the whole time we were talking. He shined them until they gleamed. They were extremely heavy, but I carried them for the rest of the trip, a labor of love. They sit on my desk now; and as I write this book, I gaze at them, remembering the moment and the man who seemed frozen in time.

With the newly purchased bookends in hand, we entered the hotel lobby whereupon Gian Carlo called out, "Signora Ferro, vieni!" I came to his hotel desk as he wanted to introduce to me another hotel manager, Paolo. He took my breath away. He bent down and kissed my hand. I was all a twitter; I actually twirled in the lobby. I could hardly speak. I blurted out that I had to change for the evening and said, "Ciao." As I gazed at his dark piercing eyes, beautiful smile, and dark wavy hair, he turned and glided away. I thought again, *Ah, Venezia.* Once again, Venice was casting her spell. Where do they come from? Are these men hired for their looks? I would love to be the casting director for Italian life. The men are simply gorgeous.

When we first arrived at Harry's, it seemed quite frenzied, loaded with tourists and large groups of partying people, weddings, and others. We did not know that Harry's had a second floor, but soon found out when we were seated there.

Harry's is quite commercial, not very Italian or old world in its ambiance. It could have passed for a tourist place on Fisherman's Wharf in San Francisco. The waiters and the maitre d' seemed to move through the routine of service with a brisk efficiency. The maitre d' marched like a Swiss doll wound too tightly. I tried to speak Italian as best I could, and then there was a ripple in the "waiter brigade." Suddenly, the captain of the waiters became friendly, charming, hovering over us as though we were favored customers. He told us about special drinks and different menu items. He laughed with us, and we laughed more. The waiters' smiles turned into grins, and we stayed until late in the evening. We came close to being their last customers of the night, returning to our hotel happy and blissful. I have no idea why the attitude changed. Was it because I tried to speak Italian while we were there? Perhaps. Provare.

Before the evening ended, we had a nightcap out on the hotel terrace that faces the Grand Canal. We made sure to say buona notte, good night, to the gondoliers. One of them was tying up his gondola, and I started to talk to him. He was finished for the evening, and I had such a curiosity about this Venetian occupation. I invited him to join us for a drink. He laughed about my curiosity and then willingly climbed over the railing on to the terrace. During our conversation about his family, he said he was married and had two daughters but was trying for a son. He also explained that typically this occupation is handed down from father to son. And that they have to take many tests and then become licensed. He also shared that a gondolier must be very strong, agile, and really skilled in steering this banana-shaped boat. Although there was one woman who tried to do the job, unfortunately, it did not work out for her. I wondered in my lifetime if there would ever be a female gondolier or a female U.S. president? I am happy to report, in August 2010, Giorgia Boscolo became Venice's first female gondolier. Well, we are halfway there; as the adage goes, "The cup is half full." He was such a lovely man, and we wished him well in his baby-making. Who knows, maybe one of his daughters will become a gondolier. The next day, I leaned out from my hotel room window, but before I could greet the gondoliers, they called out, using my name, "Signora Ferro, buon giorno!" Good morning, Signora Ferro. The Italian American blonde had arrived.

It was early in the afternoon, and we were moving slowly. The maids had not made their rounds of cleaning our place as they knew the drill by now. I am sure they saved us for last and as late in the afternoon as possible. It was simply our Alpicella ritual, same as Gianni Battista when he moved from bench to bench.

As we sauntered into the lobby, Gian Carlo looked up at us with his beautiful smile and asked, "How can I help you?" We gazed back into his beautiful eyes and murmured, "Not a thing today, but perhaps our transportation when we leave."

We felt like cinghiali with crowns on our heads, in other words, totally spoiled. After exploring and shopping, we returned to the hotel and found it was about eight in the evening, time for dinner. We went back to the Ristorante Giglio and looked for the couple from last year who met secretly once a year in Venice, the German banker and the teacher from Finland. Would there be more lightning and thunder this year? We never saw them and wondered if their "same time next year" relationship had continued. Only Serenissima, as Venice is called, has the answer.

Our waiter that night at the Giglio Ristorante was a truly inept gigolo. In between the courses of our dinner, he flirted outrageously. Then out of the blue, he offered to come and make love to me on the sofa of my hotel room while my cousin slept in the bedroom. It was not a smooth Casanova moment. I told him he was rude, and I found his behavior disdainful. My bella figura was affronted by his blatant offer. I wondered who else he might have affronted with his brutta, ugly, figura. Every year since that episode, he was absent; and apparently, someone made sure he had been removed from this lovely restaurant.

The following day, we went to the Island of Burano. Quaint and charming, Burano is noted for embroidery and handmade lace, while Murano is noted for hand-blown glass. The handiwork with lace and linen is exquisite, as it has been for centuries. As the ferry brings you closer and closer, you notice the island homes are painted beautiful bright rainbow colors. Burano is an explosion of color because the husbands would return from fishing after dark and would flash a light on the shore to find the color of their home so they could aim for it. Burano has small canals that are interspersed with rows of brightly colored houses and shops and no streets or vehicles. It is absolutely quaint and charming.

I have visited this island several times, and it is always the same. Everything is in its place, window boxes with flowers, shopkeepers and housewives cleaning the front of their homes. Burano was so clean that you could have eaten off the cobblestones. If you have time while you are in Venice, take the ferry to Burano. You will not be disappointed.

After a long day of sightseeing in Burano, we returned to the Bauer. As I climbed the winding stairs, I heard the phone ringing. I knew instinctively it had to be Roberto. I struggled with the huge key. I finally got the door open and grabbed the phone. "Pronto." It was Roberto. As I sat down on the sofa and listened to him, I noticed a huge bouquet of fabulous long-stemmed pink roses. I thanked him profusely for the roses, but he said very softly, "I did not send them." Roberto told me he could not make it to Venice because he was in Paris waiting to fly out. Business had drawn him to Hong Kong and then on to Australia. Then he said in a very serious tone, "I have life-altering changes to discuss with you and cannot share them over the phone. It is simply too complicated." Roberto went on to say that he might get back from his trip and asked where I would be staying in Milan. I told him the name of our hotel. Milan was our last stop before returning to the United States. I wished him safe travels and hung up, wondering who sent the roses. I opened the card; the flowers were from the hotel manager, the unbelievably dashing Paolo.

I have nothing else to say, except they were lovely flowers from a lovely man. Venezia, she holds so many secrets and so many surprises.

It was dinnertime, so Anita and I went to nearby Le Caravelle Ristorante. The Italian word caravelle means a three-mast ship like the Nina, Pinta, and Santa Maria. The restaurant sign has the three ships on it. Caravelle has a lovely, lush courtyard dotted with potted flowers, green plants, and fountains. The waiters are responsive and friendly. As we sat under the stars, it was as if we had entered another world, sailing along on calm seas, with sea-scented air, a gentle summer breeze, and delectable food. Anita and I dined that night, taking our time to savor the Venetian evening. We listened to the crickets, which soon lulled us back to our room. It was sheer bliss.

As we walked back to the Bauer, I wondered what would happen with Roberto and what was this life-altering conversation that we needed to have and only face-to-face. Who was this man? We'd had little correspondence.

The next day, we had the laborious task of preparing for our next stop, Perugia and the Umbria World Jazz Festival. We did not leave our room until two in the afternoon, but this time, we had an excuse. Once again, the molecular explosion had happened. The challenge was how much weight had we added to our luggage and ourselves, and this was only the beginning of our trip.

We finally left our room and took a leisurely saunter down the vicini, small alleyways, inhaling the everlasting beauty of Venice, the living museum. The sculptures, the art galleries, the opera house, the Gran Teatro La Fenice, everywhere we looked, our senses were saturated with beauty and antiquity. As we wandered through the side streets immersed in the old-world ambiance, suddenly, we came upon an erotic shop that was beyond our imagination. It had a window display that was graphic and clashed with the classic antiquities that surrounded it. It was located on the corner near the farmacia and the sea horse bookend shop. I do not know what happened to it, but it is gone now.

Venice has always been erotic but never overtly graphic. Even in its most infamous periods of history, the messages about the erotic, while clear, were subtle and had bella figura. It was in the way you held your fan or used your mask that sent the clear messages of amour between uomo and donna, man and woman. If you held your closed fan with your right hand in front of your face, you were beckoning your suitor to come with you. If you brought the handle of the fan to your lips, it meant "Kiss me." Tracing lines on your cheek meant, "I love you." Age has never been an issue with the Italians in matters of the heart, but I thought with the complex movements of love messages sent by an older woman with a fan that it must have been tough when Alzheimer's set in.

We continued walking until we came upon a side alley, where we found a young man working on some incredible Venetian Carnevale masks in a very tiny studio overflowing with masks. The artist was making them on the premises and signing them. They were different from the usual masks found in other areas, especially the main streets where the tourists go. He had made masks that sparked my imagination: giraffes, hippopotami, peacock masks blazing with sequins, and plumes three feet tall. I saw an erotic mask of a goat in black and silver. Half of the mask was silver sequins, and half was black velvet. It had horns that curled down and around and were half-black velvet and half-silver lamé with golden tips. A golden diamond-shaped filigree pin with a crystal adorned the mask in the center. There were satin ribbons to tie it. I tried it on. As I looked in the mirror, I imagined myself at the Carnevale in a black-and-white dress with my red Venetian cape swirling around my shoulders. I bought it.

I asked Anita if she had ever thought about the meaning of Carnevale or maschera. She said, "Carne means meat." "Yes." Then I added, "It comes from the Latin word *carnem*, meaning meat, and *levare*, which means to remove or put away. Consequently, after Carnevale, we put away the meat." I continued, "The English word *mascara* is derived from the Italian word *maschera*, which means mask. "Anita immediately laughed and said, "What is going on in your head now?" I looked at her and said, "I have a cinghiale theory about masks." Anita exclaimed, "Oh lord, I'm going to need a glass of wine for this!"

"I think that everyone, once they reach a certain age, forty, fifty, or sixty, depending on their wrinkles and bone structure, should wear a mask. It could be that you tipped a few too many margaritas over the years, were out in the sun and baked yourself into an irreversible prune, or perhaps you just had bad genes. Oh well. The first thing you need to do is take an honest look at yourself in the mirror and ask this question: Is it time for a mask? The other test is to ask someone you don't know. You don't do it in a bar in the dark at closing time when everyone is desperate for a date. You could send me a picture on my cell phone, and I'll tell you the truth. Once you are past your denial, you have to think in terms of masks for various seasons, for different functions, for different working conditions, and last but not least for sex appeal. For example, you wouldn't wear a BBQ mask to a funeral or a funeral mask to a cocktail party. Anita, I've got it. I think we should start a mask company in Venice, hire the Venetians to make the masks, and create a boom in their economy. Imagine, Anita, you could become the mayor of Venice, and I would be the Doge. I like it. It rings true. We'll be Mayor Anita and Doge Donna. The Genovese would take back Venice. My ancestors would be proud."

Realizing that she needed a mask, Anita followed my trailblazing example and bought one. It was fit for her new role as mayor of Venice. The mask was elegant, with a myriad of exquisite sequins: blues, greens, gold, and feathers. When we made these purchases, we felt that we were making a commitment to our new mask company in Venice, and we made a promise to debut our new masks at Carnevale. Picture this, cinghiali at Carnevale. Thank goodness we will be wearing long ball gowns to cover our hooves.

We celebrated our new masks and potential mask company and new positions as mayor and Doge while sipping our tea at the Florian. You may remember this was the caffè frequented by Casanova in the 1700s. The cinghiali had high tea with delicious little sandwiches. After tea, we returned to the hotel to refresh ourselves and to enjoy the beauty of the view on the Grand Canal. We sat until the sun began to set. We were passing time, or as we say in Ligurian, passa tempo. In our reverie, we reminisced about all we had done and seen. Our waiter, Simone, brought us compliments of the hotel, little sandwiches of tuna, egg, and green olives, called cichetti; but in Liguria, cichetti means a small drink. No wonder with these language differences the cities were always at war.

We continued our discussion about our new positions of mayor and Doge in Venice when I heard, "Signora Ferro! "Signora Ferro!" I went down to chat with the gondoliers. They told me that I was famous with them, and they all knew who I was since the other gondolier told them my name. One of the gondoliers said, "We used to wonder, when July came, if the blonde lady would call out to us, and it was you!" They were so friendly, and since they were Venetian and I was Genovese, I began to wonder in my heart why Venice and Genova had fought so much. If they had merged, they could have ruled the Mediterranean and Adriatic seas, bankers and merchants, such a powerful force. Most people do not know that Venice had Doges until 1797, and Genova had Doges until 1805. I thought we, Genova and Venice, are more alike than different, proud seafaring cities steeped in rich history. The sea is our fortress as well as our invader. We are both courageous and adventurous people. I was truly beginning to think, feel, and know on a conscious level that I am Ligurian. Io sono Ligure.

While sitting on the terrace, a couple appeared, the man dressed in a tuxedo with tails, a top hat, and a cane. The woman was wearing an elegant wedding dress with a veil. She spoke English and told us that she was an opera singer originally from South Carolina. We asked how they met. She had come to Italy to study opera. And then the story unfolded. When she got her electricity bill, it was so huge she went down to the local bar to drown her sorrows but could only afford cheap wine. A man, who would later become her husband, heard her lament and told the bartender to throw out her cheap red wine and replace it with champagne. They knew each other for five years and then married in Parma. They were recreating their wedding evening in Venice, having a drink and then going for a gondola ride. Love is so beautiful; so is Venice. It was our last evening, and it was perfect as usual. *Grazie, un grande bacio,* a big kiss.

The rest of the trip was our magical routine: attending the Umbria Jazz Festival; sightseeing through Tuscany; and returning to our nest, *il nido,* to see our relatives. Roberto, you ask? Did I hear from him? All I heard was silence.

Chapter 13

Sicily, the Resort Tour 2008

By August, after just returning from Italy, I began planning next year's trip. It would turn out to be an odyssey worthy of the Greeks. My mother wanted to go to Sicily. My daughter decided to come; and with Anita and me, it made four. We called it our resort tour. We planned a week in Sicily and then a week at a hotel in Varazze followed by the rest of the time in Portofino. It sounded delightful.

The trip would begin in San Francisco then to Philadelphia and on to Milan, with a change to Alitalia Airlines to Rome. We would change planes in Rome and continue to the Catania Airport in Sicily, a flight not for the faint of heart. We would be traveling more hours than I would want to count, assuming no flight delays making for extended layovers. A driver was scheduled to pick us up and take us to the San Domenico Palace Hotel in Taormina, Sicily, the wedding capital of Europe. Then in December, my daughter announced she was pregnant with Alyssa Rose. The group shrank to three, since Alyssa Rose planned to arrive during the trip or shortly thereafter.

Because of our early flight, we stayed in a hotel near the San Francisco Airport and had dinner to celebrate the coming fun in Italy into the wee hours. At four the next morning, there was a loud knock on our door. It was my mother. "Okay, you sleeping beauties, time to get up." We laughed and talked all the way to the boarding gate. We had our seats and were good to go. We were waiting for the announcement to board the plane. Then a passenger who had just checked in leaned over to me and said, "There is a big problem."

I launched myself over to the boarding-gate desk. I asked the clerk, "What's going on?" He pointed to his screen. There, blinking in big red letters was "Flight Cancelled." I went into my superwoman mode and immediately told the boarding-gate clerk, Riccardo, we could take a direct flight to Rome and skip Milan, even if it meant going economy. There goes all the free miles I had accumulated to bump us up to business class. Meanwhile, Riccardo and his coworker began working on our travel solution, trying to get seats and making sure our luggage stayed with us. The speakers blared out the cancelled flight information to the rest of the passengers on this full flight. Chaos! Bedlam! It was pandemonium.

We thought things were going to be fixed because he got us on another flight. We boarded and then sat and sat and sat. The weight in the cargo section of the plane was not distributed correctly and had to be rearranged, which took an hour. We finally took off. I calculated how much time we had left to make our connection to Rome from Philadelphia. It was twenty minutes. I urgently requested that a wheelchair be waiting at our arrival gate for my mother so we could move faster. This was my second request since I had called to ask for one prior to the trip.

We were in the air when the travel gods struck again. A young man on the plane collapsed, and the flight attendants thought he'd had a heart attack. They were prepping for an emergency landing in Toledo, Ohio, when they asked if there were any doctors on the plane. Luckily, there were two doctors, and they rapidly determined the young man had an anxiety attack and had fainted. So he recovered in the air, and we continued on to Philadelphia. As the doctors worked together on the young man, they discovered that they practiced in the same hospital but had never met. One was a surgeon, and one was a cardiologist. Lucky young man, lucky passengers.

I had several discussions with the flight attendant because I was so nervous about making our connection. Then the pilot announced that we would be delayed another fifteen minutes because we had to be rerouted around a thunderstorm in the Philadelphia area. He also said that it was eighty-seven degrees there, with 90 percent humidity. I was already sweating making this connection when the thunderstorm hit and reduced our connection time to five minutes. Anita and I looked at each other and said, "We're screwed." We might be roasted cinghiali in Philly or Philly cheese cinghiali.

The flight attendant came by to reassure us that we would make our fight to Rome and that there would be a trolley for my mother. As we taxied to the gate in the domestic terminal, the flight attendant announced that some passengers had tight connections and asked others to allow them off first. They even asked us to raise our hands so the others would know who we were and would lessen our chances of being trampled in the rush to get off this extremely late plane.

We bolted off the plane and scanned frantically for the trolley, which was nowhere in sight. I grabbed my mother's purse and her bag of medications and sprinted for Gate A 21 in the international terminal. As a focused cinghiale, I had determination and lots of Italian curse words for the missing trolley. To fuel the fire, it was July, muggy, sticky, humid, and just plain stiflingly hot. The terminal was packed with vacationers all heading for their gates. It was like swimming upstream against the current and all the other fish. I was frantically reading all the signs to make sure that I didn't make a wrong turn. Finally, there was the international terminal. As I approached it, a trolley whizzed by with Anita and my mother but no room for the Italian sprinter. Anita called out, "We'll get your ticket and hold the flight." They had been unable to print out our new boarding passes at the San Francisco Airport because their printer wasn't working.

I swore again under my breath in Italian and continued running. Yes, I am fluent in swearing in Italian, thanks to my father, Carlo. I can still hear my beloved father and his colorful Italian expletives, while my mother would say, "Carlo, don't say that. She's going to learn those bad words." And I did. Here are a few of my favorite pristine but colorful phrases that my father used: *brutto bestia*, "ugly beast"; *mondo cane*, "dog world"; and his all-time favorite, *porco miseria* (drum roll), "miserable pig." In order to do justice to these phrases you must have an operatic or theatrical flair and exaggerated gestures. If you are not Italian, please go, stand in front of a mirror, and practice. Then when you think you are ready, try it on a friend. If they are impressed, you are ready to go public. Bravo.

As I turned the corner heading toward the international terminal, I noticed it was getting even hotter. I thought it was all because of my running, and then an announcement was made that the air-conditioning was out of order in our terminal. Now I really began to sweat. Finally, I slid into Gate A 21, holding on to the desk and sucking air. I wondered where all the passengers were. It was empty. Squinting through my steamy sweaty glasses, I saw a small sign. The flight had been moved. It was now taking off at Gate A 25.

Another announcement was made they were now closing the door to my flight to Rome. I took a quick deep breath and began to run again. I could see Anita in the distance, holding the plane for me and began to cheer me on to run faster. God loves her. Later we found out that our original connecting flight from Philadelphia to Milan (the one we missed) had been delayed. The attendant had asked Anita if we wanted to go business class to Milan, our original plan, or go directly to Rome economy class. Our luggage was heading to Rome so Anita made an executive decision; we should follow our luggage. It was an inspired decision because our original Milan flight, which was delayed, never took off; it got cancelled. I was the last person on the plane and expected to relax in first class, only to find my seat was in economy, and we were not even seated together. All my miles saved for this trip flew out the airplane window.

I was crestfallen, like a cockatoo that had lost its mate, but grateful to be on the plane, albeit separated. Then some generous passengers said they would trade places so we could all sit together. As we buckled in, another announcement was made that we were again delayed because of the thunderstorms, and now we were tenth in line to take off. I was worried about making our Alitalia connection to Sicily, quel che sarà, sarà. I would have ten hours to think about it, and maybe the pilot would make up some air time. Hope springs eternal. What else could go wrong? I was afraid to entertain the thought.

I settled back and decided to watch a movie, only to discover that our TVs didn't work: ten hours and no entertainment, just ourselves. The flight attendants gave us our meals and drinks. We were giddy with relief and also strung out from the six-hour flight from San Francisco, the Philly connect experience, and the trip so far. We began to laugh and tell jokes to lighten our spirits. The attendant came by and said to quiet down so that we did not disturb the other passengers, who might want to sleep. She then slammed our window shades down and left. Anita summed up the message from our stewardesses from hell. "Sleep, you bastards, and leave us alone." The only bright light was one angel attendant who kept our drinks coming. She may have been medicating us to get us to sleep, and we finally did. Thank you, my angel of the skies.

We arrived in Rome, had time to eat, refresh ourselves, and shop in the airport because the pilot had made time in the air. Finally, we walked over to our gate, only to find that the travel gods still had us in their clutches. FLIGHT DELAYED. We took off an hour late. Alitalia was most gracious about the delay and couldn't wait on us enough. We landed at six o'clock in the evening on Wednesday in Sicily; our odyssey had begun in San Francisco on Tuesday at four in the morning. The driver was waiting; all we needed was our luggage, but the travel gods were not finished. They woke up from their nap and mischievously decided to hide my mother's luggage. Fortunately at the time, she wore my size clothes, but her style was for elegance and mine was sporty chic; however, she had to wear the same pair of shoes she had worn on the flight because her dainty feet were a full size smaller than mine.

Our driver, Salvatore, was like a tour guide, reviewing the history and culture of Sicily and pointing out the flora and fauna to me as I rode in the front seat. Sicily is a blend of all cultures that surround the Mediterranean Sea because she has been invaded by Romans, Greeks, Vandals, Byzantine, Islamic, Norman, Hohenstaufen, Catalans, Spaniards, Lombards, and finally the ultimate conquerors, the cinghiali Ferros. Simply, it is the most strategically placed island in the central Mediterranean. Because of this, the architecture, art, and people are a blend of all of those cultures. The people are resilient survivors and committed to an ingrained independence. Goethe thought that "To have seen Italy without having seen Sicily, is to not have seen Italy at all, for Sicily is the clue to everything."

From the backseat came the gentle sounds of snoring. My mother and Anita were unconscious, actually comatose. We climbed and climbed into the hills until we reached a wrought-iron gate that opened to the San Domenico Palace Hotel. Originally a monastery, the hotel sat on the edge of a cliff overlooking the sea. It was like a living museum; and the hotel actually gave tours, once a week, because it was filled with so many antiques and rare art pieces. Much of the furniture was hand-carved from the fifteenth century and seemed to me to have a kind of Dominican monastery style of heaviness to it. The imagery of the art was dominated by saints. The colonnade emptied into a courtyard, and the guide said that if you listened closely, you could still hear the chanting of the original monks.

Anita and I had a huge suite with old-stately elegance. Our room had an enormous terrace with breathtaking views of the azure Mediterranean Sea. The terrace was furnished with chaise lounges, tables, and chairs. When we finished admiring our suite, we went over to see my mother's room next door. Her room was equally beautiful but had one additional feature: a gigantic bouquet of flowers sitting on a beautiful antique desk with a small card leaning against the vase. As we entered, my mother pointed. "Look, I got flowers." The bouquet, staggering in size, was stunning, with sunflowers, roses, bluebells, orchids, irises, anthuriums, and gladiolas all arranged in a magnificent porcelain vase. I looked at the front of the card. The name on it was Donna Marie. I opened it. It said, "Welcome to Sicily. I'll meet you at the Genova Airport on the sixteenth. Roberto. P.S. I'll call you." And to my amazement, he did. We had the flowers moved to my room; and trust me, if Roberto had known my mother, she would have gotten the flowers, not me, because she was la scignua.

Life's events are never boring. I believe my mother, in another lifetime, was a Genovese empress and had conquered Sicily. In all of her travels with Anita and me, she had never lost her luggage. Was this a Sicilian vendetta? Since I was a little girl, she had always wanted to go to Sicily. She was fascinated by its rich history and its people. Now in her eighties, for most of the day, because of her ill health and our horrific travels, the Genovese empress was in repose. In the evenings, la scignua would light up, borrow some of my clothes, go down to the bar, and explain patiently to the bartender how to make a cosmopolitan. She had gotten the idea to drink them from the TV show, *Sex in the City*. The hotel staff had difficulty understanding her as she always spoke the Genovese dialect. I would have to step in and translate for her or, as she would put it, interfere in her conversation. Many hours of conjugating verbs were finally paying off.

The curse of the situation involving the missing luggage stems from my mother, the Genovese empress, and me, because we never believed in bringing a carry-on. Let me explain. Anita always travels with one, and she says it is her good-luck insurance. When we arrived in Rome, our connecting flight was delayed for an hour. Anita was still lugging around her carry-on, so I suggested, "We only have another short hop to Sicily, why don't you check it so you can look at the shops?" We were all exhausted from our trip and its mishaps, so she agreed and checked her lucky bag. Sure enough, when we arrived in Sicily, my mother's bags were missing. Anita had a remedy. She said that when my mother's luggage was finally found and it became time for us to depart, we should all have a carry-on because it would break the curse. It did, and we did not lose any more suitcases during the rest of the trip. Anita and her sage advice; we need to listen to her more often.

My mother rested during the day, while Anita and I explored not only the town of Taormina but also the many, many terraced acres surrounding the hotel. Off in the distance, we could see Mt. Etna belching its smoke like a signal from Vulcan. We hiked up and down the terraces and admired the English gardens, Roman and Greek statuary, fruit trees, and gardens full of roses. It was spectacular.

One afternoon, we turned a corner in the garden and saw a huge descending staircase of nearly seventy steps. At the bottom was a beautiful swimming pool with cabanas and chairs. We returned to our rooms and changed into our swimsuits. Anita put on a poufy shower cap to protect her new hairdo. She wore it with her bangs out. I said, "What are you doing?" She replied haughtily, "This is the new trend across the pond. I am establishing the Shower Cap Society of Women." She proceeded to go down to the pool, wearing it with great regal aplomb.

Lo and behold, the next day as we are sitting at the pool, less than twenty-four hours since Anita had established her new trend, a woman appeared getting into the pool, wearing a giant poufy black-and-white polka-dot shower cap. I took a picture. Anita is such a trendsetter. I never have any idea what new trend or style she will set in our travels. As cinghiali of Alpicella and as cousins, we have now decreed that the Red Hat Society is passé; and women need to join President Anita in the new, much more chic, Shower Cap Society.

While lounging by the pool and musing about the lady wearing the poufy polka-dot shower cap, we began to think about selling our own shower caps. We would have them designed in Italy and made in the United States. There would be a myriad of functions for this fashionista shower cap such as the obvious: wearing it on the plane so that the back of your hair remains in place and perfect for landing, especially in such rainy places as the state of Washington.

It could serve dual functions, day and night: for example, the day cap could double up as evening attire with snaps to add with sequins, feathers, or rhinestones, how divine. If you wanted a custom-made cap, you could provide photos of your pet, grandchildren, or even the colors of your state flag or country, no problem for us. Our cap designs are only limited by your imagination. We could even make shower caps that match your pajamas, day or evening. My cousin, President Anita, recommends you wear bangs, as it softens the look and makes one look more alluring. The cap goes from shower time to dinnertime to bedtime. Let's not forget those of you with thinning hair. You'll wear it all the time and never stress again about your "do." And for those of us with bad-hair coiffure, such as the cock-a-doodle-do style and straw style, just put on the cap. No worries.

We think the cap is also perfect for weddings. Through the years, we have traveled and have taken many pictures of brides, even two or three in one day here at Taormina. The veils that the brides wear appear lovely but often later are a nuisance. Have you ever noticed that if the veil is too long, it is stepped on constantly and becomes dirty, soiled, and torn? If it is a hot day, the bride spends copious time pushing and blowing the veil away from her face. The veil becomes a weapon of mass hair-and-makeup destruction, intruding upon the groom, preventing him from kissing the bride. We have a solution for the veil dilemma: the sublime wedding shower cap.

Matrimonially speaking, it could be the color of your choice, any material and style, so unobtrusive for the bridal kiss, never a hair out of place, or a blinding veil to mar the ceremony. Truly a blessing for the bride who knows trends that will last forever. It could become a classic wedding cap. We're now in the process of gathering focus groups across the world to see if they would be interested in wearing such a fashion piece. Are you? Drop me a postcard and give me your thoughts. Or if you would like to be in a focus group, just let me know. We value your opinion.

After a hearty laugh about shower caps, we began to muse about how perfect life seemed here away from the rest of the world. It was a beautiful sunny afternoon in Sicily. Anita and I were sitting around the pool sipping a Rossini, which is strawberries and champagne. Here we are, Americans, sitting with citizens from everywhere in the world, listening to all the different languages threading into one common cord. All was serene and blissful. Why is it we could be at peace here? Why not everywhere? Maybe we need to build swimming pools indoors and outdoors with beautiful scenery and lots of beautiful plants, and then maybe our humanity will be restored. I think the world governments should look at this proposal as a tool toward world peace. Just think: the byproduct of this would be a physically fit world. Write to your local government officials. Let's swim for world peace.

By the time the fourth day arrived with no luggage, it was time to take my mother shopping in Taormina. Shoes are always among a girl's best friends, and so my mother purchased three pairs of glitzy sandals. Then we found a lovely little dress shop with two little old ladies running it. At this point, prior to making a major purchase, Anita, "The Wise One," suggested calling the hotel to make sure that the errant luggage had not shown up: Murphy's Law. It had. It was sitting in my mother's room. The adorable shop ladies were so happy for her; it was as though they had sold $1,000 worth of clothes. That night, we celebrated with cosmopolitans. The bartender, who had now perfected the cosmopolitan under my mother's tutelage, made *la Regina Rosa del cosmopolitano di mondo*, "the Queen Rose of the cosmopolitan of the world," drink. It was a pretty good title for a woman in her mideighties.

We also shared more good news. Arrivals are much better than delays or cancellations. Anita phoned her daughter, Erin, to confirm via sonogram that Erin was eleven and a half weeks pregnant. The sonogram showed feet, hands, legs, and arms. Anita gave it the nickname Nugget because we didn't know the sex, and Nugget was now the size of a chicken McNugget. It's like kismet. I would soon be *lola*, grandmother in Tagalog, because my son-in-law Vince is Filipino American. Anita would also be a grandmother and liked the title nonna, and that would be her claim. Lola D (the initial D is for Donna) sounds so much more youthful than Nonna, but truly the word nonna has a very special meaning for me.

I have often thought about what it means to be a nonna. I think of it as a very noble title, and my nonna Maria began living with us when I was five years old. I was very fortunate to have a nonna to help raise me into adulthood and in between the terrible teens. There are certain qualities imbued in a nonna that I would like to share with you. First, a nonna makes the family number one priority in her life. Second, she will cook for you like a short-order cook: morning, noon, and night. Third, she doesn't judge you and will listen to you when you have problems or to share secrets that you don't want your family to know. Fourth, she is the person you go to no matter what time of day or night. She is there for you. Fifth, you can always see her in the kitchen with her apron on, happily cooking for more people than what exists in the household. Sixth, she loves to clean everything; even your parakeet will glisten. And most importantly, a nonna is all about unconditional love. I wish everyone had one. I was blessed with two.

Our daughters' children would be born six months apart. We are thinking, someday when they get older, we will take them with us to Italy. If they misbehave, we will send them off to their parents, and we will continue with our merriment. Alyssa Rose was expected in late July and Nugget in late January. There were no delays, no cancelations, and no returns.

My cousin and I think suitcases are such prized possessions. We fondly say goodbye to them as we depart, and with great anxiety, we look forward to their return at our destination on the conveyor belt. Nothing seems more magically mixed with fondness and anxiety than awaiting our grandchildren, who were on the conveyor belt of life. What a thought; it's overwhelming. And yet it happens all the time. This was our first time. Here we were, two cousins in Italy, knowing that a part of us started long ago in Liguria. We hope someday they will join us in our adventures in Italy, and they will create new future memories with their nonna and lola.

One of the beauties of San Domenico Palace is that when you sit on the terrace in the evening, you can look up and see the Teatro Greco, a theater, all lit up, and built thousands of years ago by the Greeks. When you look down, you can see the incredible blue-green Mediterranean Sea. The temperature was perfect, the sound of the beautiful piano music drifting on the evening air was bliss. The woman playing that night had been a concert pianist, and her gnarled fingers played with a certain but light touch. There was a young woman sitting next to her on the bench, whom she was mentoring to take her place. The older woman in her mideighties played, and the hotel gave her meals in exchange. It turned out that the young woman sitting next to her was the daughter of the owner of the shop in Taormina where I bought the baptismal ensemble for Alyssa Rose.

The next night was dramatically different. We went to our usual table, ordered our usual drink, and sat waiting to be transported to paradise, when a young man in a tuxedo sat down at the piano and began pounding on the keys. The chords crashed on our eardrums. The reverie was shattered. After five minutes of painful listening, during which no one could hear anyone else speak, I asked the pianist if he could play some Italian music, which he did; and I was so grateful. Then I left the terrace to powder my nose. When I came back into the hallway, the young pianist was leaning against the wall in a perfect James Bond pose and asked if I would meet him later. I looked him straight in the eye and said that I was returning to the terrace and told him I had a headache. The two pianists alternated each night so that one night was paradise, and one night belonged to Dante's Inferno.

Taormina is a beautiful beachside resort, the wedding capital of Europe. So many couples come from Northern Europe to be married in this breathtaking place. Our ritual was to go to a little corner bar next to the Immaculate Conception Church so we could watch the weddings; almost every other hour, there would be a wedding. A Maserati would drive up with flowers in the back window. Flowers festooned the railings of the church. There were so many weddings that we rated them. We sat at the corner table, so we could get the best photo ops and take pictures. The wedding that got our ten-out-of-ten rating was the pretend Mafioso wedding. The young men wore black suits with pin stripes, white shirts, and black caps and had cigars in their mouths. They surrounded the bride, who wore a black lace dress with a bustle in the back and had a crown of red, red roses in her jet-black hair. There were no bridesmaids. They posed for pictures near the church in an ancient archway that had a large Byzantine mosaic of the Madonna and child. They were walking, no Maserati and yes, it was an amazing sight; but then, this is Sicily. How seductive.

Sicily has its own intoxicating spirit, and unless you go there, you will never understand it. It is a rich tapestry woven over centuries by the cultural threads from many invaders that formed an ancient and eternally powerful presence, nourishing and guarding her courageous and resilient people. "Thank you, Rosie, my dear mother, for saying, 'I always wanted to go to Sicily.'" Sicily loved my mother as much as she loved it. I would encourage you to go to Sicily. You won't be disappointed. It is its own miracle.

One of the waiters, Giuseppe, escorted us all over the hotel and loved my mother. Every night he looked for her, waited for her, and brought her a cosmopolitan. When it was time to depart, he took her arm and gently, with great respect, escorted her down the stairs. He looked into her eyes with great fondness and kissed her. They had a special bond, despite the generation gap. If she had been twenty years younger, they would have been quite an item. Then it was time to leave for Genova.

As our taxi sped along the autostrada to the airport, you could see Mt. Etna billowing smoke. The taxi passed what seemed to be an interesting building. My mother asked, "Is this an apartment house?" "No," the taxi driver replied. "That is the men's penitentiary." I must say, it did resemble a large boxlike apartment complex, and it had no barbed-wire fence or guard tower.

We departed from the Catania Airport and flew to Rome, where we were to connect to Genova. We knew our luggage was safe because we each had a carry-on, but the plane to Genova was delayed one hour, and Roberto was to meet us at three o'clock. I had rented a car in Genova to drive to our hotel in Varazze since we were not staying with the relatives; consequently, we didn't have the pressure of possibly missing a connecting flight. The question of the day was, would the mysterious Roberto would be there at the airport?

Chapter 14

Summer Time in Varazze 2008

After retrieving our luggage, we headed toward the exit, where I saw Roberto. He greeted all of us and spoke to my mother in the dialect. He said he had to return to work, but that did not surprise me. He said he would be contacting us soon. It was the first time I had seen him in two years. As he went through the exit doors, he turned and looked at me; our eyes met and I thought, *Who is this man?* We never really corresponded, and yet every May, he would send an e-mail asking when I was coming to Italy. I often wondered what would happen if I never responded.

We proceeded to the car rental area and picked up our huge Volvo station wagon. Roberto called it the tractor, and I called it the tank. The gods of driving were kind; it was an automatic. When we finally arrived in Varazze, I drove round and round, trying to find the hotel; but the car seemed to have a mind of its own and kept making turns up the hill toward Alpicella. Finally, I found the hotel and squeezed into a small parking space. This hotel was not San Domenico Palace. My mother had the room from hell; it had a small bed, with sink and shower in the corner of the same room. She couldn't unlock or lock the door; so finally, the hotel manager moved her to another room that had a toilet, sink, and shower in a separate room. Our room was small, but we had a balcony overlooking the parking lot and a peek at the city of Varazze. Later that evening, we walked my mother to a restaurant in the hotel; and there, wearing a wonderful dress, she held court, talking to everyone in the dialect. La scignua had arrived.

Anita and I walked the eight blocks to the center of town, where the beachside action was happening and all the caffès and restaurants were bustling with tourists. It was July, but even with all the crowds of people, we found a delightful restaurant, Lo Spuntino, across the beach and had a fabulous fish dinner. We talked to the restaurant owner, Antonio, and told him we would return the next night; and he graciously said he would always save a table for us. Afterward, we walked the passeggiata with the other people in town. It is a promenade through town to walk after dinner and greet your friends and to be seen. Every gesture, every word, every man, woman, and family is telling the same stories as they did a thousand years ago. Boy loves girl, girl loves other boy, other boy doesn't care, and then the story continues. That's the beauty of living; it doesn't matter how many times it happens. "It is what it is," at that moment. Well, Roberto, you did come to the airport.

The next day, Anita and I were having breakfast outside at the hotel restaurant, when we looked over and saw Giacomo walking down the sidewalk. I raised my head and in my special high-pitched cinghiale voice called out his name. Gia-co-mo! He broke into a beaming smile, walking toward us as we ran toward him. After lots of hugs, we chatted for a while, and then Giacomo assured us he would take us to see Lalla Nita the next day and agreed to be our driver while we were here. It was a relief to know I would not have to drive the "tank." Giacomo was a retired boat mechanic; and anything that moved, especially with speed, was his favorite.

Later that day, we had another surprise. Cousin Piero came down to visit us at the hotel. He never leaves the hill, but there he was. We invited him up to our palatial suite where we sat on the beds and gave Piero the only chair with a cushion. He apologized that we would not be able to stay with them, but Angela's aging parents were not well, and she was caring for them. Piero spent the afternoon with us and then returned home. Piero is a lucky man. Thank heavens for St. Angela.

Late in the day, we walked down to the store to get the ingredients for my mother's cosmopolitans. It was getting close to cocktail time, and we had still not heard from Roberto. While we were enjoying our drinks, the phone rang. Surprise! It was Roberto. Time had escaped him once again, and it was close to eight o'clock at night. He said he would like to take Anita and me out to dinner. Fortunately, in the summer, everyone eats later in the evening. My mother would eat in the hotel and happily hold court. He was planning to pick us up in an hour, and I thought I'd better get a look at the weather so we knew how to dress. I went out on the balcony, and it was beginning to drizzle. It figured. Now I would have frizzy hair. Anita and I went downstairs to meet him in the lobby, but he was not there. I looked toward the hotel restaurant; and there he was at my mother's table in his elegant business suit, on his knees, talking with my mother in the dialect.

Off we went to Varazze for dinner at our new favorite restaurant, the one we had found the previous night. We had a great time and caught up on two years of conversation, well, almost.

When we left, it started to rain, and Roberto had a huge blue umbrella to cover us. He opened it. "You never know when you might need an umbrella." I still have it. When we returned to the hotel, Anita went up to her room. Roberto and I stayed downstairs to talk, and he went into detail about his personal life and what had transpired in the last two years since I had seen him.

Originally, he said he had met Francesca in the first-class lounge waiting for a flight from New York to Milan. He had conversed with her and her son Brando during the flight. He felt drawn to Brando, since he didn't have a son. He and Francesca ended up together for about eight years. She originally was returning to Italy from the East Coast to take up permanent residency there. He said that when we first met, she was still in his life and had not really moved out as he had previously told me. He said she had emotional problems, and now they were finally living separately. Francesca lived in an apartment he was renting for her in Genova. Roberto said he had quit his job in order to save the relationship so that he could be there for her son. Brando had forged a strong bond with him, even though he had a father in the United States on the East Coast. Brando did not want to live with his mother, and this was a huge legal dilemma for Roberto, even though Brando had dual citizenship. Roberto was going through the courts to have himself declared a guardian for Brando, and eventually, he did. Since resigning from a huge corporation as the CEO—and yes, I saw the website of this international corporation— he formed another company that has become very successful. He is quite the overachiever in business, but not in relationships.

Roberto said he felt as if he had known me before, and I felt the same but had some misgivings. I wondered, *Was his villa my villa in Portofino, the one I coveted near Splendido?* He said he would phone me the next day and make plans for that evening. One of the hotel staff was sweeping the floor in front of us, and it was time to say good night.

The next day, Giacomo kept his promise and took us to see the relatives. Lalla Nita was looking good. As soon as I saw her, I said, "Il Papa." And she said, "Il Cardinale." Whoopee. I had not been demoted. After several hours, I could see that my cousin cinghiali, Giacomo and Anita, were getting restless and needed to roam; while my mother wanted to stay. Cousin Lorenzo agreed to return my mother to the hotel later. We went merrily into Varazze to wander around the shops. Afterward, we went back to the hotel, and there was a message from Roberto.

The message said it was impossible for him to come that night, but he would call. Giacomo, Anita, and I went down to the hotel terrace for a drink; and with a twinkle in his eyes, Giacomo asked if we had plans for the evening. We said we had no plans and we were wide open. He announced, "Well then, we are going to a festa in Albisola, about twenty minutes away." He always knew where the parties were: dancing, drinking, and eating. The cinghiali celebrate all the saints to the wee hours of the night. We had a ball.

At the festa in Albisola, they had a big stage with couples dancing ballroom-style. We decided that we would get up there and "shake our booty." The next thing we knew, the other couples had joined us. They thought it was a new dance from the United States. Of course, we were just making it up as we went along. Maybe it was the dance of the cinghiali. We had so much fun. Giacomo is a sleeper. As Anita says, "Still water runs deep."

The next day, Anita and I sat at a caffè and had a drink and thought about last night's festa. As we mused, we watched the children play, the seagulls soar, and the cars and motorcycles race by. During the summer, every town seems to have a patron saint or a Madonna to celebrate; and the celebration is always the same trinity: eating, drinking, and dancing. I noticed that a few towns seem to adopt the same saint. I guess one town can get permission to adopt the same saint from another town. Now that is really a true form of ecumenical cooperation. I wonder if the Ferro cinghiali can adopt a saint, or if there is a saint that represents the cinghiali, sort of like the lion represents St. Mark. Perhaps Angela will be our patron saint?

Summer in Varazze is just like all the other coastal towns, and the population seems to explode. It's not just tourists. There are bumper-to-bumper baby buggies, strollers, and children playing ball with their nonne; and mothers are everywhere. Yet Italy is supposed to be at zero population. Anita and I have a hypothesis: These children and families are professionally hired sort of like rent-a-family to walk in front of tourists so that people think Italy has a baby boom because it is supposed to be the country of *amore*.

As we continued our musing, we noticed that the seagulls in Italy seemed to sing differently than the ones in San Francisco. They appear to be warming up their vocal cords with melodious bell tones as though they are going to do an opera, singing the scales. I think that some of their operatic arias might on occasion rival Andrea Bocelli.

We came to the conclusion that the parking game in Italy is just like soccer. You need excellent hand-eye coordination in spatial relations, a nimble agility to handle la macchina, a creative sense of timing, and divine intervention with the rules to win the game. It is where you take a big car and put it in the smallest spot you can find without scraping or denting it. The Italians know how to park in spaces that don't even exist. They park diagonally, on the sidewalk and anywhere they can create a space. Sometimes they park parallel, but often they block other cars. Once I parked out of the way, diagonally under a tree, only to receive a note on the car window telling me I was blocking the delivery truck. When that happened, I said to myself, *I will wait for Giacomo because there were no other parking spaces, and he'll figure it out.* Parking is skill, art, intuition, and divine intervention. Picture this: the parking area at my Varazze Hotel had twenty cars plus four or five motorcycles but only nine spaces. Giacomo did resolve my parking dilemma. He figured that he could park half the Volvo tank on the sidewalk near the entrance of the hotel and the other part on the street. It was impossible, but he did it. Italians are so ingenious.

In Italy, if there is any logical possibility that something cannot be done, it will be done. For example, the Italian love of speed and attachment to cars and motorcycles make for a survival of the fittest in an environment that only the bravest can endure. The Italian hand-and-eye coordination at top speeds is literally a gift from God. To survive driving in Italy is truly an act of God. And since the Italians are directly connected to God, they don't just survive on the road; they thrive.

Chapter 15

The Round-About 2008

We were sitting on the balcony at the hotel in Varazze when I asked my mother if she could name the five stelle. She demurred, "No, because that was on your father's side." "But, Mother, you know Stella San Giovanni, where your cousin Maria Cipresso lives. Of course, you know where my father's mother was born in Stella San Bernardo. And just to refresh your memory, here are the rest of the stelle: San Martino, Santa Giustina, and Gamergna." My mother asked me, "How did you learn all of these?" I responded, "I've been driving around here for years while you were sleeping."

Then almost as if she were clairvoyant, she asked, "Wasn't Roberto supposed to call tonight?" I said, "Yes." Then the phone rang. It was Roberto. He had received a phone call that Brando had been in a bicycle accident, head on with a car near Florence, where Brando's maternal grandmother lived. Brando seemed to be all right except for a banged-up knee. Roberto said he would not be able to come to Varazze. And then he said, "I don't deserve this." Feeling nonplused and thinking, *So what*, I said, "Why go? He has his grandmother nearby, and you have to drive a couple of hours." He paused and then responded, "I'll call you after I get more information about Brando." After I hung up, Anita, my mother, and I agreed that he was either jinxed or was making it up. He reminded me of Captain Pinkerton, but I was not Madame Butterfly.

The Robertos of the world continue to search and never seem to find that special person, even when it is within their vision and reach. And if Brando does exist, I hope he doesn't fall into Roberto's pattern, another Captain Pinkerton, only younger, while another Madame Butterfly waits for his return, as there is no returning. It is not part of the Pinkerton nature. Their world revolves around themselves.

The next day was Sunday, and we planned to go to Alpicella with our cinghiale chauffer, Giacomo. It was the Madonna Del Carmine Festa. We joined Gianni Battista Ferro. Guess where? Sitting on the bench in the late afternoon sun, lazily chatting away, I wondered, *Where was my Luenzin?* "Have you seen him?" "No," he said. Then he looked up and pointed with his cigarette. There across the piazza, Luenzin appeared. I called out his name as I hurried across to see him. Two souls were once again reunited. Every time I saw those incredible blue eyes, we connected, and in an unexplainable way, I began to understand his dialect even when my mother couldn't.

We sat on the bench, jabbering away like old friends. As I looked at the piazza and the preparations, everyone was getting ready for the festa. It was late in the afternoon, and the mist was slowly climbing over the hills. I gazed up at the white marble Rock of St. Anna. It was beaming a message to me: "You're home." Then I heard the band and saw the men with crosses and the statue of the Madonna promenading along the roads of Alpicella. They entered the church for mass, and after it was over, there was a burst of sound that broke the serenity. I heard the roar of the motorcycles and cars as young people flooded into Alpicella for the festa that evening. They were gliding like eagles as they drove round and round, coming up the hills, gracefully and swiftly landing at their destination. I hugged Luenzin one more time in the piazza, and then he turned and disappeared into the crowd.

Anita, Giacomo, and I sampled the food from the festa booths and brought it to Giacomo's apartment. We watched as the long tables filled with people, and the music and dancing began. The sun was now setting, and the DJ's music filled the air, boom da-da boom. I began to move to the music, doing a sort of cinghiali dance by myself on the balcony in the dark. Suddenly, a spotlight flashed on me, and the crowd turned toward me. The DJ got on the loudspeaker and asked me my name. I called back, "Maria Teresa." I couldn't say Donna Marie because Donna means woman in Italian. Nonna

Antonietta was smiling down on me. The crowd began to chant my name, "Maria Teresa. Maria Teresa." I went inside to get a drink of water. The crowd went wild, chanting my name; and when I returned, they cheered even louder.

When I waved, the crowd waved back; if I blew kisses, they blew kisses back. It seemed as though my ancestors were there in spirit with me. I was with my people. It was toward the end of the evening, and the crowd was beginning to leave, and so I blew them a final kiss. I wished them all buona notte, went inside, and closed the shutters. Evita and Marilyn had lived again in Alpicella at the annual Madonna Del Carmine Festa. I was exhausted and elated; I wondered about Luenzin and how these magical moments occurred on the balcony in Alpicella.

The next day, our chauffeur, Giacomo, wearing his baseball cap in reverse as usual, drove the tank northward up the coast. Albisola and Sassello are beautiful beach towns and also are noted for their ceramics that have blue and white as well as green and white designs. Later in the afternoon, we had lunch in Varazze and ordered pizzas with pesto; and the more I tasted the pesto, the more slices I ate, until I thought I was going to burst. I suddenly flashed on the nightmares my mother had the time she ate too much of it. Toward sunset as I was watching the ocean waves, I could hear my stomach gurgling and rumbling really loud. It was so loud that Anita remarked, "Your stomach, what's happening?" I should have known better. I'm just like my mother.

We were sitting on the terrace, trying to decide what to do for the evening. The phone rang. Guess who? Roberto. He went into great detail about Brando's recuperation and his condition. Brando was now fifteen. When he first came to Italy at the age of six, he was in a language immersion school and did so well that he was now in a main stream Italian school, on track to be a scientist. He was living with Roberto 80 percent of the time and the remainder of the time with his mother. Brando spends his summers with his maternal grandmother outside of Florence. After Brando's recovery, Roberto then returned to work. He said he had just finished a conference call and was tired. He said he would leave a message for us at Splendido in three days.

Roberto was planning to show me his villa. He told me that I should wear very casual clothes, as we would be riding in an ATV, an all-terrain vehicle. He usually drives an Audi. He parks by a twelfth century church called Sant' Appolinare, named after a Greek martyr.

He takes the ATV to his villa nestled in the steep hills overlooking the Mediterranean seaside. He said that he was not able to be with us on the weekend but was available on Thursday, Friday, and part of Saturday. We wondered why he was always pulled away and speculated about other women, a wife perhaps, or other possibilities. Our many hypotheses about this mystery man became bedtime fodder for Anita and me.

As we drifted into slumber land on the night of July 22, the phone rang. It was Terèsa who excitedly told us that she was about to be induced. The next day, we told our relatives that they needed to come to us at the hotel while we were on baby watch, since we didn't get good phone reception up in hills. After about three or four hours of my mother speaking the dialect with the relatives, Anita's eyes glazed over, and we decided we would go into town to buy baby clothes. That evening was quiet. We stayed near a phone, waiting for news about the baby, just like waiting for our luggage on those airport carousels. The next day, we heard that the inducing did not work, and they were going to let nature take its course. No cancellations, just delays.

After we spent all day packing for Portofino, Giacomo came down and offered to take us to dinner. Then Giacomo suggested that we drive to the festa in Santa Margherita near Portofino, an hour and a half away without traffic. It was July, high season and height of the summer tourist crush in Italy. In addition, the road was two lanes, one in and one out. It would have been madness to go, as we were leaving in the morning. So I turned to Giacomo and said, "What else is going on here?" His eyes twinkled, and he looked across the inlet at a building. We could hear music drifting across the lapping, gentle summer waves, with lights glowing and people dancing inside. "There, there is music and dancing!" he exclaimed. It was across the street and on the same side as the beach, such a lovely setting.

We walked into the club. Anita and I took a table; and Giacomo, like a sentinel guard, ensconced himself at the bar with my purse under his arm in a headlock. Little did I know that my new curly do would call to the wild beasts, and before I knew it, I was a dancing machine. I was twirling, waltzing, polkaing, and tangoing. Each man who asked me to dance had his own quirks. The first man, who spoke only Italian, was amused at my novel way of waltzing. You see, I do not follow directions well, especially from strange men. After he returned me to my cousin, a gorgeous man, handsome enough to be on *Dancing with the Stars*, dressed all in black, took my hand; and we began to dance. I was wearing my Clark shoes, and my cinghiali hooves were all over his. He soon returned me to the table.

I made a quick trip to the bathroom but in my haste went into the men's room by mistake. I had to focus on holding the door closed the whole time I was in there. As I walked back toward our table, a young man approached me and said he needed a "hot American woman." Anita told him, "There are many at the local university." Then with the snap of a finger, another man grabbed my hand and twirled me away from the young man and into a frenzied tango.

For one thing, I don't tango, and even if I could, I wouldn't do it in Clark shoes. As we moved around the floor, the older Italian suddenly crushed me tight to his chest and tried to kiss me. I pushed him back firmly, and as I felt myself going under for the third time in this dancing lake, my hand instinctively shot up in the air. I locked eyes with the young man and gave him the "save me" look. He cut in, and as he pulled me away, the older man said, "I have a reservation to dance with you later." I looked him straight in the eyes and said, "I didn't know I was a hotel."

We sat briefly with the young man, whose name was Riccardo, and he shared some of his stories with us. He said he lived in Torino, and he seemed to me to be Romanian. Riccardo was beginning to make some forward moves when I noticed Giacomo turn his hat to its driving position, backward. It was the signal. It was time to get out of there. We jumped up, gave a brief farewell to our young man, and with Giacomo walked rapidly to the exit. Giacomo had seen something and sensed danger. As we neared the exit, both the older man and the younger man were hurrying to catch up with us. The older man was saying that I owed him a dance and was begging me not to leave, while the younger man was on the cell phone talking to someone in a language no one understood. It seemed that he was being given orders to delay us for some reason. Certainly, we thought, no good reason.

All my internal alarm systems were going off, and so were Anita's and Giacomo's. We increased our speed; now we were running. The men kept pace with us all the way across the street. At this point, I was blessing the fact that I had on Clarks because we ran to the jeep and jumped in. I was in the middle, with the gear shift between my legs. Giacomo never said a thing, just threw the Jeep into first gear, and we sped away.

Once we were on the road with some distance between us and the men, Anita observed dryly that Riccardo, or maybe that was his alias, was deficient in proper gigolo skills, especially those centering on discretion. It was a wild adventure we hope never to repeat. Thank goodness for our bodyguard, Giacomo.

Morning came, and it was time to leave Varazze and drive to Splendido in Portofino. We all piled into the tank, and my challenge was to drive past my nemesis, Genova. She sucks me in every time, usually into Il Centro, the center of town. This time was no different. She sucked me in again. Then I took a wrong turn and went into a tunnel. When I emerged, the tank somehow turned toward the sea side of Genova. I had never gone this way before. I was now going on instinct. Anita remarked that Genova had changed the signs to lure me into one of her prettiest areas. In fact, I discovered later that I had unknowingly driven past Roberto's business. At the time, I pointed it out to Anita and said, "I think that is where Roberto works." And it was. I drove part of the way to Roberto's villa, even though I didn't know it was the route to his villa, and somehow managed to get us safely to Splendido. It was a scenic drive albeit circuitous. On this route, we saw beautiful hotels, museums, and all manner of places to visit and things to do in Genova. What was Genova saying? Was she trying to tell me something? What was it? Why don't you visit me?

At Splendido, suite 108 was waiting for us. It was perfectly appointed as usual with champagne, flowers, candies, and a beautifully handwritten card welcoming us home. We unpacked, and with my mother resting in her suite, we headed for the pool. As we lay back on our lounge chairs, feasted our eyes on the bay, we heaved a sigh of relief and let the stress of the last twenty-four hours fade from our bodies. It was then that I realized how badly my feet hurt. I reported this to Anita, who sniffed and said, "Well, you were the dancing queen." "Oh yes." I sighed and closed my eyes.

It had been a few years since I had met Francesco and his brother, Lillo. I was drifting, half asleep, when Lillo came up to us, saying, "Signora Ferro. Signora Ferro. Welcome back. How are you?" After the pleasantries, he said that he was going to phone his brother Francesco to tell him that we had returned. I asked where Francesco was and was shocked when Lillo said, "Kentucky." Lillo was from Sicily. He worked at Splendido during the seasons from March to November and then, having saved as much money as possible, returned to Agrigento, Sicily, to be with his parents and family.

I turned to Anita and remarked sarcastically, "Well, we haven't heard from Roberto yet. Hum, there is that opera aria, *La Donna Mobile*. It should be called *L'Uomo Mobile*." The theme of that aria is that women are like the weather, fickle and ever changing. Upon returning to our room, I could hear the phone ringing. Was it Roberto? Yes, it was. He told me to dress casually and that he was taking me to see his villa that night. There was no way for me to dress casually, knowing that Roberto would be in a beautiful business suit, so I wore a lovely sundress in green with gold sequins on it. My mother, Anita, and I went to sit on the terrace to have a drink, listen to the piano, and wait for Roberto's arrival.

Roberto is about five feet, nine inches, with curly graying brown hair, laughing brown eyes, and a somewhat predominate nose. Originally, Roberto and his family were from Torino, not from Genova, although he had lived there for many years. He was dressed impeccably in a beige and tan plaid jacket, a blue shirt with navy slacks, and brown shoes. He had a wonderful smile that lit up the whole terrace when he walked in. He is soft spoken but very animated; he emanates joy and high energy. He came up and kissed us on each cheek and immediately went to my mother to speak with her in the dialect. Anita thinks that in past years, Roberto was so immersed in building his business that he did it to the exclusion of everyone else. She is usually right and is a very wise woman.

The four of us had dinner on the terrace, and then at about ten o'clock, we headed up to Roberto's villa. We drove up the route I had serendipitously driven earlier that same day. We wound up the hills carefully. At one point, a cinghiale and her baby pigs trotted across the road. It was so dark and winding, a scary ride. We parked the Audi at the church and switched to his ATV. We then entered a road with a precipitous drop so steep and at such a rapid rate of speed that I feared we would fall off the cliff into a dark abyss. I held on to Roberto in fear for my life. Finally, we arrived at a beautiful flat piece of land filled with grape arbors, blooming rose bushes, and lemon trees.

The renovated villa was simple but elegant. He called it Lille Bergan for Norway. He had worked in Norway for many years and loved it. From the veranda, you could see little flickering lights floating out to sea. It was the fishing boats, but they looked like lucciole, little fireflies.

He showed me Brando's bedroom, which was filled with every manner of things related to soccer. He was planning a trip to New York so Brando could see his father. I wondered why Roberto was so attached to a child with no bloodline to him and why didn't he have children of his own. He said, "I have never thought about it."

Both Roberto and I love music. He knew many songs, classical, American, Italian, and operatic. He also played the guitar. At one point, I mentioned opera and Madame Butterfly. He remarked, "Oh, Captain Pinkerton, he was not a very nice guy." We had long philosophical conversations. We had many things in common. He told me that his father was a baker who loved to make cookies called Baci di Dama, the kisses of a woman. So he knew how to bake and how to cook. He promised that he would cook dinner for me, and he kept his promise another night. He made the pasta in a pot, threw in some tomatoes, some pesto; and with a small salad and some wine, we had a beautiful dinner out on the terrace overlooking the Bay of Portofino. Brando's pet cat, Lucy, named after Lucille Ball, dined with us. Ah yes, lucky Lucy.

Roberto picked us up on Saturday. He had on jeans, hiking boots, and a polo shirt; and off we went to the Vortex, Genova. We learned so much from Roberto about the history and culture of Genova. Founded in the fourth century BC, Genova's name stems from Latin, *ianua*, which means door. It was an important Roman port. The Genovese are a reserved and very proud people. Genova was the first northern Italian city to rise against the Nazi occupation and the Italian Fascist movement in World War II. They liberated themselves prior to the arrival of the Allied troops. Roberto explained the psyche of the Genovese people. He said, "The people of Genova turn their back to the sea, put their arms around their families, and trust no one else." *Ah*, I thought, *this is very true.* I could hear my nonna Maria saying, "You only trust your family, no one else."

During our touring of Genova, we went to a museum where we saw some famous ceramics by an artist named Ferro. Later we walked down an alley and saw a sign that said Vico Del Ferro; and as we rounded a corner, we saw a Vico Del Rusca, the last names of my grandparents. Perhaps Genova had been calling to me, pulling me toward her. Genova and I had become respectful friends; I no longer feared Genova, nor was she the Vortex. She and I had made our peace. Maybe Genova was using Roberto to bring me to her so that I would understand my proud Genovese roots.

While we were exploring Genova, he took us to a sixteenth-century jail. We put on hard hats and climbed down into cells carved out of stone. You could feel the despair seeping out of the walls and imagine the groaning desperation of the former prisoners. Afterward we climbed up the steep steps to the top tower of the prison. Proud Genova was laid out below us, a mysterious empress that commanded the seas and once rivaled the opulent La Serenissima, Venice. Genova has faded; but it still guards its people, embracing them with an impermeable bond linking her families, including mine. The circle was strengthened.

Roberto said it would be an early day because he had to drive to France the next morning with some colleagues for business. He brought us back to Splendido, and we thanked him for the wonderful tour and said our farewells. Maybe getting lost in Genova wasn't so bad after all. I learned a lot about her, the majestic Genova, and Roberto. I learned that while Roberto identifies with Genova, he was not born there; he was raised there. He is just like Genova, humble with a soft but firm manner. His strength was simply there. He was a citizen of the world and seemed able to move within many cultures. His mind was brilliant and his thoughts deep. Like Genova, he had understated elegance and an inner fortitude of quiet resilience.

Later, after dinner, Anita and I sat at the bar; and I had one of my journals out and was writing about our day in Genova. I wondered what Roberto's big blue umbrella represented. I began to free associate: blue skies, blue Mediterranean Sea, Portofino, protection, and family. I knew Italy and my family would protect me for sure. I thought aloud that Roberto's umbrella was significant because it was round, never ending, like a circle. I said to Anita, "It seems like I can't come up with a title for this book. It's as though these journals and this book will never end." Signore Rossi, the assistant bar manager, then said, "Signora Ferro, there is no end. It will go on and on because it is *il circolo*, the circle." That was how this book was christened.

The next morning, it was time to return to reality. We went straight to Milan. Ermes had given us excellent directions. We returned the car and checked into the First Hotel near the airport. No muss, no fuss, no dents. At the airport, we went to the lounge, and the screen showed no delays. Hurray. Then I received a text from Roberto, wishing us safe travels, so I called him. He told me he had sent me an e-mail, but my phone did not allow me to access the e-mail, and it had to wait until I got home.

While we were sitting in the lounge, Anita went to the bathroom and came back with a red hue like a Sumatra Lily. I asked her what happened this time, and she said, "I mooned the Malpensa Airport." Apparently, as she exited the restroom, a woman had come up to her to tell that her dress was caught in her bloomers. She said that she didn't think the world saw it. Anita is such a trendsetter, always on the edge. Who knows what she will trend next—shower caps, mooning airports?

I decided to phone my daughter and check on the status of Alyssa Rose. Terèsa said that she thought naming her Rose after my mother had imbued her with such stubbornness that she was simply not going to come out until she was good and ready. She was going to be just like her bisnonna, her great-grandmother, stubborn; this turns out to be true.

Other than a little turbulence, we landed safely in San Francisco. I dragged my suitcases into the house and collapsed. The next day, I checked my e-mail. The subject line: Coincidence. Roberto and his colleagues were returning from France. Roberto had been driving nonstop for more than five hours. He heard on the radio that there was a huge accident. It was the middle of the night, and their GPS had gone out so they decided to stop at a hotel and ended up just a few kilometers from the First Hotel, where we were staying. He wrote that he was starting to doubt that this was just a coincidence. I thought perhaps he was like a round-about. You start to enter the circle of traffic, and sometimes you miss your exit and go around and around and around, exiting some place you never expected.

What about the babies? My granddaughter, Alyssa Rose, decided to wait until she had a full audience; four days after we got home, politely giving us time to recover from jetlag, she arrived on August 4. Anita's grandson, Nugget, is a boy; and his name is Keith. Both babies were right on schedule, no delays and no cancellations.

Chapter 16

Benvenuta Perugia! 2009

We flew in a "puddle jumper" from Milan to Perugia. I felt like an eagle with an incredible lens as I gazed upon the wondrous landscape of Italy. The plane was so small it hovered over the terrain, revealing a patchwork quilt of the Italian countryside. I saw the Venetian Islands; the Lake District, Lago Maggiore; the Industrial Milan with all of its apartment houses; the gallerias of Liguria; and the restless Mediterranean Sea, followed by the rich soil of its agricultural center. Then the pilot turned inland, to fly over the fields of rolling bales of hay and bountiful sunbursts of sunflowers, finally landing at the tiny airport of Perugia.

The taxi driver picked us up at the airport to take us to the Brufani Palace in Perugia. The driver, originally from Assisi, told us he was named Giovanni after John the Baptist. He continued telling us that St. Francis's baptismal name was Giovanni. He said that Giovanni (St. Francis) went off to war but returned safely, only to find that his beloved mother had died. His father, grateful for his son's return and to honor his son's French mother, told his son that he should be renamed Francesco, which translates to be "French man." St. Francis took the name Francesco, which later became San Francesco di Assisi, and is known worldwide as St. Francis of Assisi.

Who knew we would learn about this famous saint from a taxi driver, only in Italia.

As we wound up to the Brufani Palace, there was Josh waiting by the revolving door as if he knew we were about to arrive. He welcomed us like special old guests. Everyone remembered us as "the girls with the brown paper lunch bag." And they were amused to see real luggage coming in the door with us. Josh escorted us up to the same beautiful corner suite we'd had the year before. When we entered the suite, we saw a Perugian chocolate house placed upon a beautiful porcelain plate as well as a large bouquet of flowers and a bowl of fresh fruit.

After we unpacked, we stood on one of the balconies and visually drank in the picture-postcard panoramic view. One by one, the cathedral bells began caroling the hours. One set would ring, there would be a brief moment of silence, and then the next church bells would ring. It gave Perugia a magical air, as if they were announcing we had returned. It was wonderful that we had returned to this special place of beauty.

We made the same reservations as we had the previous year at one of our favorite places, La Victoria Ristorante. We went exploring to see what we could find. We sashayed around for awhile and then returned to the hotel to freshen up for dinner, only to find out that our key did not work. The old skeleton keys with their enormous tassels were gone, replaced by plastic magnetic key cards. How sad. Another piece of the old world had disappeared. A nearby porter came to our rescue and opened our door.

Later pushing through the festival crowds, we tried to keep close so as not to get separated, finally arriving at La Victoria, a fabulous restaurant near the main stage in the piazza. As usual, we had an outside table so we could watch the action and listen to the music. Giuliana and her husband, the owners of the restaurant, remembered us and greeted us enthusiastically. We once again told them that we loved the food. They remembered that my family was from Liguria and offered to make us some Ligurian food for dinner, even though it was not on the menu.

As we sat there, it became unusually cold, so cold that they offered to move us inside. At this time of year, Perugia is usually baking hot. Amazingly, the Victorian cameriere lifted our table; loaded with its candles, drinks, wine, and water glasses, salads, silver, and plates, raising it all high into the air; and ported it into the restaurant near the door so we could hear the jazz. Anita and I trailed behind this caravan of furniture, food, and friends, laughing. It all seemed so magically Italian in every way, and we were charmed at the simplicity of it: one moment chilled and the next inside, warmed and happy, all within about five minutes.

The dinner was exceptional, and as we were complimenting the chef and ordering our dessert of tiramisu, Giuliana was teasing her husband about eating too much of it and that he should not have any more. Later, while Giuliana was busy elsewhere, her husband came by our table with a portion of tiramisu and, with a twinkle in his eye, gobbled it down. We assured him everything was wonderful and that his secret snack was safe with us.

We told him we would be here every night, at which point he said he would save our table for us. This was very important because with the Umbria Jazz Festival being the hottest music venue in Perugia, a restaurant like the La Victoria with a view of the performances was very scarce and difficult to get. The Umbria Jazz Festival started in 1973. It is usually held in the month of July, although there is a winter festival as well. It has featured such talents as Wynton Marsalis, Natalie Cole, B. B. King, Herbie Hancock, Chuck Corea, Eric Clapton, George Benson, and Alicia Keyes, not to mention those that I have met, including Tony Bennett, Carlos Santana, and Solomon Burke. It is held in great esteem by those aficionados of the jazz world. If you've never been there, you are missing an incredible treat.

We returned to the hotel, and once again, the key did not work. As I was struggling with the card, Anita was telling me, the Italian speaker, to go and get help; but then a young man built like a body builder came by. I asked, "Can you help me?" He said he would try to open the door. As we talked, he introduced himself as Solomon Burke, Jr. I told him our names and then suddenly realized his father was THE Solomon Burke, "the King of Rock and Soul." I just love his rendition of the song "When Love Comes to Town," and he was the jazz headliner for the next night. Solomon Jr. was like lightning; he got us right into the room. I was so grateful. I told Solomon we were going down to the hotel bar and wanted to buy him a drink if he would let us. He replied, "It isn't necessary, but since you are going down to the bar, be sure to look for Rudy Copeland, the keyboardist for their group." I asked, "How will we know Rudy?" Solomon replied, "You can't miss him. He's black, and he's blind."

When we entered the bar, sure enough there was Rudy. We approached him and said we had just met Solomon Burke, Jr. upstairs. Rudy was charming, no airs at all. When he took my hand, he felt my fingers and proceeded to describe me perfectly, right down to my hair color, eye color, weight, and height. He said, "My hands are my eyes. I am not blind. I see through my heart. I can tell you have a good heart too." I was honored to have met such an incredible human being. Then I told him he reminded me of Ray Charles, and he broke into "Born to Lose." You could have heard a pin drop. If I didn't know it, the late great Ray Charles just made an appearance at the hotel bar and sang this song to me.

He told us stories about his life and the musicians he knew. He had played keyboardist for all the greats, including James Brown. He also talked about the demons that musicians had to fight. He was a wonderful gentle spirit, but said he was tired and had to go to bed because he had to perform the next day. Solomon Burke, Jr. escorted Rudy to his room at about one thirty in the morning and then came back down. As we listened to more stories, a man from New Zealand who had been eavesdropping came over to us. He was a geophysicist attending a conference in Perugia. He had come to the Brufani to have a drink after listening to the jazz.

Then Solomon Burke, Jr. said he had a huge suite with an open bar and invited everyone to his suite. While we were there, Solomon explained that the lock on the bathroom was broken because of a domestic altercation between the previous guests. The wife had a fight with her husband and had locked herself in the bathroom; and her husband had forced his way in, breaking the lock. Stories like this interspersed with jazz and singing went on through the night; we didn't leave until 7:00 a.m. Blurry, red-eyed, and exhausted, we were escorted by the professor and Solomon to our suite.

As we were crossing the lobby to go to our room, I saw our Perugian angel, Josh, coming to work. He commented that we were up unusually early. We replied, "We're going to bed. And these gentlemen offered to walk us back to our suite." Josh immediately offered to escort us to our room, noting that we had previous trouble with our key. And so he did; the men saw the suite and left; and we got some rest. Whew, what a night.

Suddenly, I woke up in a panic. I looked at my watch and thought it was two in the afternoon. I turned to Anita, "Wake up. We've got a hair appointment in one hour." The always sensible Anita looked at her watch, which had all the numbers clearly on the face of it, and sighed with relief, laughing. "It was only one o'clock." We looked at each other. What were we thinking? We were cinghiali; we weren't thinking. So we got up and began to beautify ourselves to begin our new day and new adventure. Ah, Italy. There is always a surprise waiting for us.

Our hair appointment was with Luigi, *il gatto of Perugia*. Anita had another young stylist and came out looking gorgeous as usual. I sat down with Luigi, who suddenly said, "I have to leave. I have to leave. I have a massage appointment." He handed me off to a different young stylist. She gave me the most creative hairstyle I have ever had in my life. My hairstyle is normally parted on the right and falls in a medium-length bob, not rocket science. First, she couldn't seem to get a vision for me. She combed it this way and then that way. She used hot rollers. She used the blow-dryer, combs, brushes, everything. She teased the top of my hair into a "rooster's comb." When I left the shop, I walked back to the hotel, saying, "Cock a doodle doo." over and over. Anita kept laughing hysterically and repeating, "I'll fix it for you when we get back." But an hour later, after more hot rollers, curling iron, spray, and even water, I was still looking in the mirror and saying, "Cock a doodle doo."

In all fairness, there might have been a reason the stylist was distracted. Luigi had often asked me if I would go out with him. So while she was doing my hair, I told her that Luigi had told me he was single and in good shape because he rode his bicycle from the flatland up into the hills to work. He would say, "Feel my thighs, feel my thighs." He had told me that he lived next door to his aging mother, who lived with his brother. The stylist laughed with the other staff in the salon as she informed me that Luigi was married and had been for some time. In fact, he had three daughters. His mother lived with him, not his brother, and his single brother was the one who lived next door. Finally, she announced with some gusto, "He left suddenly because he was late to see his mistress, the masseuse." *Ah, il gatto di Perugia*. Shame on you, Luigi.

Anita and I were laughing so hard, and we were so exhausted from the night before that we passed out in our room and took a nap. We woke up about 8:30 p.m. to the music of Solomon Burke wafting up through our open balcony doors from the arena below. We had wanted to go to hear Solomon, but the evening was bitterly cold, and we had reservations at La Victoria Ristorante. We got ready and threaded our way through the crowds to our table no. 15 at La Victoria Ristorante, looking forward to another sumptuous but relaxing dinner. After dinner, we went back to the hotel bar, where some of the bartenders who knew us from years before took a double take at my "cock of the walk" hairdo and laughed. We shared our story about Luigi, and all they said was, "We told you so."

After smashing my hair into the pillow all night and with much more effort on Anita's part in the morning, my hair began to look more normal. You could say it was "crestfallen." We went to a delicatessen not far from Tom-cat Luigi's salon because we were scheduled to be in an apartment in Florence for the week and wanted to buy some wine to take with us. We returned to the hotel, carrying bottles and bottles of wine. Antonio, the bar manager, wanted to know what we were up to. He went on to add, "You two are famous in this hotel." I wondered, *Was it my new hairdo or our escapades or both?*

That night, we returned to La Victoria and watched Guliana and her husband and their Sophia Loren / Marcello Mastroianni relationship. When we returned to the hotel bar, we met a couple from Naples who spoke English. They shared the difficulty of having a profession in Italy. In Italy, one is apparently limited to those professions that your parents or other close relatives had, which was Alessio's dilemma. The couple was thinking of leaving Italy because of their concern that even though they were pharmacists, they would not be able to work in their profession because they did not come from a family of pharmacists. Anita was engrossed in assisting them with their situation and giving them sage advice. I am sure the advice she gave was excellent, but we had been burning our candles at three ends and were truly exhausted. Finally, since it was three in the morning, we said buona notte.

There is something special about Umbria, its cypress trees stretching to the heavens, the sepia colors of the landscape, the terra cotta colors of the ancient buildings somehow softened by the Italian filter that sunlight passes through in this region. This same gentle Umbrian landscape, loved by so many for so many centuries, is the same one I hold so dearly in my heart that I cannot describe it. It must be experienced in person as there are no words to describe the sunrises and sunsets in the Umbrian summers.

The passeggiata is an ancient, ageless ritual. Here it was again, people walking with their children and with their pet dogs around the piazza. When I had first visited Italy, I asked Nonna Maria, "Why they did not have pets?" She had responded, "You can't have animals if you can't afford to feed yourself or your family." It had been a long time since post-war Italy when no one could afford an extra mouth to feed. Now Italians proudly walked their dogs, their cats sun themselves on doorways and window sills, and song birds are found on balconies on lazy summer days. Even the animals seem to have their own passeggiata and rituals.

The other cultural aspect that was so memorable for me was that even in the most crowded areas, people were incredibly polite to each other. During the festival, we twisted and turned as if we were a huge crowd playing tag. There were hundreds and hundreds of people; and somehow no one stepped on any one's toes, no one pushed, no one was rude. We were almost shoulder to shoulder even when we moved in different directions, but never touching each other. At three in the morning, we were simply there to experience the beautiful music and the moment. If there were such a thing as a "crowd bella figura," the Italians have created it.

We went back to the hotel bar, and Anita did her usual job of being "queen of those who wish to dump their stories." This time, it was a small man who looked like a cross between a gnome and Albert Einstein. He regaled her with the stories of all his marriages, infidelities, and travels, never asking her for even the time of day. She wondered how she always managed to attract these poor souls. Didn't anyone ever listen to them except for her? When they encountered Anita, they had built up such a need to speak over so many years that it was like a dam bursting, and the information just flooded out with no control.

The next morning, when I looked in the mirror, I saw my hair had taken a turn for the worse. There was a rat's nest on the top of my head. I am sorry now that I did not take a picture for you. I wasn't going to waste any more time in Luigi's salon so I began packing. Florence was waiting, and I could get my hair done there. We struggled and struggled to pack the suitcase until five o'clock to no avail. Since we were still in our pajamas and the wine was gone, we knew we had to get dressed and make our way to La Victoria for our last dinner in Perugia.

Near the end of our dinner, the waitress brought a glass of beer to our table. When I told her that she had made a mistake, she said that the man a few tables away had sent the drink. I went over to him to thank him for the beer. In his raspy voice, he insisted that he wanted to meet me the next day. I instinctively knew this is not a man to play with. I thought I had just met Tony Soprano or the Godfather of Perugia. He offered to take me to lunch the next afternoon. Repeatedly and respectfully, I declined, saying we had a car scheduled to pick us up and that we were leaving the next day. I returned to our table and told Anita that it was time to go. This was an extremely influential man, and the word "no" was not acceptable in his vocabulary, especially when he makes the offer. I certainly didn't want a horse's head in my bed or Anita's. We bid our goodbyes to La Victoria's staff with hugs and kisses. And, oh yes, when you go there, don't forget to order the tiramisu. Even though years ago I swore never to eat it again, it was yummy.

Like homing pigeons with their own rituals, we returned to the hotel bar, where the bartenders opened a special bottle of wine for us and toasted us, saying that we were family. When we paid our bill the next day, there was no bar tab. It was another Italian moment. Exhausted from our partying in Perugia, we gratefully climbed into the car; and Enrico, our driver, took us to Florence.

Chapter 17

My Appointment with David 2009

At first, the fields of sunflowers were spectacular, and then exhaustion tumbled in. We nodded and napped as if we were sunflowers heavy with seeds in the August sun. The trip lasted only one hour; and then we came around the last turn and saw the ancient walls, the towers, the shops of leather, pastry, and flowers of Florence. Enrico drove to the Oltrano District, which is not far from the Boboli Gardens. We arrived at an old apartment building that looked very plain on the outside but was surprisingly elegant on the inside.

Simply appointed, the apartment was large, light, and airy with hardwood floors, a rarity in Italy. It had modern-style furniture, a large dining room, a den, a large living room, modern appliances in the kitchen, one large bathroom with a Jacuzzi tub, and lots of hot water. The apartment even had air-conditioning. Agnes, sent by the owner, was there to meet us with the keys and a large platter of pastries, which immediately went from eye to hand to mouth. Delizioso!

After Anita and I explored the apartment, we decided to go grocery shopping; and everywhere we looked, there was the temptation of leather goods, clothing, pottery, and wonderful jewelry. We discovered a grocery store about three doors down from our apartment. The vegetables were so fresh the lettuce still had a little dirt in its roots, the tomatoes seemed warm from the sun like they had just been picked, the bread was hot and fresh from the oven, and the olive oil had the fragrance of flowers. We bought all our new friends, the groceries, and took them home. We put the food away, turned our radio to some Italian music, opened our wine, lay down on the sofas, and experienced the perfection of life in Florence. There was a party on the roof of the building across the street, and if we hadn't felt so content, we probably would have invited ourselves; but we stayed home.

As I said before, life is by appointment not by coincidence. The next day, we drifted out of our apartment about noon, still on Perugia time. We were ambling toward the Ponte Vecchio to go window shopping, when all of a sudden, I stopped. I turned to look back at the apartment then looked down the street and said, "Anita, this is the street where I parked the car four years ago in that terrible hail storm." We had no clue that four years later we would be renting an apartment on the same street.

We crossed the Ponte Vecchio where all the jewelry stores were located and went into the one where I had bought my fleur-de-lys earrings four years before. I recognized Benedetta, the salesperson for my earrings. She was petite, had brown eyes, brown hair, with a warm personality and a dazzling smile. She spoke with such assurance that one couldn't help buying something from her.

I spoke my best Italian to her; and as we discussed where I was from, she said that she had been to California, to a city with a street named Park. I exclaimed, "Park Street? Alameda?" When she said, "Yes," I almost shouted, "I live there!" She got all excited because her relatives live in Alameda. We chatted for a while and tried to determine if any of her Alameda relatives knew any of mine. And yes, they did. It was like six degrees of separation or the classic "It's a small world." Who'd have thought? It was all by appointment. I told her that I was looking for a pair of earrings to go with the lion pendant I had purchased in Venice in 2007. I glanced down into the case, and there they were, a simple pair of gold hoop earrings intertwined with white gold.

Meanwhile, Anita had become entranced by a huge golden filigree heart necklace that could be worn as a necklace or as a bracelet. Benedetta did not know the price of the piece and called for assistance. The assistant manager made a dramatic operatic entrance in a deep, commanding voice. Mario was over six foot, a handsome man with puppy-dog brown eyes, a Florentine Davidic nose, and blue-black hair slicked back. However, Anita reverted to her Spanish La Conquistadora style and decided since it was our first stop, she would think about the piece and would, perhaps, come back. I have to tell you that the operatic entrance was priceless and was definitely 18-karat.

We crossed the Ponte Vecchio and continued to explore, looking at the leather goods. I met a wonderful Italian man who owned a leather-goods shop, and for the next twenty minutes, we chatted. He said he enjoyed talking to me and that he would give me a large discount on whatever I bought. It was as though we were already old friends. I bought an attaché case at a fabulously low price. We hugged and kissed goodbye and wished each other's family well. I told him I would return. His outside shop was located not too far from the museum where Michelangelo's David is located. Was this the time to see David?

I decided, "Yes." We had seen the lines of people without appointments; they were blocks and blocks long. Every day when the museum closed, hundreds of people went away disappointed. I had asked the apartment landlady how I should go about getting an appointment to see the magnificent statue of David. She gave me a number to call. I began calling. I called and called and called. I would reach someone who would tell me to hold on, only to be disconnected. This went on for days. I called morning, noon, and night. Finally one morning, I woke up and announced to Anita, "We are going to see the David today." Yes, your assumption is correct; we had no appointment, or did we?

As we sauntered past the shops walking toward the Accademia (Academy of Art) near the Piazza S. S. Annunziata, I asked directions of the shopkeepers. "Dov'è David?" A boy went by on a bicycle; I called to him, "Dov'è David?" He told us to go straight, calling out "diritto" and then right "destra," and rode away. As we continued on, we began to see lines of people so far out that the Museo was not even in sight yet. The tourists were holding bottles of water as they baked in the sweltering Tuscan sun. Anita remarked, "You think we are going to get into the museum? Look at the line. We might be out sizzling and baking with the rest of them." I shot back, "Well, we are almost there. Let's give it a try."

We arrived at an intersection, and we wondered, *Was this where we were to turn right?* Suddenly, the boy on the bicycle appeared out of nowhere, calling, "Signora, destra, destra." We turned right, and there was the entrance to the Galleria dell' Accademia. We walked up to the guards. Using my best Italian, I told the guard my story. We had come from California, and seeing David was on the top of our list. I pleaded by telling him about all the art history classes I took in college and how much I love Renaissance art and history. Then I told him that I had seen David many years ago and had promised that I would return. I told the guard, "I have been trying to get an appointment and have been calling for days, but continuously was disconnected each time." Finally, I said, "I didn't know what else to do. So I just came here." He asked, "How many are in your group?" I replied, "Only two, solo due." Then miracle of miracles, he waved us in.

As we entered the lobby and ticket area, I noticed that everyone had tickets printed with a specific time. We not only didn't have a ticket of any kind, we didn't even have a reservation time. I approached the next set of guards and began my story over again, when I noticed that the guard was looking over my shoulder at the entry-way guard, who was waving to this new guard to let us in. And then in the space of three minutes, we were inside. We could not believe what just happened. It was like a dream with a happy ending.

In a state of shock, I walked past the other marble statutes in the corridor. My heart was pounding and full of emotion; it felt surreal. Something inside my head was saying, "I've been waiting for you. What took you so long?" It had been many years since I saw David with my mother and daughter.

There he was, Michelangelo's David. I could see the pulsing veins in his hands and arms, his Florentine nose, his eyes of determination and willfulness. It was an overwhelming sensation, the highlight of my visit. All else paled in comparison with this experience. This was not a fluke. This was not an accident. This was not luck nor was this a coincidence. David and I had an appointment.

We stayed there for hours, sitting and gazing and gazing up at this incredible masterpiece. We did not see any other works of art, as it was all about the magnificent David. Suddenly, they announced the museum was closing, and we had to leave. The appointment had been completed. My heart was singing as if I had met an old friend. It warmed my soul. I know that I will someday return, for I have a future appointment with David.

Wrung-out from the heat, we returned to the apartment to recharge our batteries and to revel in seeing David. It was now about eight in the evening, and I said to Anita, "Let's go eat where the locals do." She shrugged and replied, "Why not? It makes sense." We ambled down the street, looking at the marvelous architecture and beautiful frescos. We made a point to especially look at the corners of the buildings, since usually they had a statute or a fresco of a Madonna protecting the home. As we approached one of the corners and looked up to see the ubiquitous Madonna, we were surprised to see a bust of a man with a very white face, his head tilted, holding his nose, high into the air as if something stunk. The restaurant was called Tre Cinghiali Bianchi, the Three White Boars. Obviously a sign, welcoming us! We had a delightful meal. The restaurant was filled with the local people from the neighborhood. Everyone was table-hopping and talking to each other. As we ambled back to the apartment around one in the morning, we heard the sound of drums, tambourines, and whistles. We followed the sounds and found an impromptu group playing, while others were hooting, whistling, and laughing; it was just a Florentine neighborhood block party on a hot summer night. Why don't we have these in our neighborhoods?

In the morning, the heat wave brought the temperature to almost 105 degrees. That didn't stop us. As cinghiali, we wandered the streets and encountered a wedding. The beautiful bride was sheltered and shaded under a parasol. Her dress was white lace with layers upon layers of ruffles. She and the groom were leading a long procession of friends and family to a restaurant where the reception would take place. They filled the street with their matrimonial happiness. I thought, *Imagine all the weddings that have taken place in Florence. Oh! If those cobblestone streets could speak.*

As we wandered in the sizzling heat through the different shopping areas, we discovered the Caffè Carrazza and took shelter from the relentless sun. It was around three thirty, and for the first time, we switched to beer to quench our thirst. While I was the designated driver in Italy, Anita's job was to scout out the bathrooms. Was it unisex? Did I need a key? How did the flush work: a pull, by button, a foot pedal, or automatic with a timer? The timer is a tricky one. In these cases, you had a limited time to do your business before it either flushed or sprayed the whole bathroom. Yes, I've gotten drenched; and no, it wasn't fun except maybe to those who watched when I came out.

Anita sent me back to the bathroom in the Caffè Carrazza, and I was shocked to find a most fabulous young Florentine man washing his hands. "Mi scusi, Signora," he said with one of those impossible-to-resist Italian smiles and departed. Later as we left the restaurant, I heard someone calling, "La vita è deliziosa. Life is so delicious." And so it is, even in the bathrooms of Italy.

Next stop, we headed to the Basilica di Santa Croce, where Galileo and Michelangelo were buried. Some think that Dante is buried there, but he is not. He is buried outside of Florence in Ravenna, exiled even in death. Many, many artists, sculptors, composers, and writers are buried in the basilica. On the way, we were sidetracked by Gioielleria Aurea: the Aurea Jewelry Shop. We went into the shop, and before we knew it, we had joined the lady shopkeepers' philosophical conversations on life and how fragile it is. One of the women asked us what kind of wine we drank. I replied, "Bianco." Finally, the conversation turned to jewelry when suddenly one of the women asked us to wait and said she would be back shortly. In a few minutes, she returned on her blue bicycle with a beautifully wrapped bottle of white wine in the basket for us. We kissed the shopkeepers goodbye and savored the delicious wine that night with a toast to them. I always go back to that store each time I am in Florence. Now we are on a first-name basis with Sandra and Nora. This is the place to buy jewelry and also to make a wonderful friendship.

Fortunately, near the jewelry shop is the Basilica di Santa Croce. There was no line at Santa Croce, and once again, we were waved right in. As luck would have it, it was late in the afternoon, so there wasn't much time to explore. I immediately went to Michelangelo's tomb and thanked him for David. It was an exceptional visit because we were alone; and I was able to take Anita to each tomb, giving her the history of who was buried there and what they were famous for: Michelangelo, Galileo, Machiavelli, Foscolo, Rossini, Ghiberti, Alberti, and Bartolini. We thought that because it was so hot, the tourists had taken shelter in cooler places. Florence gave us the gift of being able to view the sarcofaghi without long lines of tourists. It was as if we had our own private tour, and we had the whole basilica to ourselves.

That evening, we followed the locals and stumbled upon Mamma Gina's Ristorante for dinner. We both ordered Mamma Gina's breast of chicken layered with multisauces, a touch of wine, and fresh mushrooms. Anita had a beautiful salad of mixed greens in a large bowl prepared for her at the table, and I had the Toscana white beans happily drenched in Tuscan olive oil. We were sated, spiritually and physically. Oh, Florence. She is magnificent in all her regal splendor. I cannot get enough of this wondrous city.

When we got up the next morning, Anita announced sarcastically that it would be a fun morning: we needed to do our laundry. We still finished the laundry in record-breaking time compared with our efforts in Alpicella. After finishing about noon, we left to go to the Boboli Gardens of the Pitti Palace. It was going to be one of those scorching summer days and would hit 107 degrees. You have to climb a steep gravel hill in order to take panoramic pictures of the Gardens. I declined to climb, as I was in a black dress with black sandals. Not a good idea to wear black on a triple-digit heat day. Afterward, when Anita descended, we searched for the costume building to get ideas and a theme for Carnevale. We could not find it and finally asked a gardener, who pointed to the unmarked building immediately behind us. The Costume Museum included Carnevale costumes and also many, many couture outfits, dresses, and shoes of current Italian designers. The costumes were wonderful and gave us many ideas. I added to my theme a floor-length sleek strapless dress, half black and half white, with a red cape and red stiletto heels. I will wear opera-length gloves, one white and one black, and of course my erotic black-and-white goat mask.

Later that afternoon, we stopped to get some money from the ATM; and my card came back, saying No Funds. Anita tried hers with the same results. So I tried again, and this time, the machine ate my card. I almost fainted. Anita decided not to tempt fate and kept her card. Smart move, Anita! There was major rush-hour traffic, the exhaust fumes were overwhelming, and the heat was still over a hundred. We were tired, grimy, and sweaty. I wanted to take a bath. Here we were, six thirty in the evening, no access to funds in triple-digit temperatures.

Thanking the travel gods, on my list of critical phone numbers including international numbers, I had a friend, Alfredo, a banker with whom I do business. I had a copy of my card, front and back, with me. According to the wise Alfredo, if you put your card in the ATM and get bad news, you should not put it in again. The machine thinks you may be trying to tamper with the system, and it will always eat your card. Finally, if there is a bank and you can go inside, go there before using the ATM. It is much more secure. Alfredo fixed the problem for me, but I have learned a very valuable lesson in banking, and that is why I am passing it on to you.

On a happier occasion, with the Florentine sun shining brightly, we needed to take out the garbage; and all we had were designer bags, so we really had chic and trendy garbage. We found the bin, but it was too high for us to open the lid and get the bags inside. Then just like in the movies, a dashing young Italian man appeared and helped to put our garbage in the bin. He simply stepped on the pedal to open the bin and threw it in. Ah! Italy! There is even romance at the garbage bin. As a garbage man's daughter, I can really appreciate his help. Complementi, signore.

We usually have no purpose or goals on vacation; however, we did this time: we wanted to find the perfect tie for Alfredo's help. On our mission to find the tie, we discovered the Caffè Gilli in the Piazza della Repubblica. It was established in 1733; the décor was aristocratic and elegant. Thank goodness it was early, and we were still presentable. Somehow the heat had not yet melted us. After we sat down, we noticed that "the David" actually worked as a waiter at Gilli. He looked at me, and I looked at him, and our eyes locked. I continued to chat with Anita as I followed the "Living David" with my eyes. Each time he glanced my way, our eyes locked. Once I gestured broadly with my hand, and he immediately came over. "Does Signora need something?" Suffering under the now intimate "eye lock," I astutely responded, "Huh-um, no." "Well, if Signora needs anything, just tell me." Italian men are so debonair, like the famous silent film star Rudolph Valentino. We continued to do the dance of the Paso Doble. He was the matador, and I was the bull; he would flash his eyes, and I would flash back my smile. Finally, even though we ate as slowly as possible, we were done, and it was time to leave. We paid and were about to leave; the waiter seemed to have disappeared, but in one last delaying move, Anita decided to take pictures of the pastries.

The "Living David" suddenly appeared at my side. He asked, "Where are you going? I have a break. Please wait a few minutes. I will meet you by the side entrance of the restaurant so we can talk." I put my hand on his muscular shoulder and shuddered from the electrical currents rippling between us. And then, with as much diplomacy in my voice as I could muster, I replied, "Oh, I can't. I have an appointment to get my hair done." He said in shock, "What?" His look of complete disbelief destroyed his savoir faire, and his bella figura was shattered. He could not believe he had been turned down. But a girl has her priorities, and I was looking forward to returning my hair to its normal style.

While the rooster comb from Luigi's Salon was gone, my hair was in great need of professional services, and it was my highest priority. The living David gave me an incredulous look. He couldn't believe that a woman was choosing to wash her hair instead of spending time with him. He was stunned. As we walked toward the hair salon, Anita turned and said, "I can't believe you turned down the living David to get your hair washed." In Italy, flirtation, romance, and love are always around the corner. There would be more, or as they say in Italy, "That's amore."

On the way to the salon, we found a men's store and an amazing Armani tie, the perfect tie for Alfredo, the banker. It was a solid deep blue, handmade of 100 percent silk, subtle elegance. I loved that tie; it was definitely bella figura. Somehow we were still on time for our appointments at the salon, even though we had detoured for the tie. Anita got the fabulous hairdresser again; while I got another one who was, again, rushing off to Rome for amore. With a cigarette hanging from her mouth, she styled my hair straight as a board in thirty minutes. It looked like straw. I had gone from the cock of the Perugian walk to a Florentine broomstick and lost the living David to boot. The gods of hair had been cruel to me on this trip. Oh well, better than the Ligurian pigeon present dropped on my head that had me washing my hair in the fountain in Santa Margherita.

We returned to the apartment. I curled my straw hair and was finally ready to go to dinner about eight thirty. Wouldn't you know it? Our neighborhood had a local restaurant named Camillo's. We mused about the Camillo of Liguria and the similarities of the two Camillos. In the wake of the Florentine Camillo's death, his niece now owns the restaurant. And in Florence, there is a quote above Il Ristorante Camillo's entry: "He is now slurping his spaghetti in heaven." And so they both are, our Ligurian Camillo from Santa Margherita and the Camillo from Florence. We gave several toasts to both of them.

We were on our best behavior and got to bed by midnight, because the next day, we were returning to Alpicella. I was hoping for an automatic shift in the car, since the last two times, I had driven a stick shift. I guess the third time is the charm because I got lucky, and the car was completely automatic. Hurray! The man at the rental agency gave us excellent directions and a map. Miraculously, we got out of Florence without getting lost and headed to Alpicella. About three hours later, we arrived. No bumps, no bruises, no major dents. Life was good.

Chapter 18

Il Nido—The Nest Alpicella 2009

I tooted our arrival, and Piero came out from the garden in his red shorts. It was about two in the afternoon; and I thought we had missed the festa this year because there were no tables, no chairs, no cooking setups, and no stage being built in the piazza.

When we went inside, Angela told us that we could clean up (remember, no hot water here), have some drinks, have dinner, and then go to the festa of the Madonna Del Carmine. We were lucky and had bathed with hot water in Florence before we left. So the festa was on, and the cinghiali would kick up their hooves that night. You could "festa" your way through Italy in July and August. Who knows, maybe that will be another trip for me and Anita, "the festa tour." Of course, there are other festivals in other seasons all throughout Italy. If there is a saint, there is a party. What a great calendar that would make. Maybe if I do the toilet guide first, I could follow up with the festa calendar. And don't forget the mask and designer shower caps; cinghiali are quite entrepreneurial.

Since we had taken our baths and had our hair done, Anita and I went down to the Baccere Baciccia, where Giovanni "Gianni" Battista Ferro (no relation, so say some of the family members) sits on the bench. Giovanni buys us a bottomless glass of wine. We sit, of course, on the bench and chat. Then we are brought up on all the news since we were there last year. Here is the news: people died, and people were born. That is the news of Alpicella. It's a very simple formula. I like it.

It was time to return to Piero's for dinner. We walked back and sat with the family on the terrace overlooking the lush green valley. We dined al fresco until about ten thirty, sharing the stories of our many adventures. Then Angela and Piero announced it was time to go to the dance. The population of Alpicella has a whopping four hundred Alpicellians and swells about another two hundred or more during the festa. In the piazza, we could hear the chatter and laughter of the carefree crowd getting ready for the dance. In Alpicella, the news had traveled fast that the "cinghiali girls" had returned, and many relatives welcomed us back home at the festa. Both sides of my family came to this festa each year, which makes it so special, and we danced our little hooves off. We even formed a conga line, snaking through the tables and on to the tiny piazza, not for the faint heart as you pound your hooves into cobblestones.

In the morning, we attempted to make our coffee without scorching our fingers or having the pressure in the pot blow the lid off. We were too embarrassed to ask for our modern coffeepot purchased in Florence. Yes, we cinghiali do have our pride in not losing face or tusk. In this coffee challenge, Piero is of little help, unless Angela is in the kitchen to supervise. Three points for Angela, zero, zero, zero for the Ferro cinghiali. Later that afternoon, Piero and Angela drove us down to Campo Marzio to visit Lalla Nita and the rest of the family, her son Lorenzo, daughter-in-law Mariuccia, and sons Maurizio and Damiano.

Everyone looked so sad when we arrived. When I walked in, I expected to see Lalla sitting in the kitchen with her apron. "Where is she?" With downcast eyes, they whispered, "She is in bed." No one had warned me. This was the first time I had ever seen her looking so fragile. For me, after my nonna Maria had died, Lalla Nita was the foundation of my mother's family, the matriarch.

There was a pall in the air, and Lorenzo's eyes were so mournful. I thought, *This could be the end. Would this be the last visit?* I cried inside and tried to be strong, but the tears were welling up in my eyes. Lalla Nita was my Il Papa; she was the pillar of stoic strength that everyone had always leaned on, had taken advice from, and had looked for her wisdom.

She had always told me that I should never allow anyone to see me cry, just like Nonna Maria said to me when I was young girl. I should have been a professional crier for funerals as I can really wail and could have earned a living at the same time. The problem is that I would have puffy eyes all the time. Not a good look. I mustered up courage and put on a stoic face, then dried my tears and walked over to Lalla Nita's bedside. Sitting on the bed, I drew her close to me, and then I called my mother and daughter back in the States so they could talk to her. I kissed her and called her Il Papa and told her that she should rest, but her Cardinale would return. It was difficult to say goodbye to her and my family, but finally we left.

What was going to happen? I knew she was in her late nineties. Would she die while I was here or soon after I returned to the United States? I could not imagine my life without her, and time was not a luxury that she had left. But fate had other things in store for me and Lalla Nita.

When I returned to Alpicella, I had a horrendous headache from my tears and sadness and, yes, puffy eyes. Angela gave me some medication for my throbbing headache and recommended that I have a glass of wine to deal with the stress. Angela always knows what is best. Anita and I walked down to the Baccere Baciccia Ristorante to get a change of scenery and to readjust my attitude. Later, Angela, Piero, and Enrico, a friend of Piero's, and his wife, Rosaria, joined us for dinner at the ristorante. We had risotto with mushrooms, grilled chicken, slices of fresh tomatoes and mozzarella drizzled in olive oil and balsamic, roasted vegetables and pasta with pesto and truffles, and sea bass with garlic and olive oil. To top it all off, there was a view of the verdant valley below us, dotted with terra cotta roofs. I excused myself to go to the bathroom; and on the way, as fate would have it, I met Lalla Nita's great-nephew, Andrea, and his wife, Katia. I had not seen them in a year, and they live in Campo Marzio across the street from Lalla and her family. Quite typical in Italy, they had renovated one of the old family homes.

Later, we all moved to the tables outside to chat and to dance, and then I heard my name called again and again. This time, it was Andrea's brother Piero, the youngest brother from the Vallerga side. I was swirling in my genetic pool surrounded by my family. Everywhere I looked, I saw features, gestures, and heard voices that echoed from past generations. We danced the night away, and I floated home in the cradle of my ancestry. And yes, once again, I was with Luenzin.

Earlier that evening at the festa, I talked to Maria and Gian Piero about whether Giacomo was coming. Then like clockwork, it was 11:00 p.m., and Giacomo appeared; he was just like Gianni Battista. Giacomo had his ritual of appearing at 11:00 p.m., Gianni had his benches, and the rituals continue.

After two days of "festa-ing," we thought we'd have some time to lounge around. Our precious Piero invited us to go with his friend Enrico and his wife on their boat to view the coast along Liguria. It is such a different perspective from the sea, with its lulling serenity, rather than the autostrada, with its frenetic, on-steroid, pace. We went down the winding mountain road with Piero's accordion music blaring. I had no idea he would park so far away from the dock, and we would end up having to hike a quarter of a mile to the boat. I was so grateful when I saw Enrico, his wife, and the boat. I could have kissed them, and I did.

Watching Piero board the small boat for the first time was quite an experience; I could see the fear in his eyes. He stepped from the dock on to the boat and immediately dropped down to his hands and knees. I found out later that he had never been on a boat. And yet this is the same man who raced motorcycles and climbed mountains. In contrast to Piero, Enrico's hunting dog was "captain of the ship," sitting amidships, enjoying the sea air with a big grin on his muzzle. As we cruised down the coast, Enrico pointed out a yacht worth thirty million Euros. It looked like a battleship, gray and sleek. It did not look like the usual yacht, gentle lines, soft to the eyes, opulent, and graceful. It had six floors, with one designated for crew members only.

Enrico told us about the incident that took place a couple of nights earlier. The owners were drunk and got into a fight over who would bring their yacht into the harbor. The yacht had a captain, but the owners told the captain they would pilot the boat into the anchorage. In the process, they crashed into the pedestrian bridge, destroying it and ripping huge gaping holes above the water line into their yacht. As we cruised the area, helicopters flew over the bridge and yacht, assessing the massive damage. We returned to the yacht harbor and had lunch. The conversation turned to the damaged yacht, and we wondered how much the owners' deductible would be out-of-pocket to fix the mighty yacht. And yes, this story made the evening news for several nights and was quite entertaining.

After lunch, Enrico and his wife invited us to their mini-villa. It is nestled in the hills overlooking Varazze, with a view of the city, the hills, and the exquisite yacht harbor below. July is the month to be seen on the riviera. Many famous musicians and actors cruise the riviera from St. Tropez, Monaco, Varazze, Portofino, and the Amalfi Coast. We can now say that we have chugged-chug-chugged down the coast of the riviera. After a lovely afternoon, we said our thank you's and asked Enrico if there was a short cut back to where our car was parked. Yes, he took mercy on us and told us the shortest way back to our car, and it was all downhill from there. Without question, we had another wild ride home up the hill. We polkaed down the hill with accordion music, and we zoomed up the hill with tango music. It was so sublime, and Piero is so funny. He is a treasure. *Lui è un tesoro.*

Morning came, and Anita decided to take a bath but had to wait two hours to get tepid water, although the water tank had been turned on the day before. Me? You ask? I took a cold bath, the night before, simply because I couldn't wait to get off my feet, and I ended up with cramps in my calves while I was freezing in the tub.

Later as I sat on the terrace, I could hear the pet white goat Bianca braying, the birds chirping, and gazed at the Mediterranean blue sky. It felt like home. What a transformation from my infamous first trip. As I sat reminiscing, I wondered what had happened to Roberto. Anita thinks that Roberto lives in another universe or time dimension from everyone else and that perhaps his world randomly collides with whomever it passes in the night. Roberto's entering and exiting orbits in my life were in juxtaposition to everyone else's circling orbits. In contrast, Anita and I cannot figure out how it happens that every year when I come to Alpicella, Luenzin always appears out of thin air wherever I am. It must be by appointment. It is certainly not by random collision like Roberto.

On our last night in Alpicella, we sat out on the terrace, bidding farewell to the relatives as they came by. Gian Piero dropped in with a couple bottles of wine. You could hear the quiet of the night being broken by our chatter, laughter, and good conversation as we melded and blended our family.

It was a beautiful evening without a cloud in the sky, and then at exactly eleven o'clock, Giacomo appeared like an Italian vampire. He lives in Bersorara up above Alpicella on the way to the Rock of St. Anna, a very isolated forested area where our beloved cinghiali roam freely. When I say isolated, I am here to tell you that it is so quiet you can hear a butterfly's wings beating. Originally, it was the Ferro home, where Nonno Antonio "Mazzetta" with his two brothers, Giacomo and Pietro, and his sister Teresa, were raised. The rustic stone home was eventually divided into four units. Giacomo and another family live there, and the other two units are vacant; one is owned by a doctor in Milan and the other by Cousin Piero. The road is unpaved with lots of rocks and deep gullies from the rains in the winter. Imagine what it must be like to drive during a torrential rainstorm. Oh, no, not for me; but if I did drive there in the rain, my luck it would get stuck in the mud. According to Maria, wife of our cousin Gian Piero, Giacomo had purchased the apartment in Alpicella for his wife. She had been ill for quite some time. He thought living in Alpicella would be a better option for her in case of an emergency, less time to get down the hill. Ironically, she could not take the sound of the church bells tolling all night in the piazza right across their apartment. Unfortunately, she passed away, and Giocomo kept the apartment and Bersorara, which is his favorite. He stays in Alpicella in the winter when the weather becomes too unbearable for him. On the other hand, I wondered, *Does he have hot water in his apartment?* Maybe Anita and I could take up residence in his unused apartment, but the real question was, did it have hot water? I smiled at him and said, "I didn't know you had an apartment in Alpicella." He said, "Come on, let's go." I thought, *This is by appointment, not coincidence.*

Like a bunch of teenagers, we all jumped into the two little cars; and in less than a minute, we were in the apartment, except for Angela, who stayed home, smiling like the Cheshire cat. She knew I was on a mission seeking hot water. Anita and I thought it was complete bliss, a five-star apartment. When the apartment building was renovated, this apartment served as the model for people to view as they sold the other four units. I discretely slipped into the bathroom, shut the door, and turned the tap in the tub. Eureka! Hot water! The Marines have landed. When I told Anita, she wondered if we could stay there. So I asked. "Of course, you can stay here," Giacomo replied. If he only knew we would be his permanent tenants in July. I'm sure this was a relief for St. Angela, as she would have fewer Ferros to take care of in the summer.

Giacomo's apartment overlooks the center of a small piazza (piazzetta) in Alpicella. From there, we could zoom down the hills to the riviera, shop, party, and generally enjoy the whole area. I envisioned great visits in the future. I was picturing Monte Carlo, a good hour and a half away in one direction, and Portofino, another hour away in the opposite direction. What could be more perfect? Joy filled the summer air, and the Ferros laughed and hugged. Then it was two in the morning, and we were leaving that same morning at ten.

OMG! Suddenly, it was ten, and we needed to go. I was driving toward the piazza when a garbage truck decided to pass me. It must have been a sign from my father because we were on a stradino (a very narrow road), and the truck blocked me from seeing the driver behind him. After the truck passed, I saw the other car coming. The driver was Giacomo. He had appeared in the morning. Not just at night. We paused, hugged with our eyes, and he said, "Remember, the apartment is yours. Come to visit anytime." Woo hoo! It was by appointment, our appointment.

On the way to Milan, there is a left turn out of one of the tunnels that marks the departure from the coast and goes toward the east into the central part of Northern Italy. As I saw the Mediterranean Sea disappear from the rearview mirror, tears welled into my eyes. How could this happen? All I knew was that now I had one part of my heart in California, and the other part remained in Liguria.

We dropped the car off at the airport and took the shuttle back to our hotel. We always stay at the same place because it is very close to the airport. It is clean, has a bar, a small restaurant, and that is it. As I lay there trying to sleep, I kept wondering why it was never easy for me to leave Italy. I know my grandparents emigrated from Italy in order to survive. I am eternally grateful for my American lifestyle, but Italy keeps beckoning to my heart. On my first trip, my father and I had made a pact never to return to Italy, but here I was again and would be again and again returning to the homeland of my ancestors.

The next morning, Antonio was there to take our luggage. He worked for the First Hotel as a porter. Antonio is a young, spry jovial man. The first time we stayed at the hotel, Antonio had adopted us and went out of his way to make sure that we got where we needed to go. He drove the hotel van, with me following, so that I could gas up the rental car. He had me follow him to the car rental return place at the airport so I would not get lost as I had before. He gave me sage advice about driving in Italy. He made sure that I was able to perform the mundane simple tasks all tourists must do. And he also made sure, just like Angela, that I practiced the phrase, "Scusi mi, sono persa dov'è l'autostrada?" Excuse me, where is the autostrada? This time, he told us that he came to work early so he could wish us goodbye. He had seen our names at the reservation desk, and he knew that this was the time of year we usually came. We wished him well, and he told us to have a safe flight home.

Having successfully negotiated our way once more with Antonio's assistance, from the hotel to the boarding gate, we boarded Lufthansa. We were so grateful to be on this flight because the plane was clean, had excellent customer service, polite flight attendants, great food and drinks, and the movies were recent releases. And most important, Lufthansa ran on time, which is critical for making connections, nothing like our infamous trip to Sicily on the "Dante Inferno Airline."

As we were ascending, I looked out the porthole and saw the airplane wing glistening in the bright blue sky filled with fluffy clouds. It still amazes me how a bolted chunk of steel can fly. It's beyond cinghiali senses, and that's okay by me. Some things are better left alone.

Ah! You may be wondering what happened to Roberto? Niente! Nothing! Sometimes we perceive things that may not be real or true, never exactly knowing everything, curious about some things, and accepting of other things we don't seem to care about. Why is it that we try to make sense of things that have no logic? Maybe the universe is teaching us a lesson that all things are not revealed or perhaps they are, but for whatever reason, we do not want to see them for what they really are or are not.

On this trip, we had so many days, evenings, and hours of laughter. Sometimes we could not explain the wondrous events that occurred. How was it that we were able to see the David, when the lines in the blistering sun were curling around block after block in Florence, or meeting Solomon Burke, Jr. just because I couldn't open the door to our hotel room? These are inexplicable and illogical moments, but somehow by appointment. When I am in Italy, something transcends the commonplace.

Thanks to the travel gods, once again, we had a beautiful landing in the City by the Bay. While I was deplaning, my cell phone rang. My daughter was picking us up. I hoped nothing had happened. I looked at the phone, a missed call. It was Roberto. What was my universe trying to tell me?

Chapter 19

The Apartments 2010

Gazing at Alyssa Rose while she slept in my arms, I had conflicting thoughts about my next trip to Italy. I knew that I would have my mother with me, but probably not Anita or my daughter. I thought it might be wonderful to rent an apartment on the Isola Giudecca, an island across San Marco, Venice, to begin writing my book. Perhaps I would also rent an apartment in Recco, a village in Liguria. In addition, it was important that my mother spend a week with her relatives in Stella San Giovanni, while I would spend that week in Alpicella. It was just the two of us, the non-navigator and her driver. Rose was thrilled to go, even though she had become fragile and needed someone to lean on when she walked. She was now in her late eighties.

We arrived in Italy without a hitch or a hiccup. As we boarded the vaporetto and sped across the Grand Canal, we could see the Isola Giudecca in the distance. On the island is a massive compound of buildings called the Hilton Molino Stuckey; our apartment was next door to it. The original owner of the compound, Signor Stuckey, used the buildings to produce grist mill until World War II. After World War II, the island became desolate and rundown, but in the 1990s, it had a resurge when international movie stars and famous personages discovered the island and renovated buildings and grounds. The Hilton renovated the mill and opened it as a hotel in 2007 and kept the ambiance of the island, maintaining the original brick structures.

Luckily for my mother, our apartment had an elevator in spite of only being two stories. It also had free vaporetto service, compliments of the Hilton Hotel, to go to and from San Marco. The apartment, filled with glorious antique furniture, had a huge bouquet of flowers in the center of the dining room table. Yes, from Roberto. He planned to be at the Genova Airport to meet us later the next week. The apartment was an all-glass affair overlooking the Grand Canal, with unparalleled views of Venice, the Piazza San Marco, and all of the boats and business of the Venetian day. When I stepped out the front door and walked down the small canal street, I first came upon the Hilton with all of its amenities, and then a series of shops containing everything anyone could want to buy. Isola Giudecca gave me a serene peacefulness that was different from the constant daily hubbub found in Venice.

I had just begun to explore the neighborhoods connected by the little bridges when I discovered a small shop where a man was making Carnevale masks. After watching for a while, I asked him if he would make a mask for me. The mask is baroque, with swirls of silvery and white sparkles, and is fastened to a carved handle about sixteen inches long. On the right side is a large red flower with vines curling around the top of the handle as though they were holding the mask tight to it. It is an elegant mask, and I can imagine a woman peering at a potential lover through it and flirting in that special way during Carnevale as only the Venetians can do. Now I had the vision of my full Carnevale costume, thanks to the Costume Museum in Florence; and this shop had given me another possible mask to wear, so I could change them for the different parties. Tutto a posto.

I was truly immersed in the Venetian culture because the island was where many Venetians lived and few tourists came. I began my day sipping my espresso, watching the Venetian boats conduct business, the flower boats, the UPS boats, the fruits and vegetable boats. The early morning garbage boats, both recycle and regular, had entourages of Venetian seagulls swooping while wearing their Carnevale masks in a Mardi Gras dance. It was like observing the inner workings of a watch; the timing, the rhythm, and the dance of life on the Venetian water were so intricate. I wondered how difficult it must be in the winter months with the cold and the storms from the Adriatic Sea. Of course, the Venetians had centuries to perfect their seamanship, and no doubt the rhythm of the Venetians remains uninterrupted. We could take a cue from the Venetians. When we have our first rains in California, we act as if we've never seen rain before and don't know how to drive in it.

It was one of those Venetian evenings that happen every so often and felt as if we were living a dream. My mother and I were having dinner in one of the intimate restaurants outside on the patio of the Hilton when we noticed a beautiful couple dining at a nearby table. They were having a leisurely dinner, dining con amore. He had movie-star looks: over six feet tall, tanned face, dark curly hair, impeccably groomed in a double-breasted suit. He was oh so continental in his style. She looked about twenty years younger, runway model looks, a statuesque six feet tall, two-thirds of which seemed to be her legs, which dropped out of a very short, body-hugging black dress. Her long blonde hair curled slightly as it rested on her shoulders. They began with the antipasto and slowly consumed many courses, including lobster, which they ate sensuously, licking their fingers, never losing eye contact. Then suddenly, they gulped down their dessert. He could not stop checking his watch, and she could not sit still. Abruptly, she jumped up and literally ran with him to a waiting vaporetto. He helped her board the boat and stayed there as her vaporetto departed, but did not wave to her as he stayed on the dock. I turned to my mother and asked, "Why isn't he returning to his table or leaving?" My mother kidded back, "Maybe he's got another hot date." Within minutes, another stately woman closer to his age, wearing a wedding ring, appeared. He then greeted her cordially with a brief hug and a kiss on both cheeks. Ah! The wife had arrived. I know this because I asked the waiter. Venezia is such a seductress. We had watched the Casanova drama unfolding before us, and we had ringside seats.

The next day, my mother and I decided to take a gondola ride and explore the canals of Venice. As we boarded the gondola, the gondolier asked us our names. When I replied, "Cognome Ferro," he yelled to a man wearing a beautiful white linen suit, walking along the side of the canal, "Hey, Ferro, here is your cousin." He pulled the gondola over, and soon my mother and the man were conversing in Italian, she in her Ligurian and he in his Venetian dialects. Would this have happened in San Francisco or New York? A taxi driver pulling to the side because one of their customers had the same last name as someone he knew walking on the sidewalk? I don't think so. It is the allure of Italy that life takes a break from business to live in the moment. Or as my father would have said, "The way Genovese beat the Venetians was to marry them. Better to make love than war."

Another late afternoon while my mother rested, I wandered down to a bench near the water facing the Grand Canal and San Marco Square in Venice. While I was sitting and writing in my journal, an elegant elderly Venetian couple strolled slowly by; they were on a passeggiata. The couple had an old-world elegance about them; they were impeccably dressed. The woman walked on the outside next to the water, holding on to the man's arm, balancing and supporting him in a protective but gentle manner.

As they neared me, the man suddenly stumbled slightly. The woman was unable to stave off his fall, and so I reached out and pulled him on to the bench next to me. They were effusive with gratitude. While he recovered, they told me that they had been married over sixty years. He had owned two stores, one in New York City and one in Venice, that made and sold fine clothes. This was certainly borne out by the way they were dressed that day.

They told me the story of the island. The island was decimated during World War II and lay ignored and dormant for almost forty years until the 1990s. A few Venetians built homes on it during that time, but no one was really interested in it until it was discovered by the international set and the Hilton Hotel chain. Now it has become an exclusive resort but still not well known to the average tourist. As the man and his wife said their goodbyes, he turned to me and said with a twinkle in his eye, "You're not really Ligurian. You are a Venetian." He took my hand and said, "You will always be my Venetian angel." To this day, I treasure this memory. Forever they will be the couple who symbolize true love in sickness and in health. They emanated bella figura.

For years, my mother and I had a ritual of getting our hair done, especially when we were on the move in our travels. We found it quicker to get our hair done at the same time. I made appointments at the Hilton Salon, and the hotel called in Fabio from Padua. To get to us, Fabio had to take a bus, two trains, and then the vaporetti. Fabio had his own salon in Padua but came to the Hilton on specific days. He was forty minutes late, but when we heard his travel saga, we understood; and my mother and I were his only clients that evening. Fabio gave me the most fabulous hairstyle. He took over an hour to cut and style my hair, and he named it the Masai cut. He twisted it, spun it, his scissors flew over my head in a way that has never been repeated. When it was over, my hair was glorious. In fact, when my mother came out from Fabio's masterful handiwork, all I could do was gaze at her new coiffure. She looked younger and more vibrant. Fabio asked me to sponsor him to the United States. Unfortunately, I could not, but he said that there was another couple from San Diego that might. I hope he got a sponsor because he will be very successful. We christened him with many kisses on the cheeks and renamed him Fabulous Fabio, "Fabio Favoloso." Our fabulous hairstyles were confirmed that night at dinner as people complimented us on our hair; even the waiters remarked. We felt like Venetian glamour queens, but tomorrow we would fly into the arms of its ancient rival, Genova.

Before we left for Italy on this trip, I had my usual conversation with Alfredo at the bank to share my itinerary in case I had any fiscal fiascos. He said that he was going to Italy with his lady friend. I told him that if he was there when I was, we would try to meet up and have some dinner. As luck would have it, we met in the Genova Airport. I suggested that Alfredo and his girlfriend postpone their train trip and stay with us. I had rented an apartment that was part of an old villa in Recco. It had four bedrooms and plenty of space to roam.

When we walked through the airport doors with our baggage, Roberto was standing there, waiting for me and my mother. We all hugged and kissed, but something inside me said things felt different. Remembering the gorgeous bouquet in our apartment in Venice, I thought maybe he was preoccupied with work or Brando. We loaded the baggage into the minivan and Alfredo, who was very practiced in European driving, followed Roberto, who was on his motorcycle, to the villa. Thank goodness for Roberto and Alfredo as the road up into the hills were screamingly skinny and snakelike narrow. The entrance to the grounds had an electronic gate with a code. I punched it in, and the gate swept open. We went down a steep gravelly makeshift driveway, and if our brakes had not worked, we would have been instant close personal friends with the other occupants in the villa.

We entered the villa apartment through huge hand-carved doors. Straight ahead was a living and dining area with a kitchen that opened on to a beautiful terrace with a view of the Golfo Paradiso (the Gulf of Paradise). A washer and dryer were in a pantry in the kitchen. The kitchen had no oven, which didn't stop Alfredo, who loved to cook while his girlfriend loved to sleep. Looking to the right, we saw a master suite for my mother with its own bathroom. Looking to the left, we saw a guest bathroom and another bedroom. We walked down the hallway and saw two more bedrooms and an additional bathroom.

At the end of the hallway was a family room, which could be used as an additional bedroom and a big terrace. The accommodations were luxurious, with a view of the Golfo Paradiso from the private terrace. Nearby were the tennis courts and the swimming pool.

That evening, we went to Rosa's Ristorante in Camogli, a small seaside town about fifteen minutes away. Reservations were difficult to get at Rosa's, but Roberto was able to get us a table for five. When we arrived at Rosa's, the owner soon discovered that my mother was fluent in Ligurian and had the same name as the owner of the restaurant; and we were bonded. The chef came out of the kitchen to meet my mother. He was the son-in-law of Rosa, the owner. They refused to let us use the menu but insisted that we just tell them what we wanted. My mother began by telling him about the dishes that her mother made for her as a child, dishes I never knew existed. Oh my, the food began to flow from the cucina of that ristorante. We ate, we drank, we laughed, we basked in the stunning view of Portofino Bay, and we savored the morsels that passed over our palates and warmed our Italian souls.

The stunningly beautiful town of Camogli has a harbor edged with little shops that stay open quite late in the summer. The beaches are pristine, and at night, lovebirds come to sit on the shore to smooch and nestle in the sand. The word Camogli in the Genovese dialect is Camuggi. Ca a muggè means literally "house of wives." If you think about Ca = casa = house, mogli = wives, it seems to make sense. Camogli is a romantic place, and in the summer, it beckons the heart and soul to sigh.

Our Chef Alfredo was inspired by the chef at Rosa Ristorante and every day went down to the local market to find the freshest ingredients for his dishes. He found the best shops for fresh fish, vegetables, and fruits. He even found an organic wine shop, where he bought bottles for a euro each and then was able to refill them each day, a local practice, for a few euros more. One evening while I was assisting Alfredo in the kitchen and he was putting together a dish with basil, he asked if I knew how the basilicas got their name. I didn't know, so he told me the story.

There once was a woman who cooked for a priest and was always looking for ways to make the priest's food better and different. One day she found some basil in the garden and decided to add it to the dish with garlic and olive oil. The priest summoned her to the dinner table and asked her what she had done to the food. She thought she was in trouble, but the priest exclaimed that the fish was wonderful and a miracle to eat. When she told him about the three ingredients she used, he said it was the holy trinity for food. As he was rhapsodizing about the taste of the fish, he declared that, in fact, some churches should be elevated, like the fish; and instead of just being called churches, they should be called basilicas because they are of a higher order. That is the story of basil and how the basilica got its name, according to Chef Alfredo. Don't you just love fairy tales and folklore?

Our week in Recco was one long party. We would get up mid morning and go out to explore the towns in the surrounding areas. About six in the evening, Alfredo's friend, the sleeping beauty, would awaken from the previous night's dancing. Chef Alfredo and I would be in the kitchen, music playing, lots of laughing and lots of cooking. In the evenings when Alfredo was not in the mood to cook, we would go with Roberto to Splendido, and my mother would hold court. After Alfredo and sleeping beauty departed, my mother connected us with a taxi driver named Gianni from Camogli, recommended to her by the Rosa Ristorante. He would pick us up about seven for dinner at Splendido. Gianni loved speaking the dialect with my mother while I sat in the back seat, enjoying the magnificent scenery of the Ligurian Coast.

One Sunday morning, eight o'clock arrived with my mother standing over me: "Get up. We're going to the relatives." I snapped and must have said something unacceptable to her because a few minutes later, I heard the door slam. By the time I got dressed and went out to check on her, she was nowhere in sight. I searched the grounds, the tennis court, and the pool area. I looked everywhere with no results. Standing outside, I heard the fateful sound of my front door slamming shut like a coffin for the last time. I was locked out! I had my new cell phone with no phone numbers. No keys! It was Sunday morning, and everyone had been out celebrating the night before as there is always a festa somewhere in the summer. Even the church bells had taken a break; the only sounds were the happy song birds chirping. I was not happy. How could she have gotten past the electronically controlled main gate? I searched for about two hours. She was nowhere on the grounds. How could she have disappeared?

I talked to the man from Milan in the downstairs apartment and brainstormed what might have happened and told him that I had managed to lock myself out. He called the fire department. They arrived with sirens blaring, waking up the whole compound. They were able to use a tool to get the doors unlocked. Their tool looked like a thin piece of black plastic. They kept shimming it back and forth in the crack of the door until it unlocked and opened. While they worked to get it open, I was sweating bullets that they would damage the massive antique doors, and I would have to pay for a new set on top of losing my mother. Miracles never cease; the door unlocked. No damage. The firemen came in to my apartment to verify my identity, and I showed them my car rental agreement and my passport. Then they asked for a tour. I was so relieved to get back in the apartment that I gave them a grand tour. Still shaking, I called my daughter in the United States in a panic. The nine-hour difference made it the middle of the night, but Bella (sometimes I call her Santa Terèsa) immediately figured out my mother must have gone to the relatives; and she was right. She calmly said, "You know Noonie. She's probably with the relatives. She went to Lalla's house." But how?

My mother was never short on brains. She had gotten a groundskeeper to call Gianni, the taxi driver. The groundskeeper took her to the front gate in his little truck and opened the gate when the taxi arrived. Within the hour, she was sitting in Campo Marzio with her relatives, sipping coffee and eating pastries, while I was in complete disarray. By the time the situation resolved itself, I was totally relieved and completely emotionally exhausted. I called Roberto to tell him what had happened with my mother and had to let him know that I was the only one he needed to take to Alpicella for the Madonna Del Carmine Festa. This was the last festa that my mother ever attended.

In Alpicella, Giacomo met me, Roberto and Lalla Nita's son, Lorenzo, at the apartment. I stood on the balcony and listened to them talking in Ligurian. Then I could not believe my eyes; there was Luenzin and Piero walking arm and arm toward Giacomo's apartment. I called out to Luenzin as he stretched out his arms, beckoning me to come to him. While Piero was saying, "Mi cugina. Mi cugina," I was blowing kisses to them. They were coming to visit me. I continued to watch Roberto interact with my relatives, including Piero and Luenzin. I looked down at the tables in the piazza to see all of my mother's relatives starting to arrive.

Roberto had another commitment and was not going to be with us at the festa. He always seemed to have so many extra obligations. This time, he had a headboard for a bed that Brando's grandmother had asked him to deliver to a stranger in Genova. Obviously, his attachment to Brando was extremely strong, and maybe it would be just a matter of time until Francesca moved back into the villa. He said he would come back in several days and take my mother and me back to the villa, which he did. We said our goodbyes. I went out on the balcony; and then he came around the corner, stopped the car, gazed up, and smiled at me. I looked at him, gave him a big smile, and waved; but I knew all that truly mattered was my family in Italy and those that I loved at home. I turned my back to the sea and went back into the embracing circle of my family.

Over the next four days, I became the "Julia Child" of Alpicella. Since Giacomo did not have an oven, I cooked everything on four small burners on the stove top. Here are some simple recipes that you might enjoy and are, in my opinion, foundational to Ligurian cuisine. Many of these recipes have been contributed by family and friends. Mille grazie!

Chapter 20

Buon Appetito! Recipes of Family and Friends

Pesto: Basil Sauce

This is a basic sauce you can probably find in any recipe book, but it is essential to Ligurian cuisine.

The basil is different in Liguria. The fragrance is much more pungent, and the flavor is stronger than what you can get in the grocery stores here in the United States. I recommend that you grow your own so that it is fresh. I grow mine in pots by the kitchen window.

Ingredients:
    3 cups packed basil leaves
    3 large cloves of garlic
    ¼ cup grated Parmesan-Reggiano or Romano cheese
    ¾ cup to 1 cup of olive oil, depending on the thickness you want
    ¼ cup toasted pine nuts
    Salt to taste

Directions: The best way to make the pesto is to crush and grind the ingredients by hand with a mortar and pestle. Finely mince the basil leaves and crush with a mortar and pestle; add the finely minced garlic, which you have mashed into a paste; add the grated cheese; and begin adding the oil little by little to mix all ingredients until they are thoroughly blended. At this point, add the minced and ground-up pine nuts. Blend all ingredients until smooth. Be sure to taste the pesto to adjust the seasoning. I recommend that you use your pesto right away. Fresh pesto is the best.

Pesto is a versatile topping. It can be used on fish, chicken, veal, vegetables, pasta, with oil and vinegar for salad dressing. I haven't tried pesto gelato yet; you might, and let me know.

Insalata di Bandiera d'Italia—Flag Salad of Italy

This is an easy recipe. Even I can make it! Use your imagination as there may be other ingredients you wish to add.

Ingredients:
> 2 large beefsteak tomatoes, sliced into 8 slices, ½ inch thick
> 2 fresh mozzarella di buffala (baseball size), cut into 8 slices, ½ inch thick
> 8 large basil leaves, plus some smaller for garnish in the center of the platter
> ¼ c. extra virgin olive oil
> ¼ c balsamic vinegar
> Sea salt and coarsely ground pepper

Directions: Arrange the ¼-inch-thick slices of tomato, top with a slice of cheese, then place a single large basil leaf on top. Sprinkle with balsamic vinegar and let marinate for 30 minutes, and then sprinkle with extra virgin olive oil.

This colorful salad represents the three colors of the Italian flag: green, white, and red.

A suggestion by my friend Deborah: chop all the ingredients into one-inch pieces, add some chopped red onion, and toss all of it with olive oil and balsamic vinegar then seasons with sea salt and pepper. For those who love anchovies, she recommends laying an anchovy across the top of the salad above but under the basil leaf.

Notes:

Another name for this dish is Caprese salad.
I am thinking of putting some on my facial wrinkles and my varicose veins because I noticed that the people of Liguria look very young, and they do seem to eat a lot of pesto.

Uccelletti: Nonna Maria used to call this "Little Birds"

Ingredients:
- 4 thin slices of veal scaloppini (1/4 lb. each) or pounded breast of chicken ¼-inch thick
- 2 oz. of unsalted (if possible) mozzarella coarsely chopped
- 2 oz. prosciutto (very fat) coarsely chopped
- 4 sprigs Italian coarsely chopped flat leaf parsley
- ¼ c freshly grated Parmigiano-Reggiano cheese
- Sea salt and freshly ground pepper to taste
- ¼ c All-purpose flour
- 2 tbsp. light virgin olive oil
- ½ c dry white wine, preferably Pinot Grigio

Directions: Place the veal slices between two wet sheets of waxed paper and individually pound them very thin, pat the pounded slices dry, and place them on a board; and if the mozzarella is unsalted, salt the veal slices and add pepper. If the mozzarella is salted, as is usual in the United States, then leave out the salt. Put ¼ of the mozzarella, prosciutto, and parsley mixture on each slice of veal. Sprinkle each slice equally with the grated Parmigiano-Reggiano cheese. Roll each slice of veal into a cigar shape. Tie with string. Spread a thin layer of flour on the board. Roll the uccelletti in flour to coat very lightly. Heat the olive oil in a heavy skillet on medium high and sauté until golden on all sides, about 8 minutes. Sprinkle with salt and pepper, add the wine, and lower the heat. Let the alcohol evaporate slowly, perhaps 10 minutes, stirring frequently. Remove the uccellitti from the pan and rest them for 5 minutes. Cut the string off, add toothpicks for wings, move to the serving dish, and top each one with the sauce from the pan. Serve hot.

Sauté diced celery, carrots, and onions with mushrooms of choice in olive oil add wine and cook to reduce for 15 to 20 minutes. You may finish the sauce with an ounce or two of butter if desired. Either serve on the side or drizzle over the platter of uccelletti.

Zuppa di Tortellini: Tortellini Soup

Just like Cousin Maria Cipresso makes in Stella San Giovanni (4 bowls or 8 cups)

Ingredients:
  1 ½ c. tortellini, 1 large breast of bone in chicken with skin (more flavor)
  3 carrots, chopped
  3 stalks celery, chopped
  1 large white onion, chopped
  Mushrooms, optional
  ¼ c. chopped, packed, Italian flat leaf parsley
  Add water 2 inches above the chicken and vegetables to begin
  Salt and pepper to taste

Directions: Place the parsley and chicken in a pot with water 2 inches above the chicken. Bring to a boil, reduce the heat, and simmer for 2 hours, checking the water level from time to time to make sure the broth is kept 2 inches above the chicken. Add the carrots, celery, and onion; simmer for another hour. At this point, you could add some Italian seasoning if you wish. A teaspoon would do it, rolled between your hands as you throw it in. Remember, you're being Italian. Now the vegetables should be soft but slightly al dente. Add salt and pepper to taste.

Divide the broth. Keep the chicken and vegetables and half of the broth in one pot and the other half, clear chicken broth, in a second pot. Throw the tortellini in the second pot with the clear broth and cook for 8 to 10 minutes or according to the instructions on the box. It can be shorter if the tortellini is fresh and longer when it is dry. When the tortellini is done, the soup is done. Correct the seasoning and serve with some grated parmigiano and a dollop of pesto in the center of the bowl. Pour yourself a glass of vino and enjoy!
For the first pot, with the chicken and vegetables, remove the chicken from the pot, remove the bones and skin, shred the chicken to bite size pieces, return it to the pot, correct the seasoning, and serve. Another glass of vino is warranted here.

Dolce di Crema: Sweet Cream

This is a basic cream sauce and can be used in a variety of ways so use your creativity.

Ingredients:
   For the Crème:
   2 c. milk, or ½ milk and ½ heavy cream
   1 whole egg
   3 egg yolks
   ½ tsp. vanilla
   ¼ c. sugar
   ½ tsp. lemon zest
   For the topping:
   2/3 c. sugar
   4 tbsp. water

Directions: Preheat oven to 300 degrees. Warm a small Pyrex baking dish by setting it on the counter with very hot water in it and keep it ready. Blend milk, eggs, vanilla, sugar, and lemon zest; set aside. In a saucepan, slowly stir 2/3 c. sugar and water until it turns golden brown and caramel-like. Pour the hot water out of your now-warmed baking dish and pour the caramel mixture into the baking dish and distribute evenly on sides and bottom. Pour in the milk mixture over the caramel lining. Place the dish in a rectangular cake tin filled with an inch of hot water. Place this combination in the oven and bake at 300 degrees for 1 ¼ hours. It should look creamy and custardy when done.

Note: Aside from being delicious by itself, this custard can be used in a variety of dessert dishes.

Note: Serve with fresh fruit in season such as strawberries.

Torta di Riso: Rice Casserole

Contributed by Susan Cecconi Jacoli

Ingredients:
   2 c. rice
   4 c. water
   4 eggs
   1 medium white onion, diced
   1 large clove garlic, minced
   ½ c. Italian flat-leaf parsley, chopped
   1 c. grated Parmigiano cheese
   ½ c. olive oil
   1 tsp. minced dried rosemary
   ½ tsp. dried marjoram
   ½ c. Italian seasoned breadcrumbs

Directions: Preheat the oven to 350 degrees. Combine 2 cups rice with 4 cups water, bring to a boil, cover, and turn off the heat for 20 minutes. While the rice is cooking, grease a 9 X 9 pan with olive oil and sprinkle all sides with breadcrumbs. Add 2 tbsp. olive oil to a sauté pan over medium heat and sauté the minced clove of garlic. Add 1 diced medium white onion and sauté until the onion is translucent. Meanwhile, beat 3 of the eggs in a bowl and set aside. Add the chopped parsley to the onion and garlic mixture in the pan with the rosemary and marjoram and sauté for a minute or two more. If the onions are now translucent, add them to the cooked rice and mix. Now add the three beaten eggs to the rice and onion mixture in the bowl. Next, put the mixture into the breadcrumb-lined pan. Beat the remaining egg and spread on top of the casserole mixture. Cover with the grated Parmigiano cheese and bake in a 350-degree oven for 20–30 minutes until a knife comes out clean.

Enjoy this traditional Genovese treat.

Figasette: Little Focaccia

Contributed by Maria and Gian Piero Ferro of Alpicella
Given to my late Uncle Tom and passed down to my cousin Anita

Ingredients:
  1 ½ packages of dry yeast
  1 c. milk
  3 large or 4 medium russet baking potatoes
  1 ½ lbs. unbleached all purpose flour
  Fine salt
  1 bottle of light olive oil or corn oil

Directions: Boil and skin potatoes. When cool, mash them finely. Dissolve the yeast in very warm milk. Mix potatoes with the yeast mixture. Mound the flour on a board, making a hole in the center. Pour the potato mixture into the center. Add a little salt. Mix to a soft texture. Knead into dough. Spread flour on the board and put dough ball on the board. Cover with a cloth until it doubles in size. It may take up to two hours.

In a deep pan, place lots of oil. Heat well.
Cut chunks of the dough into the size of a small drinking glass. Flatten the chunks to ¼-inch thick. Let rest on floured board for 10 minutes. Then drop chunks of dough into the hot oil and, when golden brown, turn the figasette over. Remove from the oil when the second side is golden brown. Drain on paper towels. Sprinkle with fine salt.

Note: Figasette is dialect for the Italian word Focaccette and roughly translates to "little focaccia." The French word is "fougassette" and is a specialty in Grasse and Cannes.

Biscotti: Twice Baked Biscuits or Cookies

Contributed by Cousin Anita from Nonna Antonietta

Ingredients:
- 1 c. butter
- 2 c. granulated sugar
- 2 tbsp. anise seed
- 1 ½ tbsp. anise extract
- 2 ½ tsp. Vanilla
- 2 c. coarsely chopped almonds
- 6 eggs
- 5 ½ c. all-purpose flour
- 1 tbsp. baking powder

Directions: Preheat oven to 375 degrees and prepare cookie sheets by greasing them or covering them in parchment paper. In a separate bowl, mix the flour with the baking powder; set aside. Then with an electric mixer, beat the sugar, butter, anise seed, anise extract, vanilla extract, and nuts then beat in the eggs one at a time. Now stir the flour mixture gradually into the sugar mixture; blend thoroughly. With floured hands, shape the dough into flat logs, about 2 inches wide and ½-inch thick. Bake for 20–30 minutes. Dough will have a slightly cracked top when done.

Remove loaves from the oven and let cool slightly on pans until you can touch them. Use a serrated knife; cut the loaves on the diagonal into ½–¾-inch-thick slices. Arrange the biscotti cut side down on the baking sheet. Bake again at 375 degrees for 7–10 minutes then turn them to the other side and bake another 8 minutes until pale golden. Transfer the biscotti to racks to cool completely. These can be prepared 2 days ahead and stored in airtight containers. They can also be frozen. This recipe makes about 5 dozen.

Rabbit Cacciatore

Serves 4

Recipe by Maria Vaccarezza Calegari

Submitted by her daughter, Janet Calegari

"Mom used to make this on a spring Sunday. I thought it was chicken and wondered why I could not find the wings. I didn't want to eat the Easter Bunny."

Ingredients:
  1 large rabbit
  2 to 5 tbsp. olive oil
  1 chopped medium onion
  1 chopped green bell pepper
  3 large plump peeled and seeded tomatoes
  1 c. sliced mushrooms
  1 chopped clove of garlic
  2 tbsp. chopped celery
  ½ c. red dinner wine
  Chicken stock (If needed)
  1 tbsp. minced Italian parsley
  A pinch of rosemary
  Salt and pepper to taste

Use a large rabbit cut into serving pieces. Using a medium-high stove, heat 4–5 tbsp. of olive oil in a heavy pan, add the pieces of rabbit, and brown them on all sides. Add one chopped medium white or onion of your choice and one green bell pepper, chopped and seeded. Also, add one clove of garlic, chopped, 2 tbsp. of chopped celery, a pinch of rosemary, salt and pepper to taste.

When the vegetables are beginning to brown, add three big plump peeled and seeded tomatoes, coarsely chopped. Then add 1 tbsp. minced parsley and ½ c. red dinner wine. Cover tightly and let simmer slowly on low for 40 minutes until the rabbit is tender. Add chicken stock if liquid cooks down. Add 1 c. sliced mushrooms and continue cooking for an additional 15–20 minutes.

Crab Cioppino

Recipe from Lido Christofani

Brother-in -law of Aunt Eleanor, sister to Maria Vaccarezza Calegari, who cooked this every year for the Peninsula Duck Club and for our family and holiday time. Serves approximately eight hungry Italians

Ingredients:
>   4 medium live crabs (you may have the butcher quarter them)
>   1 lb. prawns
>   3 lbs. clams
>   1 cup olive oil
>   1 ½ c. dry white wine
>   4 c. lukewarm water
>   5 cans of 18-oz. Del Monte tomato sauce
>   2 large onions, chopped
>   2 large plump tomatoes, chopped
>   6 cloves garlic
>   1 bunch chopped Italian parsley
>   1 tsp. rosemary
>   1 tsp. allspice
>   Salt and pepper to taste

Chop two large onions, six cloves of garlic, parsley, 1 tsp. of rosemary, and 1 tsp. of allspice; chop 2 large plump tomatoes.

Add 1 cup of olive oil to a very large pot. When it is very hot, add onion and garlic and cook well. Then add parsley, pepper, salt, tomatoes, all the spices, and 1 ½ c. of dry white wine. Keeping the fire high, add 3 lbs. clams. And when the clams open, add 4 medium live crabs and 1 lb. prawns. Stir well. The clams must open for the juice to drain into the sauce. Discard any unopened clams. The live crabs can be quartered by the butcher ahead of time.

Add five cans of tomato sauce and 4 c. of lukewarm water. Cover and cook 20 minutes at fast boil. Serve with garlic bread or sour dough. Serve leftover sauce, if you are lucky enough to have any, over spaghetti the next day.

Nonni Tina's Gravy

Mother-in-law of Eleanor Vaccarezza Cavallero

Tina used to make homemade spinach tagliarini and serve this with it. Delicious! Tina was a cook for the Artichoke Nursery near Carmel, California, for ten years.

Ingredients:
- ½ lb. ground beef
- 6 chopped chicken livers
- 2 whole chicken wings
- 1 large chopped onion
- 2 stalks celery chopped
- Handful of porcini mushrooms soaked in ½ c white wine for 30 minutes
- 1 tbsp. flour
- 2 tbsp. olive oil
- Handful Italian Parsley
- 1 tsp. chopped fresh rosemary
- 1 tsp. thyme
- 1 tsp. fresh marjoram
- 1 bay leaf
- Salt and pepper to taste
- 4 cans of 10-oz. Del Monte tomato sauce

Into a pot with 2 tbsp. olive oil, sauté a large chopped onion with two stalks of chopped celery and a handful of chopped Italian parsley, add fresh rosemary, thyme, fresh marjoram, salt and pepper to taste, and cook till brown. Add a handful of porcini mushrooms soaked in white wine. Add ½ lb. ground beef and the chopped chicken livers, sprinkle 1 tbsp. of flour over the mixture for thickening, and sauté until done. Now add two whole chicken wings, add 1 bay leaf, 4 cans Del Monte tomato sauce. Simmer 1 ½ hrs. Remove chicken wings and serve.

Angelo's Gravy

Served at the Peninsula Social Club (Angelo was a friend of Aunt
Eleanor)

Ingredients:
    1 ½ lbs. ground beef
    4 cans of 10-oz. Del Monte Tomato Sauce
    ½ onion
    4 chopped cloves of garlic
    1 ½ celery stalks chopped
    1 bunch Italian parsley chopped
    Porcini mushrooms
    1 can chicken broth
    ½ tsp. oregano
    ½ tsp. thyme
    ½ tsp. sage
    ½ tsp. basil
    ¼ tsp. powdered cloves
    Salt and ground pepper to taste
    Add a pinch of red pepper flakes
    2 bay leaves

Cook ground beef over medium heat; set aside. Sauté onion, celery,
garlic, and spices together in the same pan (without cloves). When
the onion is translucent, add the cooked ground beef back in, add
the mushrooms, then add the cloves; ¼ tsp. is the MOST you add of
cloves because it is very pungent and will overpower the other flavors.
Now add the tomato sauce and the chicken broth and simmer for 2
hours. Salt to taste and serve over pasta or gnocchi.

A note about stuffed zucchini and focaccia: I have not included my stuffed zucchini recipe because I never ever measure when I make it; and I know that each time, it is not a precise action. So if you want stuffed zucchini, you'll have to come to my villa as soon as I sell enough books to buy one. As for focaccia, the best in the world is Ligurian and is called focaccia col formaggio di Recco. It is exceptional; and if you were able to speak to my mother or my nonna Maria, they would tell you that it is impossible to make it here because it is dependent on the Ligurian air and the water, which is more different there than any other place in the world.

Final note:

These recipes have not been tested by me, but all have been passed on to me by my friends or family members. As you know, when recipes are handed down, sometimes they undergo a metamorphosis. Try, provare, whatever recipe catches your eye; and if it turns out the way you like it, feel free to change it to become yours.

My humble suggestion:

Get thee on an airplane and go to Genova, Varazze, Recco, Camogli, Santa Margherita, any of these places, and sample the focaccia. In the dialect, we call it figassa.

Chapter 21

The Zigzag Tour 2011

I called Anita. "I'm looking at the itinerary for our 2011 summer trip. Sit down and prepare yourself for a wild ride. We're going to zigzag all over Italy." She laughed. "Does this mean I have to have two carry-ons to ensure the arrival of our luggage?" I said, "Maybe, because first we're going to fly to Venice, then fly to Rome, then fly to Genova, get a rental car and drive to Alpicella, then back to Genova, then fly to Naples, take a hydrofoil ferry to Capri, then back to Naples, then to Genova, and then finally home to California." I heard Anita suck in her breath. "Are you kidding? Is this for real?" We became skilled at balancing precarious piles of our luggage with aplomb. We learned each flight is its own adventure, how to remain optimistic when the flight is delayed while trying to make a connecting flight. We learned to take our lumps along the way and to surrender to the gods of travel. We let fate take our hands and just roll with it. I always said to Anita, "Did you bring your carry-on?" It's our insurance, our rabbit's foot. As long as you bring it, our luggage will arrive. And it did.

We landed at Marco Polo Airport in Venice and proceeded to the Bauer Hotel. Gian Carlo was there, greeting us with open arms and telling us that our usual suite, number 156, was waiting; but if we wanted a different suite, we could have it. Anita knew we loved our suite for many reasons. One, as you may recall, it had its own very windy staircase, and we loved waiting for room service and making bets as to whether the waiters would make it up the stairs or would we hear a crash. We always knew they would make it. But if we were supposed to do the same, I can guarantee you the room service food would be all over us in a hot minute. Two, it had a walk-in closet I coveted and wished for in my own home. Three, I loved leaning out the window and talking to the gondoliers. The hotel staff always placed gifts in the room: Prosecco, flowers, candy, and little mementos. We could see people in the other old-world hotels across the small canal, and we would wave to them. It was our own special neighborhood. We felt as if everyone knew us, and we knew them.

Our surprise this time was that Gian Carlo had called the chef of the hotel and wanted us to meet him. The chef, Giovanni, was youthful in his appearance, perhaps in his early forties with dark curly hair and jet-black eyes. He was small in stature but very muscular, and he had a smile like sunshine. He invited us to please dine at the restaurant, and we told him that we would make reservations. I had a conversation in Italian with him. I was thrilled that he understood me, or pretended to, because he did speak English.

In our room, we opened up the bottle of Prosecco and ate the canapés. Now we were fortified and ready to visit our favorite shops. Anita, over the years of Venetian excursions, had become the queen of glass jewelry. We immediately went to her favorite shop, whereupon she became entranced by the beautifully handmade jewelry. The shop owner, who made the jewelry, filled us in on all the local gossip. With packages in tow, it was our first evening in the piazza to enjoy the people and some wine. We returned to the hotel to prepare for dinner, and there were gifts on the table from Chef Giovanni for me. One was a beautiful box containing the crystal head of a lion, the lion that protects Venice, and it reminded me of my beloved dog Moe. In addition, there was a book of risotto recipes collected from the 101 top chefs in Italy who cooked at the leading hotels. Chef Giovanni came from a family of cheese makers and is known for his Risotto al succo di carota, arancia e puntarelle. Obviously, he had to be an extraordinary chef, being featured in this book. Immediately, I made reservations to celebrate our last night, a grand finale for us with the chef; but we had several nights to go.

Now that I had the risotto cookbook, we embarked on a riso (rice) hunt in Venice. I asked a shopkeeper where we could buy some riso to take home. He directed us to a shop many bridges and canals from the hotel. When we arrived, it was chiuso, closed. We just kept meandering and thought we might find another deli along the way that would have riso. Yes, we did find a deli and bought some rice. It was within two blocks of our hotel, in the opposite direction from the original route given to us. We didn't regret one step of our journey through the back streets and alleyways in Venice. We saw things we never would have seen, such as infant specialty shops with baptismal gowns, silk shops with hand-embroidered blouses and handmade handkerchiefs; it was fortunate to take the "road less traveled." Now I know exactly where to get my riso in Venice, just around the corner from the hotel.

We were in Venice for four nights and would watch the construction of a huge stage in San Marco Square for the Casanova Ballet performance. We watched the dancers practice and finally saw the dress rehearsal on our final night. Casanova, the actor, was handsome and matched his role. While completely engrossed in the play, we realized it was eight-thirty, and we were due back at the hotel for our special dinner at nine. We called and told Gian Carlo our predicament. He pushed our reservation to nine thirty for us to have time to change, which was fortunate, because when we entered the restaurant, there was Chef Giovanni in full regalia, wearing his chef's hat; and all the waiters lined up with the maitre d' just for us.

We were ushered to our table, and the dinner began. Each plate was recommended by Chef Giovanni. It was an amazing two-and-a-half-hour experience. We felt like royalty. My memory of the dinner dishes has faded from all the wonderful vino; but I know the dinner included a wonderful soup, an exquisite risotto, and a succulent fish dish, followed by divine desserts. We said our heartfelt goodbyes to the chef and the staff. Ciao, Venezia.

The plane departed San Marco Airport, landing in the Eternal City of Roma an hour later. I hadn't been there since Bella had the offer to be the young Sophia Loren in a movie. We were going to stay at the Hassler Hotel above the Spanish Steps, a former Austrian Palace turned hotel, just like the Bauer in Venice. The room we had, I think, had been formerly occupied by Audrey Hepburn when notified of her Academy Award nomination. I had seen the *Vanity Fair* magazine picture that showed her on a balcony with our same exact view. The rooms are Art Deco in colors of red, black, and white; but the real beauty is being able to sit on the balcony and view the city at sunset. From the balcony, I could see the majestic Vatican City in all its splendor and pomp. St. Peter's Basilica, the centerpiece surrounded by ethereal landscape, is simply a wonderment of grandeur extraordinaire.

Across the street from the hotel was a trattoria in the Piazza della Trinità dei Monti, which we made our home for drinks and dinner. We met the owner, Roberto, who resembled Humphrey Bogart. We also made friends with his lovely wife and the chef. When I travel to Rome alone, I always make a point of having my dinner and drinks at this trattoria. The owner always escorts me to my hotel at the end of the evening. One evening, as the pianist at the trattoria was playing, Roberto sang, and I joined him in my cinghiale voice. We went from table to table serenading the patrons as the wine flowed, compliments of the house. Another evening, when I went to the ladies' room, the door got stuck; and I found myself pounding on it in the loudest way possible, hoping to get someone's attention. The pianist heard me and came to the rescue; but when he opened the door, he didn't let me out. He came in, shut the door, and came toward me. Luckily, Roberto saw what happened and came immediately to the rescue. When I returned the next year, the pianist was gone.

When in Rome, you must become a tourist, and that is just what we did. On a sizzling hot July day, we took a bus with a guide. It was so hot that Anita recommended that we wear a hat; wise woman, sage advice. The Hassler had some good ones. They look like white straw but are really recycled paper fedoras with a band that advertises the Hassler Hotel. With hats on and the scorching-summer sun pounding upon us, we went to the coliseum. The temperature was at least 107, and Anita's hat couldn't take the sweat or the heat; it was wilting like a parched flower. At the end of the tour, the bus dropped us off, at least eight to ten blocks from our hotel. My Italian internal GPS clicked on, and Anita and I started walking. Some of the other tourists, having no idea of which direction to take, asked to join us; and our little band of withering tourists walked toward the Hassler in triple-digit heat. Thank heavens my Ligurian GPS worked, and we made it back safely. Happily, no one had a heat stroke.

When we returned, two of the women in our group invited us for drinks. A quaint little place near the Spanish Steps had misters for cooling the air. The lesson here is that when you travel, you must keep your doors open because you never know who you are going to meet. During our conversation, we discovered that they had had the flight from hell, and their luggage had been missing for several days. Anita shared our philosophy that they needed to always have a carry-on because it protects the luggage, which always arrives when the carry-on amulet is present. We also shared Anita's philosophy that the suitcases seem to shrink because the clothes have acquired additional Italian air molecules that make the contents heavier, and this has nothing to do with what you bought or what you are trying to stuff into the poor overloaded suitcases. I love Anita's hypotheses. I think she should win a prize in physics and common sense.

The next day, we spent most of the afternoon ordering bottles of wine to fortify ourselves so we could defend our clothes against the villainous Italian air molecules. We knew we had to take a taxi to the airport in the morning and tried to behave ourselves that evening at Roberto's trattoria. Proudly, I am happy to report we did.

Prior to boarding the taxi, I channeled Mary Tyler Moore as I twirled in a circle, blowing kisses and promising to return to Rome. When I finished twirling, another taxi cab driver came up to me and said, "I love you, and so does Rome. Promise you'll come back." Every time I go to Rome, I throw my three coins in the Trevi Fountain; and every time I've done it, I've returned to Rome.

After a serene flight from Rome to Genova, we got the rental car, a small SUV. It was perfect; it was an automatic. As we drove across a narrow bridge, a car came the other way. I moved toward the guardrail, and whack. There was another scrape, but nothing like Siena. Thank goodness I always have insurance. Upon arriving in Alpicella, we noticed that in spite of the altitude, we had brought the heat wave from Rome with us. Giacomo helped us unload our luggage into his apartment, and then we took up residence downstairs at the little bar and sipped wine.

It was even hotter the next day. Giacomo decided to cancel our plans. He didn't want to drive to Savona, a beautiful seaport city twenty minutes north of us. He went home instead, to cook frittatas, one for us and one to bring to Gian Piero and Maria's for dinner that evening. We wondered why he was going to cook in the heat wave. No rational explanation on his cinghiale thinking, but like the men of Alpicella, we sat on the benches.

We met two men sitting near us on the bench. One was a chicken salesman, named Mazzetto; and the other one, Carlo, was retired from the steel industry, with a wife who was still working. They were engaging in the age-old pastime of "shooting the breeze in the afternoon" with a small glass of wine. I looked at these conversations as an opportunity to practice my Italian and learn more about Italy and its culture and mores. Then, as they bought us more glasses of wine, the chicken salesman said he wanted to give me a gift, a baby chicken. I explained that I wouldn't be able to get the chicken on the plane, so he offered to give me a puppy from his farm in Alpicella. He had obviously never flown a day in his life and just didn't understand why I couldn't take an animal back to the States on the plane. He was impressed because I was speaking the dialect, and that's why he wanted to give me the live gifts. It was great fun, and they were very gracious gentlemen.

Giacomo returned with his two frittatas, made with zucchini, breadcrumbs, eggs, and parmesan cheese. We went back to the apartment to eat with him and share our adventure about the chicken salesman; and afterward, we walked up the cobblestone road to Gian Piero and Maria's for dinner and delicious homemade wine. We weren't very hungry, but we loved the company and the conversation.

When we left, Giacomo announced we should go to a guitar festa at Cogoleto. It was now eleven at night. When we arrived well over an hour later, the guitarists were playing American rock music. Wow, we thought, this is great; but within a short time, it was over. Giacomo thought the night was young, turned his baseball cap around backward, and said, "Now that it's over, let's try a different road to go home." We wondered what that meant. The desolate road was in utter and complete darkness. Giacomo was driving at breakneck speed on hairpin turns with brief stops to let the cinghiali cross the road. He had music blaring into the darkness, another polka. This did not calm our nerves. We were convinced we were going to die or at least wet our pants.

Once in the distance, I saw some lights. They turned out to be from a monastery. Where were we? It was all forest, no houses, nothing but a black abyss. It seemed like we were driving for hours, and just as we were reaching the heights of our anxiety, there were the lights of Alpicella, twinkling in the distance. We were home, safe and sound. I kissed the wall of the apartment. We were so pumped with adrenalin that we sat and had some wine to calm us down so we could sleep. Usually, no one sleeps in Alpicella because the church bells are right there ringing every fifteen minutes, but that night from sheer fear and exhaustion, we slept soundly.

It was now the weekend of the festa. The long tables; the chairs; the booth for tickets; and, near the restaurant outside, the cooking area were being prepared where they make the Figasette. A small stage was being built for the DJ. All this was visible from the best seat in the house, the balcony at Giacomo's apartment.

Later Sunday afternoon, we went and joined the procession with the crosses, the small band, the priest, and the Alpicellians. This would be the first time we walked in the procession with the Ferro cousins just as our nonni (grandfathers) did with all of their relatives. One of the young men carrying one of the crosses was the same young boy I had seen walking along the side of the procession for many years. I had watched him grow into a man, now in his mid twenties. Then to add to our Ferro genetic pool, we had a surprise. Giuseppe Ferro, a cousin we had never met, joined us in the procession; he is the brother of Gian Piero.

When we returned to the church for mass at the end of the procession, all the Ferros sat together. It was amazing to think that the grandchildren of three brothers—Antonio, Pietro, and Giacomo— were together for the first time and sitting in the same church for mass at the festa. Antonio, my nonno, was the first child baptized in the new church on December 27, 1883, two days after the church was consecrated on Christmas Day. I was so elated I had made sure to have my camera, and I took a rare picture of the Ferro clan. Then the celebration began, the music played, and I was immersed in my family and felt surrounded by love and belonging. When I'm really old and frail, I will remember Alpicella and its festa, and it will always put a smile on my face. But now it was time to continue our zigzag tour and fly from Genova to Napoli.

In the morning, we wound down the hill to Genova and on to Napoli to catch the ferry to Capri. We did not have time to stay in Naples on this trip. Among the things we missed and will put on the list for another trip was the Naples National Archeological Museum established in 1585, which has a collection of artifacts from Pompeii. The museum also has one of the world's best collections of Greek and Roman artifacts. We understand that the underground walking tour, called "Napoli Sotteranea," includes ruins from Greek and Roman times. Under the San Lorenzo Maggiore Church are the ruins of a Roman market. Napoli is noted for its hand-carved Nativity scenes. While pizza is not necessarily an ancient artifact, it was created in Naples, as was their world-famous Margherita Pizza named for Queen Margherita and commissioned by the Royal Palace of Capodimonte. If you have the opportunity, take a trip to Napoli and don't forget to order a Margherita pizza.

When we neared the Port of Naples, our taxi driver told us to take off our jewelry and put it in a safe place. The driver also told us not to linger and to get a ticket immediately for the ferry that was leaving very soon. He said, "I will wait to see that you get safely on the ferry, and then I will leave. Recently, we had trouble here." It was like having a taxi angel guarding us. I got the tickets and gave the taxi driver a big wave, and off we went to Capri.

The Isle of Capri was swarming with crowds of tourists. The only cars were the white open-air mini-taxis. The hotel staff was there at the dock to pick up our luggage. We went separate from our luggage and had our own taxi to take us up the winding hill because the taxis are too small to accommodate both passengers and luggage. Upon arriving, we saw one of the most breathtaking hotels, the Quisisana Hotel. The hotel was built in 1845 as a sanatorium, and its name means "Here one heals." Our sunlit suite was understated elegance with its white walls, white marble floors, and sea blue and white furnishings that emphasized the sapphire blue of the sea we could view through the floor-to-ceiling windows.

That evening while at the bar, we saw the "Toreador Act," an older woman with money and a younger man paying homage to her. She was upset with him, and the scene was quite dramatic. They were the center of attention, and the whole bar their audience. She ordered him around; and he scurried quickly, trying to please her without success, as if she had a tight leash around his neck. We wondered what was this all about; relationships can be so complex.

The next morning at the buffet breakfast, the young bull from the previous evening entered alone, looking quite sheepish, disheveled, and hung over. We wondered if there might be a subsequent show later that evening, but alas, we didn't see them together again. I wonder if he got stuck with the hotel and bar bill. Ouch!

While we were exploring the shops, I practiced my Italian. I asked the local shopkeepers what Capri was like in the winter months. Some of the locals said that it can be quite foggy and cold in the winter, but hey it's not like Buffalo, New York. Many of the stores carried famous designer labels such as Alberta Ferretti, Dolce & Gabanna, Ferragamo, Prada, and Loro Piana, to name a few. The shopping areas of Capri looked like the inside of *Vogue* magazine brought to life. In our wanderings, we came across an art gallery where a Ligurian woman had made mosaics from tiny pieces of glass. Her study had been the mosaics of the Vatican. She was amazing in her dedication to a precise and intricate form of art. Her passion was exhibited by the beauty of her mosaics.

One of the things that this island is noted for is its handmade sandals, and there are lots of sandal shops. They measure your foot, and you select the materials. I bought sandals that were made within an hour. Years ago, on a previous trip to Capri with my mother and daughter, there was a shoemaker who had made espadrilles for Jackie Kennedy Onassis. He had photographs of himself with Jackie O, posted along with other celebrities. I bought a pair of espadrilles made of deer skin. To this day, they are comfortable, and I love wearing them in the summer. Geppetto would be proud of the shoemakers on the Isle of Capri.

That evening, we discovered the Palm Restaurant, a beautiful place elevated above the street, landscaped with palm trees wrapped with tiny twinkling lights. The staff was gracious and full of joy, and exuded professional pride in their work. Capri is like a rare jewel; the summer breeze is so sensuous, and the people are kind and gentle. I wish we could bottle and sell Capri as a potion to sprinkle on those who are negative and obnoxious, transforming them into lighthearted and enchanting Capresians.

When I talked to the local people who live in Capri, they always expressed their love for this island. I was told this repeatedly from the people in the stores as well as the hair dresser. They told me they had been there for generations, just like Alpicella. Capri is its people. Capri is simply a seductive synonym for love and happiness. The Capresi have a proud, close-knit community like the Ligurians. Yes, they work hard but are grateful to live on such a spectacularly beautiful island.

The next day, we explored the grounds of the hotel and noticed the workers were preparing for a wedding. I asked the security staff what was going on, and he told me there was to be a wedding for some royals of Italy marrying some royals of England. We hung around and got to see the wedding, and I even took pictures of the bridal party. The bride wore an exquisite Italian gown with simple lines, and the groom was in a perfect Ascot. The English women were wearing wonderful gowns with fascinators in their hair; while the Italian women were draped with colorful Dolce & Gabbana, Valentino, and Armani designs, with shoes by Gucci, Jimmy Choo, and impossibly high stilettos. It was designer heaven. They had a luncheon but no dancing or music that we could see or hear or crash.

Our fantasy bubble suddenly burst as we realized that we needed to pack to return to Genova. We were now in the danger zone from shopping; the second expansion zipper was undone on our suitcases. Also, we needed to arrange for a taxi to meet us at the ferry dock in Naples to get us to the airport. When we were finished with arrangements and packing, our reward was getting our hair done and making reservations for a fantastic dinner at the hotel to celebrate our time in Capri.

We really dressed up for dinner. The Capresi were there in their finery, and even some of the guests lingering from the wedding were at the restaurant. The maitre d' came over to greet us and announced proudly that he was our cousin. I asked him, "How can that be?" He said, "There is a small village outside of Naples where everyone is a Ferro. My mother's name is Giovanna Ferro." He then gifted us with dessert, but reality was facing us, and it was time to go to our room and rest up for the long trip home.

The next morning, we said our farewells to the hotel staff, and everything went off seamlessly without snags. When we arrived in Naples, Anita spotted a limo driver with a sign showing the name of our hotel, and on the back side of the sign was our name. She is good at reading in reverse since she is an elementary school teacher. While he drove us to the airport, he was in a heated argument with his girlfriend. The louder he yelled into the cell phone, the faster he drove. Thankfully, we arrived safely and made our flight from Naples to Genova. When we landed in Genova, I went to the ladies' room and got trapped in the bathroom. Yes, again. At least there was no pianist this time as I pounded and pounded on the full-length door. I even got to the point of ramming it with my body, trying to get out. Finally, another woman in the restroom reported it to security, and someone came to pry the door open. If I am not tripping, I am somehow locked in bathrooms. Is there some kind of symbolism here?

It was now early evening, and we went to the terrace of the Grande Savoia Hotel to have a drink. Rooftop views are always the best. This one was panoramic, with all of Genova laid out below us; and in the distance, the sea was filled with white cruise ships. We chatted with our wonderful waiter, Fillippo Fascist; of course, I had to ask how he got the name. It turns out that his father had changed his last name during World War II to make a political statement and kept it. He had been working at the hotel for more than thirty years. He decided to give us a history lesson on Genova. He pointed out certain monuments and where Christopher Columbus was born. He pointed toward the hills where there is a little town named Chiavari and told us that this was where Frank Sinatra's mother was born. Sinatra's father was Sicilian, and his mother was Genovese; so while most fans think that Sinatra was a 100 percent Sicilian, his beloved mother,

Dolly, was Ligurian. So Frank was half Ligurian. Those Ligurians sure get around.

When I returned to Italy with my mother two months later, I would get to know Chiavari very well because I would have to take my mother by ambulance to the hospital, but that's another story.

In the morning, we checked in for our flight. I recognized the clerk from the previous year and mentioned my mother to her. She remembered helping my mother and commented on Rosa's elegance, bella figura. It seems that the Ligurians have a special intuition that gives them a sense of recognition for one another. It's like a sixth sense of just knowing.

All went well at the airport until Anita noticed that our flight number matched the sign showing the flight to Monaco. I thought that perhaps we would be going to Monaco on the way to Munich. Well, that's another route; and then we thought we'd better check and found out that this Monaco was Monaco di Baviera, which is Munich, not the Monaco of France. The Ligurian dialect had struck again. As we sipped our champagne at thirty thousand feet, life felt good because I knew I would be coming back with my mother in September, and Italy would be waiting for us.

Chapter 22

My Mother's Last Trip 2011

Ironically, what drew me back to Italy originally was my mother's dangling of the Côte d' Azur carrot: Nice, France. Nice is an Italian hour and a half drive from where my relatives live, but when I'm driving, it is two hours. I had thought that Nice had always been French. I never realized that it had been Italian, or that Giuseppe Garibaldi was born there while it was in the Kingdom of Piedmont and Sardinia, an independent Italian state within the Ligurian region. It is one of the most valuable pieces of real estate in the world and was ceded to France in the Treaty of Turin by the Sardinian king and Napoleon III, only one year before the Risorgimento united most of Italy. Whatever the history is, Nice is one of my favorite places on earth to visit.

Trips to the stelle originated when my mother was in her forties and was determined to find her roots and unite with her side of her Italian family. Rosa had her own Risorgimento. The first time we went to Italy in 1971, I had made the pact with my father to never return. Rose had only the name of a town, Stella San Giovanni, and the name of her first cousin, Maria Ferro Cipresso, but no address. We had stayed at Nonna Antonietta's childhood home with the dirty stone floor and the single swinging lightbulb hanging from the ceiling. It was the one with the vegetables cooling in the boxes by the bathroom toilet and the beady red-eyed rats. On that first trip to Italy, my mother was convinced that if she could get to Stella San Giovanni, she would find her family. Nonna Antonietta had told her it was too far to go and had given her dire warnings about the rocky dirt paths over the hills, but my mother was a Vallerga-Bertuccio.

My father and I had had it with finding our roots. We had already experienced dirty stone floors, cows under the floors, and beady red eyes staring at us at night. We stayed with Nonna Antonietta's sister Teresa and Giorgio and refused to venture further. We didn't care about finding any more relatives. My mother was single-minded when she got an idea in her head, and not even Italian tradition and warnings from others could stop her. I left for Paris; and my father happily stayed with his Aunt Teresa and Uncle Giorgio, while my mother went in search of her relatives. Over the course of many years and many dinner conversations, I have heard my mother recount the story. Against her mother-in-law's warning, she marched up the dirt road in search of the bus going to Stella San Giovanni. She found a bus and asked the bus driver if it went to Stella San Giovanni. Speaking the dialect, she told the bus driver she had come all the way from California and was trying to find her cousin. The bus driver said, "Yes, the bus is going to Stella San Giovanni." She then told him she was looking for her cousin, Maria Cipresso. He pointed to a woman sitting near the back of the bus and said, "There is your cousin, Maria Cipresso."

What were the chances she would be there at the right hour, on the right bus, and that her cousin would be on the bus that day? I would say that it was by appointment. Some would call it destiny or fate. My mother had found her root in her cousin Maria. Maria became the conduit to my mother finding her relatives on both her mother's and father's side.

A couple of years ago, Maria and the Stella San Giovanni relatives made the trek to my mother's home in Alameda, California, for Easter. At that time, I was still working but would soon retire in May. Each day, Maria and my mother would cry over the passing days and how little time remained for their visit. I was touched by their love for each other. One afternoon as we sat on the deck overlooking the water, overcome by emotion, I told them that I would bring my mother to Italy in September. I kept my promise. She had dangled the Côte d'Azur carrot in front of me, and I would return the gift.

In September 2011, we flew to Nice and took a taxi to the Hotel Martinez in Cannes. The taxi driver asked if we were going to the "boat show," which turned out to be the most prestigious international yacht sale in the world. The yachts looked like huge floating houses and hotels. We checked in and got settled into room 611, which had a view of an interesting nightclub called La Chunga. When you say "La Chunga," you must lower your voice register to a lower range. Why? You'll find out.

My mother took a nap, and I went wandering La Croisette. Since my mother had turned eighty-seven years young, I asked the hotel to make us a dinner reservation at the Palm d'Or Restaurant in the hotel. The hotel and restaurant had been sold out for weeks, but the concierge moved mountains and must have pulled in most of her chips. She got us a reservation in honor of my mother's age and birthday. I was thrilled and knew that my mother would relish this surprise.

The Martinez is an art-deco hotel on La Croisette, where everyone did the "passeggiata." La Croisette was also THE place to be seen. The Martinez is one of the hotels where the jet set stayed on the riviera. From the balcony of our room at the Martinez, we looked down at La Chunga, a nightclub. We had heard that the waiters wore red shirts because flamenco dancers wear red. We were curious.

Established in 1958, La Chunga is open twenty hours a day, seven days a week. La Chunga means "the Difficult Woman." La Chunga was a barefoot flamenco dancer who danced the zambra mora, a style of flamenco dancing, made famous by Micaela Flores Amaya. Ms. Amaya was La Chunga. She danced the zambra mora barefoot, with finger cymbals, in the 1950s. She wore street clothes and kept the traditional serious facial expression adopted by most flamenco dancers.

As we dressed for dinner, we kept talking and chatting about La Chunga. The word was intoxicating. Rose glammed up for the evening in a long skirt with large sequins that sparkled like little mirrors. She had on great makeup and hairstyle. She exuded bella figura. We found a wonderful little restaurant on La Croisette, called Mt. Vesuvius, with great Italian food; remember, Nice was Italian at one point.

As we strolled back to the hotel and neared the nightclub, the music pulsated and permeated the night air, making it difficult to hear. The enormous crowd outside swayed to the throbbing music and blocked our passage. My mother was entranced. It was like a moth to the flame. Slowly but regally, leaning on my arm, wearing the hotel slippers to cradle her swollen feet, she shuffled into the center of the layers of people waiting outside. The "Red Sea" parted as if Moses had arrived; but no, it was my mother. Rosa made her way into the jammed nightclub. She told me to go over to the bar, saying, "Don't worry about me. I'll be fine." What was she doing? What could she be thinking?

I timidly stayed near the cash register not far from the entrance. I was trying to figure out the situation. The throb of the music was hypnotic. The scents, the way people were dressed, and the constant semiaccidental bumping of bodies created an unbelievable sexual tension in the dimly lit room. Slowly, my eyes got used to the light. I worked my way through the steamy room to the middle of the bar and finally got a place and a drink. I found that people would look and then look away, peering over their drinks with a kind of half-lidded look, a sort of inviting predatory gaze. The cleavage was low, and the stilettos were high, but not everything was as it appeared.

I looked across the room to see if my mother was all right. Not only was she all right, but someone had given her a beautiful chair, and she was holding court with a cosmopolitan in hand. On a table nearby, a gorgeous tall honey blonde woman in her early twenties was dancing and stripping. When she got down to her lingerie, her friend lifted her up off the table and carried her away. I asked the waiter if this was part of the show; and in a sultry voice, he said, "No, it was just a La Ch-un-ga-a-a moment."

A handsome Frenchman at the bar turned to me and said, "I like to f@#k. Do you?" I turned my back to him and ignored him. He tapped me on the shoulder and apologized in impeccable English. I told him he was rude, and I thought he had very sad eyes. With contrition, he said, "I know. I do. You are right. I fail at relationships." I thought, *What a line.* He went on to say that he was ashamed of himself and admitted it was just a clever line to use with me; after all, I was wearing a red dress. It must have been a "La Chunga" signal for availability. It was a simple cotton dress with a modest neckline, accessorized with low-heeled sandals. There was no comparison with the women there with their plunging necklines, high stilettos, and dramatic makeup and hairstyles. He changed his attitude and told me that my smile radiated joy. He bought me a drink, and I listened to his tales of woe and all about his failed relationships. I was in my counselor mode. He was quite wealthy and lived in Cannes. I thought he must be a regular because he knew all the waiters by name, and they knew him. He was basically a lonely man in his sixties who looked like Yves Montand, an Italian-born French actor. We danced under the spell of La Chunga, and he treated me with courtesy and respect. I kept glancing at my mother. It was amazing how she was still holding up, a cosmopolitan in one hand, gesturing like the true la scignua she had come to be. We had just gotten off the plane from San Francisco that afternoon, and it was now 3:00 a.m.

The club was obviously not a tourist trap and seemed very popular with locals who lived in the area, but in spite of that, I still kept up my guard. I went to check with my mother to see if she was ready to return to the hotel. She gave me an emphatic no. She was thriving on the energy from the young people who surrounded her.

She was talking with Alain, a young handsome Frenchman. Alain was a yacht salesman who lived in Switzerland and came from great wealth. He had an Italian grandmother, and because of this, he was drawn to my mother and felt an endearment for her. He said she reminded him so much of his nonna, and then he invited us to be his guests at a gala preview party for the yacht sale, a private invitation-only soiree.

The plan, he said, was that a pontoon bridge and platform with multiple decks would be built over the water and decorated. The event included dinner, drinks with music; and then the very grandest, most prestigious, and outrageously expensive of the yachts would be paraded in front of this group of select clientele. My mother told him that we could not go because it conflicted with our Palm d'Or dinner reservations. She teased him and kiddingly said that he should reserve the top three yachts for her to purchase, telling him that she would give one to her granddaughter, another to me, and save one for herself.

It was Alain who shared with us that La Chunga was the place to meet and/or pay for an evening. We thought we saw a madame with a few of her girls and watched as they interacted, perhaps making contacts and arrangements. It was now four in the morning, and the music had morphed into a medley of big-band selections and other numbers great for dancing. La Chunga was organized into multilevel tiers for those who watched and dined and those who danced. As we scanned the dance floor and perused the various dancers, we noticed that many had beautiful figures, faces, hair, and clothing, but that some of it might have been smoke and mirrors, illusions.

Alain escorted us back to the hotel at five am. Thank goodness we were close to the hotel. I looked at my mother's swollen feet in her

Hotel Martinez slippers and knew she had overdone it. But at her age, why not, perché no? No sooner had our heads hit the pillows than we felt we were in a Federico Fellini film. Life has its reruns, and the morning would bring one.

Many years before, when my mother had dangled the Ritz Carlton Cannes carrot, we had stayed up until three in the morning. We slept until the maid knocked on our door, which I thought had been in the middle of the night, but it was one in the afternoon. We had planned to go to Grasse before the perfume factory closed that afternoon. Now like a rerun, it was one in the afternoon again; and this time, our driver was due to pick us up at two to take us once again to Grasse. It was déjà vu. We raced around the room, rushing through our toiletries to get ourselves put together. We blamed it on the spell cast by La Chunga. How can life repeat itself? Well, it just did.

There are many perfumeries in Grasse, one of the most famous, the Fragonard Perfumery. We watched through the laboratory windows and learned how perfume is made, delighting in the variety of fragrances concocted from flowers like lavender, rose, gardenia, jasmine, and exotic blooms from all over the world. There are fewer than two dozen "noses" in the world. "Noses" are in charge of developing the scents. If you are one of the "noses," you can never drink or smoke. Afterward, the driver took us to the old part of Grasse where we saw the Notre Dame du Puy Cathredral, little boutiques, smelled the freshly baked bread, and looked at the mouthwatering pastries. We went to a café and ordered some French pastries, which are so delicate, so flakey, and so imbedded with butter that it is almost like eating butter itself. We tried a daub of our perfume while we waited for our desserts to be served. I had a strawberry savarin, and my mother had an éclair. We sipped French champagne, while we filled the air with our new scents from the Grasse Perfumery.

That evening, we dressed in our finest clothes in preparation for Rosa's belated gala birthday dinner at the hotel's famous Michelin two-star Palm d'Or Restaurant. We used the hotel's private elevator up to the restaurant. A hotel escort in front of the elevator confirmed our reservation. Another escort walked us to the maitre d'. Our balcony table had a panoramic view of the yacht parade. We could see the gala platform for the yacht party stretching out on the bay, with its sparkling decorations and music. As we dined, the music from the gala floated up to us interrupted, at intervals, by the tooting horns of each yacht as it was described for potential buyers. We had the best seat in the house for this annual September event. The evening closed with a short walk back to our room. We felt sublimely satiated by the succulent meal and the incredible fragrances we experienced in Grasse.

Lounging by the pool the next day, I was convinced that my true calling after retiring might just be "to do nothing." La Chunga came to mind, and I thought perhaps we should go back for dinner. After sunning for several hours, I returned to the room. When I opened the door, my mother asked, "Are we going to La Chunga for dinner tonight?" "It's your party. Let's go." When we arrived that evening, the waiter recalled that we had practically closed the place down two nights before and gave us a wonderful table with a full view of the dance floor. The best, however, was when the chef came to our table and asked what we would like to eat. He said with such confidence, "You name it, I will make it for you." I think la scignua had cast her spell. We were in the perfect catbird seat for people-watching in one of the best shows in Europe. Then the madame made her entrance, and the ladies of the evening came out to work their spells. The throbbing beat returned, hypnotizing us again, drawing us into the intoxicating flamenco fantasy of La Ch-un-g-a-a-a.

A singer took the stage, recalling the old café scenes of France in those classic movies with stars like Simone Signoret. The singer sounded like Edith Piaf. She was followed by a guitarist who could play absolutely everything from classical music to rock, to jazz, to tango. Later on came the belly dancers. Yes, belly dancers. La Chunga's entertainment seemed to have a new act every hour. We were transported to another time and place beyond imagining. We were having another incredible evening, but at one thirty, my mother began to fade; and it was time to go home. As we bid our au revoirs and bonne nuit, good night, to the waiters, we could see the ladies of the evening still had a sparkling bon vivant air as they waited to dispense happiness for a price.

The culmination of the late evenings at La Chunga had caught up with my mother. She was not feeling well so she rested most of the next day. Can you imagine keeping up this pace at eighty-seven with a load of medications in you? While she rested, I kept the economy going and went shopping. The stores had clothes made in France and shoes made in Italy, female heaven. I bought a pair of black peau de soie five-inch stilettos. When I put them on, I immediately began to worry about getting a nosebleed from the altitude; but I looked down and whispered, "Hello, lover." And we were bonded for life. Once I had the shoes, I searched for the rest of the outfit and found an extraordinary charcoal linen sundress with a bolero sweater. Both of them had tiny buttons that blended the outfit, even though they were not a set. The best was that the store was going out of business, and the outfit was a bargain. I returned to the hotel and showed my mother my treasures. The effect was miraculous. Her sparkle returned, and she demanded to know if the stores were still open.

Picture this. Rose was dressed in a frilly little peach-colored blouse with a long black skirt accessorized with her Hotel Martinez slippers. Holding on to my arm for balance, she leaned forward and shuffled as fast as she could toward the store. She was in fashion paradise, especially as the store was closing and everything was on sale. We moved slowly back toward the Martinez, me balancing her on one side and lugging the many bags on the other side. I was a pretty pack mule, a cinghiale in disguise. Rose donned her new outfit. The dress was tea length made of the lightest silk that floated in the air. The fabric was imprinted with swirls of bright turquoise, hot pink, and gold on a black background. It had clear sequins scattered all over it with three rows lining the V-shaped neckline, and a row on the hem that caught the light as she moved. It met the scignua fashion requirements, three-quarter-length sleeves and glitz. As every woman knows, with a new dress, one simply had to be seen; so off to La Chunga we went. That night, the chefs outdid themselves with a black truffle risotto that melted in our mouths—a gift from the chef—followed by a coquette di diavlo. The entertainment was a fabulous virtuoso violinist. All was superb. After all, it was La Ch-un-ga-a-a.

Our French soireé was soon to be over. We were to fly to Rome and connect to Genova. When we departed Nice, we noticed a sign in the departure area that read, "Kiss and Depart." The taxi driver explained that many lovers fly in and out of Nice, and this was France's au revoir to them. I wondered why we don't have designated places in our airports for one last kiss. We need to take a lesson from Nice.

The Stella San Giovanni family was waiting at the Genova Airport to pick us up. My mother was staying with Maria Cipresso, and I was staying in Alpicella. When we arrived in Stella San Giovanni, Giacomo came to take me to his apartment. Before I left, I announced that I would cook the next night and invited the Cipressos to come to Giacomo's for dinner. When I offered to cook for everyone, I had forgotten that Giacomo did not have an oven or a microwave, only four small burners. Life does have its challenges, but I've learned to be flexible and creative.

I intended to make a breaded chicken, sliced sauted potatoes, and fresh green beans. I prepared an antipasto of cold cuts and cheeses with a secondo piatto of ravioli for the pasta and had, thankfully, bought the dessert earlier. We had seven for dinner. I had planned to bake the chicken, but no oven. I had planned to microwave the green beans, but no microwave. It all turned out, but with only four burners, I was juggling with little room to spare. Giacomo was on close supervision of the process. Finally, everything was in its place, tutto a posto. I raced down the hill to get my hair done and returned with plenty of wine. As I cooked and sipped, the dinner got better and better.

I realized the next day that I'd better invite the Ferro side for dinner. You've got to give equal time to both sides, whether they want to eat my cooking or not. I asked Maria, Gian Piero's wife, to make the gravy because I did not want to compete with perfection. I walked from one family house to another to invite them all to come to Sunday dinner with me in the apartment. I would have several days to recuperate from the previous dinner.

Sunday arrived, and as I stood out on the balcony prior to prepping the meal, what lay before my eyes horrified me. There in the back of a pickup truck were the slaughtered bodies of a mother cinghiale and her three babies. I had never seen cinghali butchered before, and it was dreadful. Giacomo assured me that our family did not hunt or kill cinghiali. It was a massacre of our namesakes. Piero had told me about the time he had allowed a mother cinghiale to eat all of his crops rather than harm it. It saddens me to think that this magnificent beast would be hunted and killed. I did not know it was opening day for cinghiali hunting season.

As I cooked, I could hear the cars, SUVs, and trucks coming up the hillside for the Cinghiali Hunting Festa. I went out on the balcony and saw they were parked all helter-skelter. There must have been more than sixty cars. I wondered how they would ever find a way to get out of their grid lock. All the men and a few of the women wore hunting outfits. Some had outfits that looked as if they had only been out of the boxes a few minutes, pristine. It was definitely a male bonding event of major proportions. The "hunters" went into the lodge next door to Giacomo's apartment, and soon I heard them singing. It was obvious to me that the real hunters were the ones who had showed up much earlier in the truck with the dead cinghiali. It still haunts me.

As my relatives arrived for supper, I suspected there may have been an undercurrent of disbelief that the Italian American relative was going to cook dinner, but the joy of the family gathering overrode any doubts. Fortunately, all went well, and the dinner was a success. Gian Piero's wife, Maria, came up to me after the dinner; and I swelled with pride when she told me I was a good cook. Her compliment was a big deal to me, and I couldn't help thinking that somehow I had fooled them all. Thank you to all the cooking channels, my nonne (grandmothers) and my mother.

After dinner, as we stood on the balcony watching the cinghiali festa slowly winding down, I saw cars leaving within a few minutes and then poof! They were gone. No one hit anyone, no one beeped their horn, and it was done effortlessly. This reversing departure dance of the chaotic parking system is pervasive in all of Italy. The parking dance in Italy is replicated nowhere else that I know of in the world. It is as though they are like birds connected, knowing without speaking or overtly communicating when and how to move, an internal GPS system.

Oftentimes I have wondered why Italians park so chaotically. I thought of my cousin, Giacomo, who after turning his hat backward drove with such wild abandon at reckless speeds up and down the winding roads in the hills of Liguria. Could it be that when these fearless Italian drivers came to their destination and finally stopped, with gratefulness to God for their safe journey, they simply stopped and left the car where it was parked at any angle and in any place? When I am in Italy, I seem to channel Giacomo and drive with verve and energy, and upon arriving at my destination, throw myself out of the car, toss the keys to whoever is there, and head for the vino to decompress from the autostrada experience. Who cares where the car is. I'm here and safe. The trip is done. The beauty of it is that Anita was usually there to catch the keys. Saint Anita.

I have heard from my friend Deborah that the only exception to this chaotic parking is in Assisi. She had been there recently and thought that because Assisi is holy ground, there was a higher order for parking. It is the only exception she has observed. I wonder if the reason Italians eat, drink, and linger in the caffès and restaurants until the early morning is that secretly, unconsciously, they think when leaving very late, they will come out to the parking and find that all the other cars will have left, and they will be able to get in their car and simply drive away. This is a wonderful theory, unscientific, but it lends itself to blind faith.

The cinghiali festa was ending and so was the Ferro dinner. It was the last evening my mother would be in Alpicella. I went out on the balcony again to get a breath of fresh air, and there below I saw my mother's family: Giuseppe, his brothers Andrea and Piero (Pero), with their families. I called out to them. They had come to the festa and were able to see my mother one last time. Usually, we were there in July, but this was September. Who knew there was a cinghiali festa and that Giuseppe would come all the way from Milan to be there? You might remember he was the one who taught Bella how to waltz. By appointment, the family on my mother's side had gathered for one last farewell visit with Rose.

Giacomo would chauffer my mother and me to Casanova, and it was our last time to see Lalla Nita. She was staying at the home of her daughter Franca. Even though Lalla Nita was mentally sharp and lived another year, we would not be back before she passed at age one hundred. Our last words to one another were, "Il Papa, ti amo." She replied, "Anche io, Il Cardinale." To this day, I cannot say these words, when I think of her, without a huge lump in my throat.

Lots of tears were shed, with many hugs and goodbyes, and then it was time for Giacomo to drive us to Santa Margherita. By the time we got to the Miramare Hotel, my mother was wheezing and having difficulty breathing. She had contracted bronchitis, and I asked the hotel manager to call a doctor immediately. Quickly, the doctor came to our room and prescribed a myriad of medications. He spoke the old world Ligurian dialect; and yes, again, my mother charmed him. Lucky for me, it was an easy walk along the seaside port, with gorgeous beaches, to the local pharmacy. As I walked the vico, toward the pharmacy, I looked down the alleyway; and there it was, Colombo Ristorante, where poor Camillo had worked. I brought the medicine back to the hotel and then headed back to the ristorante. In his honor, I decided to have minestrone soup, and I'm sure Camillo was beaming from above.

My mother was resting almost all of the time, and I was alone. In the evenings, I went to the hotel bar. I was the only person there with the exception of the bartender, Marco. I asked if he knew Camillo. He was astounded. "You knew Camillo." He said that Camillo was one of his dearest friends and asked how I knew him. I told him the story of that fateful night when Camillo died but deleted the "fatal kisses." He said he was the one at the hotel who gave Anita an ice pack for her eye, but he had never seen me. Then he said, "You were the one who stayed with Camillo and would not leave him alone in his last hours? All the drinks are on the house. You even forgot your purse that night, and the ambulance driver found your purse and returned it." Marco told me that he was the one who called for the ambulance and police that night. I had made a steadfast friend, another appointment. He checked on my mother and on me for the rest of our visit. I now have a permanent friend in Santa Margherita and all because of Camillo.

When we checked into Splendido, my mother was still frail and weak. Ermes and Luca were there to greet us as well as Carlo and other members of the staff. It was great to see them. Oh, how time had flown. After we settled in, I went to the pool to lounge and gaze at the glistening blue-green Mediterranean Sea. I reflected about how strong my mother used to be, like a mountain goat climbing the hills with no problem, shopping and carrying boxes and boxes of purchases and heavy suitcases filled with clothes and shoes. She used to stay up all night, dancing and drinking and partying. She was the toast of Portofino and every place she graced with her presence.

The following evening, she seemed to be a little bit better, so we dined on the terrace. It was to be her last dinner at her favorite corner table. Suddenly, there was a huge clap of thunder, a blinding flash of lightning, followed by torrential rain. Within seconds, the waiters came, picked up our table, and rushed it inside; and within minutes, we were dining again, watching the steady stream of rain from the beautifully appointed dining room.

She slept well that night and felt well enough the next day to go out, walk around town, and look into some of the shops. She put on her favorite leopard blouse, and we took the hotel shuttle down the hill. We had a drink at a nearby caffè and conversed in the dialect with the women who were always by the port with their linen tablecloths, bibs for babies, and various other handiworks. After window shopping, suddenly, my mother stumbled and fell on the cobblestones. Immediately, several people ran over to assist me in lifting her up. They even brought out a chair from a nearby hotel, the Splendido Mare. As I watched her grab her knee, I knew she was injured. Fortunately, in Portofino, an ambulance is available instantly as it is located at the harbor. It was Saturday evening, about seven o'clock. What now?

Luckily, Carlo, the Splendido restaurant manager, had come down the hill from Splendido on business and saw us. He immediately made arrangements to get my mother back to the hotel using the local ambulance. Whereupon he called Ermes, who made calls and secured an orthopedic surgeon who came to the hotel within twenty minutes. The doctor said while he did not think the knee cap was broken, she did need to go to the hospital and have X-rays. He made arrangements for an ambulance for the next morning to take her and me to the hospital in Chiavari. The hotel brought a huge antique hand-carved chair with a red pillow on it into the lobby to carry my mother up to her room. They placed the chair on a luggage carrier, pushed it into the elevator, and down the aisle to our suite she rolled. The next morning, they used the same throne on wheels to take my mother down to the ambulance. It was quite an elegant and innovative method of transportation. My mother was a trooper, even though she was in excruciating pain.

Soon she had charmed everyone at the hospital with her sparkling personality and Ligurian dialect. The care was superb. She was X-rayed with an infrared light, and it appeared that nothing was broken; but there had been general tissue damage, and her arthritis was inflamed. They wrapped her leg and released her. My heart was full of sadness. I knew la scignua would never return to Portofino.

While waiting for the doctor to check her, I reminisced with other patient family members about my experiences in Italy and the stories my nonne had told me about how they dealt with medical problems when they were children. They had no doctors available then and had adopted healing rituals. I remembered once when Anita had a sty, my nonna Antonietta took off her wedding band, warmed it with a candle, sprinkled it with holy water, and placed it on the sty. She then uttered prayers in her dialect as she held the ring on the sty, and within a couple of days the sty was gone, or maybe not. When I was young, I asked my dad about this ritual. He shared that Nonna Antonietta had done something similar with a man on the farm who had been burned accidently when the gasoline ignited, while he was fixing a tractor. The man's arm was not healing; and so she performed the healing ritual with the ring, candle, holy water, and prayers. Within a few weeks, the man was healed, and there were no scars.

Many stories in Italian folklore reach beyond what we cannot touch and see. Some call it superstition, but many say it is a belief in a higher power. My great-great-uncle, the uncle of my nonna Maria, was considered clairvoyant. My nonna Maria told me that when she was a little girl, one night, he woke up in the middle of the night from a dream, jumped out of bed, and ran next door to my nonna Maria's parent's home. He woke the household and told Nonna's parents that their twin daughters were in danger. Alarmed, their mother went in to check on them and found them burning with fever. The "doctor" was called, and it turned out they had spinal meningitis. They did not die, both recovered, but one was mentally impaired. Albina had the mind of a child for the rest of her life. Her twin sister, Giuseppina, took care of her for the rest of their lives, never marrying and living in the family home in Pero.

This gift of clairvoyance has been strong in my family for generations; and often we sense things that we did not, could not, know otherwise. As I sat in the waiting room, I knew that my mother would not be returning to see her relatives. It was her last trip. I cried silently.

Splendido sent a taxi to retrieve us from the hospital. The taxi driver and my mother became friends by the time we got back to the hotel. She said she would call him for future driving needs, and he said he would bring her some funghi (mushrooms) just harvested by his family, which he did. Upon our return, the hotel had flowers and champagne for us. My mother returned to the room and proceeded to keep the room service staff busy. I am still not sure how many gelatos she ordered. The phone rang; it was Ermes calling on his one and only day off to see how my mother was doing. With my mother ensconced comfortably in the room, I went down for dinner, knowing that she would soon be the queen of room service. She and my daughter had had many years of practice. Bella is quite skilled, thanks to her nonnie.

As I entered the terrace restaurant for dinner, my face must have been quite somber because the staff was acutely attentive. One of the waiters twirled me around to the tarantella music, and they all took turns coming over to talk to me. I was given a corner table at dinner where my mother, my daughter, and I had dined with her dolly Rose Marie when my daughter was eight years old. After dinner, I continued the three-generation ritual and went over near the piano to listen to Vladimar play. I sat at the bar, where years before Signor Rossi had bestowed the title of the book, *Il Circolo, The Circle*. The Splendido staff was doing its best to make my evening special, and they did, even though I knew things would never be the same.

I will always remember my mother as the complete picture of a matriarch. She simply commanded attention with sequins sparkling on her clothes, perfectly coiffed hair, and makeup. My mother was the epitome of bella figura, and she will always be la scignua in Portofino.

It was time to pack and bring la scignua home. They gently sat my mother on the throne and rolled her down to the lobby. When the taxi driver arrived, he gave my mother the funghi, and she cried. She knew without saying a word that she would not be returning. I said nothing, my heart was breaking, but I knew she would become upset if I cried. It was the only time my mother cried when she left Portofino.

We were on our way to the Grand Savoia Hotel, and just as we got to the hotel, who did we see walking down the street coming toward the Savoia? Giacomo! What a surprise! He was there to help me get my mother into the hotel. I had phoned him when the accident occurred to tell him about the hospital trip, but I never told him our travel schedule, so he must have checked with the hotel staff. It was another part of the connection of my family; we are there for one another.

My mother was quite content with the hotel room; and as long as she could have room service with minestrone soup, pasta with pesto, a gelato, and a cosmopolitan, she would continue to be happy. She told Giacomo and me to go out and enjoy Genova. "I'll be fine. Go out and explore Genova. Maybe you and Genova will become friends." So we did. We wandered the streets, looking at the shops and people. One man had marionettes and was playing the violin. The street vendors were selling flowers and fruit. The tour guides were selling walking tours. The atmosphere was carefree and beautiful on a late September day.

Since Giacomo was a widower, I had been giving him lessons in flirting. By happenstance, we encountered a widow who owned a custom T-shirt shop in Genova. I told Giacomo to give it a try. He did, and they exchanged phone numbers; but later, Giacomo said it was too far to drive. And yet for us, his family, here he was in Genova. He knew all the women in the shops in Varazze on the riviera but always had a reason why each one of them was not acceptable. The relatives always asked how I was doing with coaching him, and I always responded, "Cosí, cosí" (So, so). He was a work in progress. That's what cousins are for, to help one another.

The next morning, we needed to get up at five thirty for our nine o'clock flight. I was not sure how I was going to do it all. But I did, and with my mother in a wheelchair. There we sat and sat. The flight was cancelled because of mechanical difficulties. We were in the airport eight hours and missed our connecting flight from Paris to San Francisco. Later that afternoon, Air France found a flight to Paris and put us in a small "no star" hotel on the outskirts of the city.

Our rooms were so small we had trouble opening our suitcases. We felt that we needed to escape, so I told my mother we should go downstairs and have a drink. On the way down, I had an epiphany. I decided we should go into the City of Lights, Paris. I asked the staff at the desk to make reservations at Fouquet's Restaurant. The clerk told me it was impossible. I asked the clerk to please give me the phone number for Fouquet's, and I would get the reservation. Fouquet's Restaurant was established in 1899 and was considered quite well known to the Parisian society. I dusted off my Brigitte Bardot voice and convincingly told my story of woe about my mother's dire situation to the restaurant manager. He listened then paused for a brief minute and said, "Madame, you have reservations tonight for ten thirty." Merci beaucoup!

Remember the old saying, "When you get lemons, make lemonade." So we did. I told Rose, "Put on your best outfit, the one from Cannes with the swirling polka dots and puffy sleeves in black, white, and magenta, and your black silk slacks and Splendido slippers." She illuminated joy, which I will never forget. Fouquet's is on the corner of the Champs-Elysèes and Avenue George V. The driver took us everywhere, and I was able to take pictures of the Eiffel Tower all lit up. It was an incredible moment that I will forever treasure. We were able to enjoy the splendor of Paris. The Fouquet lived up to its glitz-star reputation. Happily exhausted, we returned to our "hotel" about three in the morning and made the flight home.

My mother was adopted at thirty-three thousand feet by the Italian-French Air Steward who was born in Nice and spoke Ligurian. It was by appointment. He assisted her in every way, and she had her own personal valet. He sang to her in Ligurian because he belonged to a professional singing group. As we touched down in San Francisco, they announced that the pilot was retiring after over thirty years of service. Rose was the last passenger off the plane, because of her wheelchair need. As we deplaned, an honor guard had been formed on both sides of the jet way for the pilot. They started to applaud as the retiring captain emerged closely behind us. I turned to the captain and said, "I also retired recently. Congratulations." My mother turned and looked up at me, saying, "Isn't it wonderful? They really must have liked me." Of course, they did. Everyone always did.

The Postscript

In February 2012, Lalla Nita passed away at the age of one hundred. That same year, as a special gift, I brought my mother on a European cruise for her birthday; she was wheelchair bound. She was able to see, for the last time, her beloved Taormina and the dangling carrot of the Côte d' Azur. Her great-grandson, my grandson Valentino, was born that same year in July; and Anita's grandson Cody was born in August. My mother ascended into heaven to be reunited with her family and friends in February 2013. As Giovanni "Gianni" Battista would say as he sat on the bench in Alpicella, "That's the news."

Epilogue

I have learned so much about myself from the many years of traveling to Italy. I am proud to be the granddaughter of immigrants and blessed to have had a home embraced by loving parents. I have been nurtured by the courage and love of my family, and I wish to offer these truths to you that I have learned and I know are in my heart.

Ligurians are survivors. We are like a cluster of grapes. We hold on to each other dearly. If we cannot protect one another, we hope the vines, the sea, and the rugged terrain will protect us. We turn our back to the world and rely on each other. We have fought for what we have, against the weather, the land, and the invaders. We have ancient minds, going back many, many centuries. We have learned to live with the others who invaded us, to be assimilated and yet not assimilated. We are true to our heritage. It thrives in our DNA and the history, the legends and the stories passed down through the generations. It is never ending—*il circolo*, my Italian circle.

Memories engraved in my heart:

- All the trips to Italy with my mother, daughter, and cousin filled with laughter and so many adventures.
- Piero, wearing his red shorts, happily tilling the summer soil in his vegetable garden.

- Giacomo turning his baseball cap backward as he swiftly speeds up and down the hills of Liguria.
- Gianni Battista moving precisely, like clockwork, from bench to bench to bench.
- Luenzin stringing the lights around the chapel of the Rock of St. Anna. And, oh! Those electric- blue eyes.
- Lalla Nita, my Il Papa, and I will always be Il Cardinale.
- My grandparents, *mi nonni*, my gratitude and love for your heroic spirit to leave your homeland to create a new life in this country.
- My mother, forever you will be la scignua.
- My father, you still make me laugh when I recall your emphatic pronouncement, "Rose, don't unpack." And then she summarily ignored your command.
- I am standing on the balcony of Alpicella with my cinghiale hooves pitter-pattering blissfully to the music of the festa.

The Little Alps of Heaven and the Crown, My Ligurian Roots

The Family Tree
Liguria, Italy

(Grandparents)

Antonio Ferro	Antonietta Rusca	Edoardo Bertuccio	Maria Vallerga
(Alpicella)	(Stella San Bernardo)	(Montessoro)	(Pero – Pe')
1883 – 1959d	1893 – 1982d	1890 – 1952d	1900 – 1985d

(Parents)

Carlo Ferro	Rosa Bertuccio
(Alameda)	(Alameda)
1918 – 1984d	1923 – 2013d

(Children)

John Anthony Ferro	Donna Marie Ferro
Oakland, California	
1943 -	1947 -

Family Members and Their Relationship to Donna Marie Ferro

California, United States

Carlo Ferro	Father	Alameda, Bay Farm Island
Rosa Bertuccio Vallerga Ferro	Mother	Alameda, raised in Oakland
John Anthony Ferro	Brother	Alameda, California
Terèsa Ferro Guarino	Daughter	Alameda, Bay Farm Island
Anita Ferro Paullus	First cousin, daughter of Tom Ferro (Uncle of Donna Marie)	

Italy

Edoardo Bertuccio	Grandfather (maternal side)	Montessoro
Maria Vallerga Bertuccio	Grandmother (maternal side)	Pero (Pe')
Antonio Ferro	Grandfather (paternal side)	Alpicella

Antonietta Rusca Ferro	Grandmother (paternal side)	Stella San Bernardo
Pietro (Piero) Ferro	Cousin (paternal side)	Alpicella
Giam (Gian) Piero Ferro	Cousin (paternal side)	Alpicella
Giacomo Ferro	Cousin (paternal side)	Alpicella
Giuseppe Ferro	Cousin (paternal side)	Alpicella
Maddelena Vallerga Perata	Great-aunt, mother of Lorenzo and Franca	Pero (Pe') Campo Marzio

(Lalla Nita, Il Papa) Husband Francesco Perata; sister to Maria Vallerga Bertuccio, my nonna Maria

Lorenzo (son) and Mariuccia Perata Cousin and wife (maternal side)		Campo Marzio

Lorenzo's sons:

Maurizio Perata	Cousin (maternal side)	Campo Marzio
Damiano Perata	Cousin (maternal side)	Campo Marzio
Franca Perata Damele (daughter) and Gianni Damele	Cousin and husband (maternal side)	Casanova

Franca's son

Elviro Damele	Cousin (maternal side)	Campo Marzio
Lorenzo and Olympia Ferro	Cousin and wife (maternal side)	Campo Marzio

This Lorenzo is the son of Pietrina Vallerga Ferro and the nephew of Lalla Nita and my nonna Maria

Lorenzo's (a.k.a. Lance) sons:

Giuseppe Ferro	Cousin (maternal side)	Campo Marzio
Andrea Ferro	Cousin (maternal side)	Campo Marzio
Piero Ferro	Cousin (maternal side)	Campo Marzio

Zerbio and Maria Ferro Cipresso	Cousin and husband (maternal side)	Stella San Giovanni

Maria Ferro Cipresso is the daughter of Pietrina Vallerga Ferro and the niece of Lalla Nita and Nonna Maria

Daughters:

Giovanna Cipresso / Gianni Curletti	Cousin (maternal side)	Stella San Giovanni
Maddelena Cipresso (a.k.a. Milena)	Cousin (maternal side)	Stella San Giovanni

Translation of a Few Words

Genoese (*Zeneize*) is a dialect of the Ligurian language, the one spoken in Genoa. Ligurian is listed by Ethnologue as a language in its own right. In its differences from standard Italian, Genoese is somewhat similar to French. The language is not dying out, and while the major speakers are older, many young people speak it as well. The spellings have never been regularized, and the Zeneize spellings here are from native speakers.

Zeneize	Italian	English
peia	*pera*	pear
limun	*limonè*	lemon
arnugnin	*albicocca*	apricot
uga	*uva*	grape
ca'	*casa*	home
ovu	*uovo*	egg
figgeü	*bambino*	child
lalla	*zia*	aunt
barba	*zio*	uncle
cüjin	*cugino*	cousin

andemmü	*adiamo*	we go
muè	*mamma*	mother (mama)
puè	*papa*	father (papa)
ujello	*uccello*	bird
gianco	*bianco*	white
jonü	*giallo*	yellow
spussa	*cattivo odore*	bad smell
spegetti	*occhiali*	eye glasses
paccugo	*pasticcio*	mess
stria	*strega*	witch
erbuu	*albero*	tree
vegiü	*vecchio*	old
zuena	*giovane*	young
fre	*fratello*	brother
so	*sorella*	sister

Glossary

Italian	English	Italian	English
Il circolo	the circle	*gallerie*	tunnel
nonno	grandfather	*nonna*	grandmother
l'isola	the island	*assunta*	assumption
Liguria	coastal region of Northwestern Italy	*tigre*	tiger
faccia fritta	fried face	*lago*	lake
stella	star	*furba*	cunning
tutto a posto	everything is fine	*vecchio*	old
corona	crown	*città*	city
chiuso	closed	*il cacciatore*	the hunter
colombo	dove	*sciopero*	strike
teste dure	hard heads	*provare*	to try
il nido	the nest	*punti*	points
bisnonna	great-grandmother	*farmacia*	pharmacy
torte	cakes	*uomo*	man
culo	butt	*cinghiali*	wild boars

Ferro Coat of Arms

FERRO

**If there is food, wine,
and dance,
we'll be there.**

Cousins Giacomo, me and Piero
walking out on to the balcony in Alpicella

Finito

The End

Edwards Brothers Malloy
Thorofare, NJ USA
April 28, 2015